# ROBERT LUDLUM

Robert Ludlum. Photograph courtesy of Henry Morrison, Inc.

# ROBERT LUDLUM

## *A Critical Companion*

Gina Macdonald

CRITICAL COMPANIONS TO POPULAR CONTEMPORARY WRITERS
Kathleen Gregory Klein, Series Editor

Greenwood Press
Westport, Connecticut • London

**Library of Congress Cataloging-in-Publication Data**

Macdonald, Gina
    Robert Ludlum : a critical companion / Gina Macdonald.
      p.  cm.—(Critical companions to popular contemporary
writers, ISSN 1082–4979)
    Includes bibliographical references (p.     ) and index.
    ISBN 0–313–29971–4 (alk. paper)
    1. Ludlum, Robert, 1927–  —Criticism and interpretation.  2. Spy
stories, American—History and criticism.  I. Title.  II. Series.
PS3562.U26Z78   1997
813'.54—dc21      96–50289

British Library Cataloguing in Publication Data is available.

Library of Congress Catalog Card Number: 96–50289
ISBN: 0–313–29971–4
ISSN: 1082–4979

First published in 1997

Greenwood Press, 88 Post Road West, Westport, CT 06881
An imprint of Greenwood Publishing Group, Inc.

Printed in the United States of America

The paper used in this book complies with the
Permanent Paper Standard issued by the National
Information Standards Organization (Z39.48–1984).

10 9 8 7 6 5 4 3 2 1

*To the English teachers of the new Russia—*
*may our paranoia have less*
*foundation in fact*

ADVISORY BOARD

# Contents

# Series Foreword

The authors who appear in the series Critical Companions to Popular Contemporary Writers are all best-selling writers. They do not have only one successful novel, but a string of them. Fans, critics, and specialist readers eagerly anticipate their next book. For some, high cash advances and breakthrough sales figures are automatic; movie deals often follow. Some writers become household names, recognized by almost everyone.

But novels are read one by one. Each reader chooses to start and, more importantly, to finish a book because of what she or he finds there. The real test of a novel is in the satisfaction its readers experience. This series acknowledges the extraordinary involvement of readers and writers in creating a best-seller.

The authors included in this series were chosen by an Advisory Board composed of high school English teachers and high school and public librarians. They ranked a list of best-selling writers according to their popularity among different groups of readers. Writers in the top-ranked group who had not received book-length, academic literary analysis (or none in at least the past ten years) were chosen for the series. Because of this selection method, Critical Companions to Popular Contemporary Writers meets a need that is not addressed elsewhere.

The volumes in the series are written by scholars with particular expertise in analyzing popular fiction. These specialists add an academic focus to the popular success that these best-selling writers already enjoy.

The series is designed to appeal to a wide range of readers. The general reading public will find explanations for the appeal of these well-known writers. Fans will find biographical and fictional questions answered. Students will find literary analysis, discussions of fictional genres, carefully organized introductions to new ways of reading the novels, and bibliographies for additional research. Students will also be able to apply what they have learned from this book to their readings of future novels by these best-selling writers.

Each volume begins with a biographical chapter drawing on published information, autobiographies or memoirs, prior interviews, and, in some cases, interviews given especially for this series. A chapter on literary history and genres describes how the author's work fits into a larger literary context. The following chapters analyze the writer's most important, most popular, and most recent novels in detail. Each chapter focuses on a single novel. This approach, suggested by the Advisory Board as the most useful to student research, allows for an in-depth analysis of the writer's fiction. Close and careful readings with numerous examples show readers exactly how the novels work. These chapters are organized around three central elements: plot development (how the story line moves forward), character development (what the reader knows about the important figures), and theme (the significant ideas of the novel). Chapters may also include sections on generic conventions (how the novel is similar to or different from others in its same category of science fiction, fantasy, thriller, etc.), narrative point of view (who tells the story and how), symbols and literary language, and historical or social context. Each chapter ends with an "alternative reading" of the novel. The volume concludes with a primary and secondary bibliography, including reviews.

The Alternative Readings are a unique feature of this series. By demonstrating a particular way of reading each novel, they provide a clear example of how a specific perspective can reveal important aspects of the book. In each alternative reading section, one contemporary literary theory—such as feminist criticism, Marxism, new historicism, deconstruction, or Jungian psychological critique—is defined in brief, easily comprehensible language. That definition is then applied to the novel to highlight specific features that might go unnoticed or be understood differently in a more general reading of the novel. Each volume defines two or three specific theories, making them part of the reader's understanding of how diverse meanings may be constructed from a single novel.

Taken collectively, the volumes in the Critical Companions to Popular Contemporary Writers series provide a wide-ranging investigation of the complexities of current best-selling fiction. By treating these novels seriously as both literary works and publishing successes, the series demonstrates the potential of popular literature in contemporary culture.

Kathleen Gregory Klein
Southern Connecticut State University

# Acknowledgments

I owe a debt of gratitude to a number of people who made this book both possible and better. First of all, my deep thanks go to Robert Ludlum for kindly granting an interview and providing information that would allow this text to be informed, accurate, and up-to-date about his life and work. My thanks also go to his vigilant agent, Henry Morrison, for arranging the interview.

I can never thank Andrew Macdonald enough for his repeated assurances, loving support, and sound advice. He not only read the text in progress and made valuable suggestions, but also discussed ideas and concepts that have made this book far better than it would have otherwise been. He wrote the section on *The Matarese Circle*, contributed to the discussions of *The Chancellor Manuscript*, provided insights about paranoia, and served as a critic and advisor throughout the writing process.

My thanks also go to Barbara Rader and Kathleen Klein of Greenwood Press, whose enthusiastic support made this book possible, and to Greenwood senior production editor Liz Leiba and my Loyola colleague and friend Raymond McGowan, both of whom provided valuable editorial guidance. Pat Doran of the Loyola Library went to enormous lengths to help me find obscure but necessary articles and books, Ron and June Foust provided insights into Ludlum's psychoanalytical approaches, and

John Mosier shared valuable sources about conspiracy theories. Elisabeth Gareis of Baruch University and Loyola language experts Paulina Bazin, Robert Dewell, Andrew Horton, Ellen Plaisance, Aida Trau, and Thomas Zamparelli helped me better understand Mr. Ludlum's foreign vocabulary and references. Paulina Bazin translated Tatiana Nekriach's article "Zagadki populiarnosti" and provided insights into Russian attitudes toward the novels of Robert Ludlum.

# 1

# The Life of Robert Ludlum

The habits we develop . . . stay . . . with us. . . . You [the writer] have to know about past history or you have no frame of reference for what is happening now—how exaggerated or dangerous or relatively unimportant a current event might be.

Helen MacInnes, *Counterpoint*

## CHILDHOOD

Robert Ludlum was born in New York City on May 25, 1927. His upper-middle class parents, George Hartford Ludlum (a businessman) and Margaret Wadsworth Ludlum, soon thereafter moved to the suburban community of Short Hills, New Jersey. In 1934, when Robert was only seven, his father died. Robert's maternal grandfather, however, an English silk importer, had left his family wealthy enough to afford a series of private boarding schools in Connecticut for Robert. Wadsworth had introduced the Jacquard loom to the United States, a device with a mechanized chain of perforated cards for weaving figured fabrics, and the income generated from that invention ensured his grandson a comfortable youth and a college education.

Ludlum began grade school at the Rectory School for boys in Pomfret,

Connecticut, then progressed to the Kent School, and later to Cheshire Academy. These schools helped shape his vision of the world. He has described the Kent School, at the time he attended, as a "proselytizing organization run by fanatics" (Skarda 306)—little wonder that tyrannical organizations and political and religious extremists people his novels! In contrast to these negative influences, assigned readings at Cheshire Academy taught him a love of history that has remained throughout his life.

When he was a teenager, acting and the theater became consuming interests, wielding an influence that has been lifelong. Ludlum told Ron Blase of *Chicago Tribune Magazine* that, while in high school, he wanted desperately to be an actor. He performed in a number of school productions and at sixteen managed to obtain a part in a long-running Broadway show. He says he felt "like a kid running away to the circus" ("Ludlum, Robert," in *Current Biography* 248). In 1943 he played Sterling Brown in *Junior Miss* by Jerome Chodorov and Joseph Fields, and joined the play's national touring company later the same year. He played Haskell Cummings in the same play on tour, in 1943–1944.

At the onset of World War II, while *Junior Miss* was playing in Detroit, Michigan, Ludlum crossed over to Toronto to enlist in the Royal Canadian Air Force. Clearly underage, he was rejected. He recalls filling out the papers for training as an aircraftsman when a sergeant major shouted his false name; his hesitant "Yes, er, no" answer ended his pretense and his enlistment chances (Baxter and Nichols 51). Upon graduating from Cheshire Academy, however, he forged his mother's signature to join the United States Marine Corps. He served two years (1944–1946) as an infantryman on duty throughout the Pacific, and spent three days assigned to combat intelligence before being transferred out. His military career was uneventful. Sent first to Mishima, Okinawa, and later stationed at the Pearl Harbor Transit Center, his duty assignment was that of librarian. Patricia Skarda describes the Ludlum of this period as "an impetuous, high-strung young man" (306).

The Marine Corps seems to have been a mixed experience for Ludlum. On the one hand, he was, by choice, fulfilling his patriotic duty. On the other hand, the tedium, the routine, and the authoritarian chain of command were not what he had expected when he enlisted. A private when he entered the Marine Corps, he was a private when discharged in 1947, a status Ludlum jokingly calls unique. The Corps did, however, help shape the mature adult and the writer he would become. It taught him enough judo to protect himself in barroom brawls and to enable him to teach it. It also taught him about weapons, large and small, injuries, and behavior under stress, all of which he later drew on for his novels. Ludlum wrote a book about his South Pacific experiences, but lost it while celebrating his discharge. He told Christopher Hunt of *Travel & Leisure* that he got "loaded" at San Francisco's Top of the Mark and woke up on the Oakland ferry, minus wallet, manuscript, and identification (126). He jokes wryly that his lost early adolescent novel was really *The Naked and the Dead.*

Ludlum enrolled as a theater major at Wesleyan University in Middletown, Connecticut. There he met his future wife, Mary Ryducha, from New Britain, Connecticut. He graduated with a B.A. degree and honors in theater in 1951, and received the New England Professor of Drama Award for his student efforts the same year. His memories of this time center on effective teachers, especially Ralph Pendleton, who insisted that Ludlum study the historical background of the plays he hoped to produce or perform in (Skarda 307). Pendleton also made Ludlum understand his own inadequacies as an actor through teaching him to look deeply at the play of language, image, and dramatic thrust in the works of playwrights like Lillian Hellman, Arthur Miller, and George Bernard Shaw. On March 31, 1951, shortly before graduation, Ludlum married Mary, to whom he later lovingly dedicated his first book—"For Mary: For all those reasons she must know so well." His love for Mary is ongoing, and she has shaped his image of the quiet, supportive heroine whose sensitivity, love, and courage provide the nurturing base Ludlum's heroes need to carry on.

## ACTING AND PRODUCING

After college Ludlum took up acting as a serious career endeavor and was moderately successful as a professional actor, performing both in regional theater and on Broadway. Ludlum and his wife (under the stage name of Mary Rydé) both performed in New England repertory theaters. Ludlum regularly performed stock parts in summer productions at the Canton Show Shop (Connecticut, 1952), the Ivoryton Playhouse (Connecticut, 1953), the Cragsmoor Playhouse (New York, 1954), and the Olney Theatre (Maryland, 1957). His New York roles included a soldier in Fritz Hochwalder's *The Strong are Lonely* (1952), the third messenger in Shakespeare's *Richard III* (1953), Spartacus in Robert Montgomery Bird's *The Gladiator* (1954), a policeman and later Cashel Byron in George Bernard Shaw's *The Admirable Bashville* (1956), and D'Estivel in Shaw's *Saint Joan* (1956). His steady work was in television production, however. He joined both the American Federation of Television and Radio Artists and the Screen Actors Guild, and appeared in two hundred television plays and productions for *Studio One, Kraft Television Theatre, Omnibus, Danger, Suspense,* and *Robert Montgomery Presents.* He was in *Treasury Men in Action* (1952), received awards and grants from the American National Theatre and Academy for various performances in minor roles (1959), and played featured roles as a murderer and a lawyer. Nonetheless, Ludlum was never given a highly demanding role and never achieved star recognition as an actor.

As a young actor, Ludlum was a "closet writer," who secretly wrote a number of television shows and plays in the hope of playing a role he had created; producers, however, repeatedly found him the wrong type for his own creations and he received no public recognition for these efforts (Kisor 24). Eventually bored with the actor's lack of control over his own role and over the integrity of the complete production, he sought more demanding work with wider choices for employing dramatic materials. Besides, he recalls, "a lot of people kept saying I would make a hell of a producer. I got the message: get off the stage" (Baxter and Nichols 51). By the late fifties, he left acting for producing. During this period his family was growing. His son Michael was born in 1952, and Jonathan the next year.

In 1956 he brought *The Owl and the Pussycat* and a revival of *The Front Page* to Broadway. *The Owl* starred an unknown actor named Alan Alda, later famous for his starring role in the television show *M\*A\*S\*H.* In 1957 Ludlum became the producer for the North Jersey Playhouse in Fort Lee, New Jersey. In 1960, with funding from the Actors Equity Association and the William C. Whitney Foundation, he established a successful theater in a suburban shopping center in Paramus, New Jersey—for which his name was entered on the Scroll of Achievement of the American National Theatre and Academy. The Playhouse on the Mall in Paramus was the first year-round shopping-center theater. It attracted an audience of more than 140,000 during its first eight months and featured Hollywood and Broadway stars as well as television personalities. Productions ranged from classics like *Hamlet* to the then scandalous *Who's Afraid of Virginia Woolf?* to the offbeat one–act plays *The Tiger* and *The Typist* of Murray Schisgal. The theater flourished through the sixties, and Ludlum produced more than 370 plays. His daughter Glynis was born in 1962.

Ludlum quickly discovered that avant-garde plays and daring productions frequently led to financial failure, and that successful producing meant a steady stream of old chestnuts. He would aim a string of conservative favorites at the lowest common denominator in order to finance the more intellectually and theatrically challenging plays. However, when he did produce something really good, he confesses, "you could shoot a moose in the lobby for all the people who ever came" ("Ludlum on Ludlum"). Furthermore, stage production meant distracting problems—everything from unions to lighting—that had nothing to do with the final product. Sick of such distractions and wanting more personal control over his materials and opportunities for greater creativity, in 1970, after twenty years in the theater—seven of them operating his own theater—Ludlum had had enough. "It was all make-believe," he said, "and I couldn't stand it anymore" (Block 25). Audiences didn't want to be challenged; they wanted the comfort of the familiar—preferably frivolous comedies. At the age of forty-two, Ludlum once again made a dramatic career change: he turned seriously to writing. The choice of the spy thriller genre allowed Ludlum to deal seriously with political concerns: to explore both international and national political movements and to play off contrastive political values (Russian versus American; hawk versus dove; conservative versus liberal). His wife encouraged him in this risky endeavor, telling him, "If you don't do it now, you're going to regret it as long as you live" (Kisor 24). Today Alan Alda jokes that Ludlum's skill in negotiating contracts and his inventive trick of "rattling papers into the phone" while claiming to have found a way to cut an actor in for a percentage should have been a clear indication of his potential skill at writing spy stories (Baxter and Nichols 51).

To support his family until he could make a living as a writer (his two sons were ready for college), he did television and radio commercial voice-overs. He was in demand to do dialects and advertised everything from Tiparillos to Tuna Helper. His wife laughingly calls him the king of toilet bowl commercials, for a three-word Plunge commercial done for a demo-tape—"Plunge works fast"—paid for his oldest son's second year of college. Ludlum jokes about this in *The Road to Omaha* (509), wherein the lead actor claims that his voice-over commercials, "including one for a rotten cat," sent one of his children through college, although he can't remember which one. After writing a successful first novel, Ludlum at first continued this lucrative sideline, supplementing his book royalties with voice-overs. His real goal, however, was to make writing his sole means of support.

## THE NOVELIST

Ludlum based his first novel, *The Scarlatti Inheritance* (1971), on the outline for a short story begun ten years before. Publishing a new author is always a gamble, and only after ten rejections did the book finally reach press. Henry Morrison, the New York literary agent who still handles Ludlum's books and who serves as the model for Ludlum's fictional agent in *The Chancellor Manuscript*, recognized the promise of this first effort and encouraged Ludlum to keep trying publishers until someone (in this case, World Publishing) accepted it. Morrison remains Ludlum's agent, and trusted friend; their agreements are sealed with a handshake, and strangers find Morrison in the role of the Minotaur who tenaciously guards Ludlum's privacy.

Despite attacks on the plot as "kitsch" (*Time* E3), the story as "lurid melodrama" (Levin 49), and the characters as thinly drawn, most critics recognized the novel's compelling power. Even as a neophyte writer, Ludlum knew how to create suspense and how to intrigue readers, and his storytelling skills have been praised by critics then and since. The book became an immediate best-seller and a Book-of-the-Month Club alternate selection. That success began a lucrative and satisfying career, which has brought Ludlum greater fame than his acting career ever did. He quickly followed his first book with two espionage thrillers set in suburban America, *The Osterman Weekend* (1972) and *The Matlock Paper* (1973). His books from this point on have been regularly at the top of the best-seller charts, with sales averaging 5.5 million copies and up.

By the mid-seventies his soaring success enabled him to write full-time, and his new income meant that he and his wife could travel widely, personally researching his novels and enjoying a new occupation. Paris quickly became a favorite city and the scene of some of Ludlum's most detailed descriptions. After *The Chancellor Manuscript* came out in 1977, the Ludlums, who had been living in Leonia, New Jersey, bought a two-hundred-year-old clapboard farmhouse on Long Island Sound in suburban Connecticut and had it sumptuously renovated. Then they bought a second home in Florida to escape the northern winters, swim, fish and play tennis. They enjoy a quiet life, visiting old friends—among them, Jason Robards and, until his death, Pat O'Brien—as well as professors from the local universities. Acquaintances describe Ludlum as "friendly but somewhat reserved," with a "self-deprecating manner" (Baxter and

Nichols 50); he is a charming raconteur, amusing but committed to se-rious political concerns. He is a family man, devoted to his wife and three children. (His son Michael, a classical guitarist, heads two orches-tras, performs, records, and teaches privately. Jonathan became a pilot and a successful entrepreneurial businessman, commanded a Colorado Search and Rescue Team, and now works as a financial consultant. Glynis studied music at Vassar and Northeastern in Massachusetts and works in the field of music.)

Success gave Ludlum the means to live well and the freedom to travel, but did not change his life much—at least not at first. People did not know his face and did not bother him in public, but his writing even-tually brought out the "crazies" and threats to his children necessitated precautions to safeguard his family. Impressed by the stunning white-sand beaches of the Caribbean, the Ludlums vacationed so regularly that they finally bought a house in St. Thomas. However, they found life there too seductive. They still visit, but Ludlum finds it easier to concentrate in less enchanting places.

Ludlum initially was comfortable doing promotional appearances, but by 1988 their toll in time and energy—a forty-day, thirty-seven-city od-yssey for one book—made him try publicity tapes instead. For *Icarus Agenda*, a two-hour interview with Dick Cavett resulted in a publicity tape broken into 2- or 4-minute clips distributed to seventy-five cities (Flashner 32). Thus, he could meet publicity needs conveniently, without loss of time.

Ludlum has no pretensions to being a documentarian or a historian; first and foremost he is "a storyteller." "I use imagination to build certain forces to credibility," he says, and adds, "I always work from the what-if-syndrome. It's fun" (Kisor 24). He is a workaholic, finishing one book only to begin another, but he enjoys the creative experience: "That's the most joyous part, when locks begin to fall into place" (25). Today "one of the most popular living authors [writing] in the English language" (Baxter and Nichols 50), he is a household name, with books sold in every drugstore and airport.

## THE INFLUENCE OF LUDLUM'S ACTING EXPERIENCE ON HIS WRITING

Ludlum the writer has learned a lot from his experience as actor and producer, especially how to involve his audience, hold their attention, and whet their appetite for more. Acting taught him a great deal about characterization, about setting a scene, and about how a good story works. It also taught him discipline, and a willingness to rewrite what does not work. He believes that theater people in general are more "willing to make changes and explore alternate routes" and that they do not confuse "initial inspiration with Holy Writ" (Block 26). Understanding Ludlum the writer means understanding Ludlum the actor, in love with the stage and theatrics.

The conversations of his characters echo the dramatic patterns of stage diction. His heroes are not the silent men of Hollywood stardom—like Gary Cooper or Clint Eastwood—men of glum expressions and a nod or two. Instead, they talk to themselves and to others, and punctuate their action with expressions of shock or outrage: "Oh, my God!," "Madness!," "Insanity!" Ludlum acts out all of his characters as he writes them. Having acted in and produced plays by George Bernard Shaw, Ludlum uses Shaw as a touchstone for defining his artistic goals. He believes with Shaw that leaving an audience in shock effectively gets a point across, but advises tempering shock with entertainment to make readers come back for more (Kisor 24). Thus, Ludlum balances serious concerns with the familiar genre patterns that sell books.

Ludlum's talks with intelligence officers confirmed his sense that good spies must be good actors, and that sometimes they may be so lost in professionally assumed roles that they become confused about their genuine identity—a fact he makes effective use of in the Bourne series. A key strategy of his secret agents, both amateurs and professionals, is to use acting trade stratagems to create disguises. His killers adopt the clothing and demeanor of ordinary workers—painters, telephone repairmen, delivery men—to enter a building unnoticed; his heroes on the run dye their hair, don fake mustaches, alter their gaits, and change body language to evade pursuers. Sometimes the disguises are intentionally theatrical—an expensive and rather outrageous white coat, a colorful neck scarf, and a large felt hat pulled low over the face—to facilitate a switch while the "tail" concentrates on the highly visual details of dress. Other times, minor changes prove significant. Master illusionist Jason Bourne, for example, without either props or make-up to assist him, simply thinks through a character role he plans to adopt—the appropriate walk, stance, gestures, and facial expressions—and then moves into the part: a young man of action is suddenly transformed into the old and frail or the bookish and nonthreatening. The theatrical training of a master spy, David Spaulding, helps him read faces, judge reliability and honesty, and dissemble—skills that save his life. Ludlum's military men define skill at disguises as "adaptability" and "protective coloration," as do his international terrorists; one of them so skillfully shifts her roles that her determined pursuer has a passionate affair with her, unaware of her true identity.

Theater and acting metaphors are an integral part of Ludlum's thinking and writing. To capture the difficulty of maintaining a deep-cover operation role, Ludlum compares the agent to "an actor in a never-ending play": one wrong move can "bring the curtain down" (Kisor 24). His Secretary of State in *The Road to Omaha* is enchanted that "actors can be anybody they want to be" (289) and can convince other people that they are not who they really are; the concept inspires him to create a task force of actors to take on the toughest tasks of espionage. Another *Omaha* character describes actors as "the most bled and most misunderstood human beings on the face of the earth—especially when unemployed" (307). Other characters speculate on soldiers as actors without proper professional training for the parts they must play (367), and on the ties between art and life. One suggests wars mounted as "civilized productions," with the armies made up of actors, the action choreographed, and an "international academy of the theatrical arts" set up to judge the merits of "the individual and collective performances" (366–67).

The strong cinematic quality of Ludlum's novels no doubt reflects his long experience with production. Asked if he ever wanted to act in a movie version of one of his own novels, Ludlum self-deprecatingly laughed, "Oh, no, I want them to be successful" (Klemesrud 38).

## LUDLUM'S WRITING PROCESS

A serious storyteller and entertainer whose style has always been popular with readers and difficult to duplicate, Ludlum spends long hours to produce an intense final product, cutting, revising, and sometimes writing four or five drafts. He has worked to remove the staccato sentences, one-sentence paragraphs, liberal use of exclamation points, italics, sentence fragments, rhetorical questions, and mixed metaphors reviewers complained of, realizing that many of these early, discarded techniques were attempts to bridge the gap between the nuances and inflections of the stage and the flat tonalities of the novel. With so many successes behind him, rewriting is now less arduous for Ludlum, and reviewers are kinder. Nonetheless, most of his novels still take at least three drafts: one to get down the ideas, another to cut and focus them, and a final version to polish the writing and produce a clean, crisp text. He told Lawrence Block in 1977 that he found rewriting a time-consuming "agony" and hoped to someday complete a book in one or two drafts (26). Today, he sees revision as inevitable and necessary, and good writing as an ongoing process, a struggle to capture nuance and meaning. Furthermore, he feels committed to his readers and is proud of writing in a suspense novel tradition. "I've got to be as good as I can be for the people who buy my books," he told Henry Kisor in 1982 (25).

Ludlum's writing schedule is rigorous. His wife affectionately calls him "Bobby Dawn" because he is an early riser (he usually gets up between 4:15 and 4:30 A.M.). After feeding his cats, walking his dog (like his 1980s golden retriever Jasper), and drinking his coffee, he gets to work before 5 A.M. and works straight through until 10 or 11 A.M. He tries to reduce distractions and concentrate fully during this period. After five to seven hours he begins to tire, but with an hour's rest he is ready to review his morning's efforts. The rest of the afternoon and evening he relaxes, but his mind is still focused on the direction and plotting of his novel. He told Skarda that he conscientiously edits out overly melodramatic phrases and overly sentimental sections (308). He goes to bed early (8 or 9 P.M.). While in the midst of a book, he follows this schedule seven days a week in order not to break the flow of his developing narrative (Block 26). With this schedule, he can turn out an average of 2,000 words (approximately ten pages double-spaced) a day (Kisor 25).

When he began his writing career, he relied on a yellow pad and pencil, and scribbled away in hotel rooms and aboard planes. He even jotted down ideas that came suddenly while driving, but a near car accident convinced him to switch to a cassette recorder. He writes wherever ideas strike him, and prefers the convenience of a yellow legal tablet to a typewriter or computer. That way, he says, nothing stands between him and his writing. His wife typed his first three novels, but he hired a typist once his royalties began coming in.

Ludlum's novels begin with an idea that provokes or disturbs him. He thinks "arresting fiction is written out of a sense of outrage" (Block 26). Consequently, he searches for an "underpinning of reality" (26), a recent event where the official explanation might hide a very different reality— a possible conspiracy beneath the surface. He asks, "What would happen if someone was given extraordinary power in an unelected position, as Henry Kissinger was during the Watergate crisis?" or what if "certain secretaries of defense" took on more than their defined responsibilities? (Kisor 24). He looks at the U.S.-aided overthrow of the freely elected Allende government in Chile, for example, and speculates about levels of State Department involvement, pushing what is known into the realm of "what if." Ludlum believes that this approach provides his efforts immediacy and realism, and allows a personal statement about political or historical matters. His formula, he told Kisor, is "ounces of truth" and "pounds of fiction" generated by an "active imagination" (24). His topics are the nightmare possibilities behind the headlines:

- The Nazi legacy perpetuated in modern German youth organizations (*The Holcroft Covenant*, 1978; *The Apocalypse Watch*, 1995);

- The amorality of international financiers (*The Scarlatti Inheritance*, 1971; *Trevayne*, 1973; *The Cry of the Halidon*, 1974);

- Drugs on campus, pushed by admired authority figures (*The Matlock Paper*, 1973);

- The vulnerability of public figures (the Pope in *The Road to Gandolfo*, 1975; the American president in *The Scorpio Illusion*, 1993);

- The Nazi-like methods of J. Edgar Hoover, his possible assassination, and his secret blackmail list (*The Chancellor Manuscript*, 1977);

- The conflict between hawks and doves in the late 1960s and early 1970s (*The Gemini Contenders*, 1976);

- The rise of international terrorism (*The Matarese Circle*, 1979; *The Bourne Identity*, 1980; *The Scorpio Illusion*, 1993);

- The rise of fanatical cabals (*The Parsifal Mosaic*, 1982; *The Aquitaine Progression*, 1984);

- CIA activities in Southeast Asia (*The Bourne Supremacy*, 1986);

- Censorship in China and a Hong Kong threatened by the Red Chinese (*The Bourne Ultimatum*, 1990);

- The question of American Indian lands and Indian militancy (*The Road to Omaha*, 1992).

In general, his villains are secret groups that wield power behind the scenes and negate a democratic heritage, whether they are the Mafia or other crime organizations, multinational big businesses and monopolies, or the more traditional "bad guys" of spy fiction—terrorists, fanatics, Fascists, and Communists. Ludlum's signature three-word titles sound like code names used to shut out those not privy to the conspiracies they define and the secrets they convey.

After choosing a general topic, Ludlum reads current news reports and personal memoirs to acquire a solid factual base and the perspective of actual on-the-scene participants (Block 26). He consults training manuals, books on weapons, and "tradecraft" about the techniques of espionage. With three former college roommates in intelligence (one is the Inspector General of the CIA) and members of British MI-6 among his acquaintances, he sounds out experts in clandestine organizations or operations about their work. Of course, such people tend to be reticent, but when he theorizes about possibilities, they will say "yes" or "no," or maybe even criticize an idea as too simple or too silly, although Ludlum quips that they never say a hypothetical conspiracy idea is "too complex." In fact, as he demonstrates in his plots, "complexity" is the essence of the espionage game. With facts at his fingertips, he then speculates about how he would behave or would like to behave in certain situations.

Ludlum has hopscotched the globe to verify descriptive details and to capture mood and place. His travels provide verisimilitude, as does using foreign words appropriate to his characters. Ludlum prides himself on his use of French, Italian, and Spanish, and finds that in real life a smattering of a foreign language opens doors to useful sources of local information. He remembers his and Mary's first trip to Paris, and his first attempt to communicate with a Frenchman in French. Shaking with trepidation, he approached a newspaper kiosk and asked the attendant for a postcard of Paris (*Monsieur, s'il vous plait, donnez-moi la carte de Paris*); instead of the rebuff he feared, he received congratulations on his worthy effort at communication (Hunt 126). Since then, he has frequently employed international vocabulary in his novels, particularly French, German, Italian, Chinese, and Russian.

The more successful his novels, the more time Ludlum and his wife have spent visiting scenes of future action to experience ambience and local color. In one embarrassing early instance (in *The Aquitaine Progression*), failure to check a Paris location resulted in a confusion of Sacre Coeur with Notre Dame; Ludlum has been very cautious ever since to be accurate about place and scene. A visit to the former residence of the late J. Edgar Hoover (in 1974, two years after his death) while seeking background information for *The Chancellor Manuscript* resulted in an eerie experience with government agents emerging from the bushes and questioning his right to take Polaroid pictures; eventually they accepted his story that he was considering buying the house (Klemesrud 38). Furthermore, travel meant for vacations has frequently turned into working travel. For instance, the Palatine gate in Rome inspired Ludlum to include it in *The Parsifal Mosaic*, while a visit to the Greek island of Mykonos so overwhelmed him with the blinding white light reflected on the waterfront and the intense white of its sunlit buildings that in his next book, *The Aquitaine Progression*, he included both daytime and nighttime chases through the island's twisting streets (Hunt 126). He enhances his memory of terrain with photographs he takes of possible location spots— as he did in Corsica. Amsterdam, Geneva, Rio de Janeiro, Rome, New York, Washington, and, of course, Paris recur in his fiction.

Once he has the germ of an idea, Ludlum prepares an outline that fuses fiction and reality. At the same time he draws on his acting experience to develop a believable central character, one based on how he personally would (or would like to) react in the fictionalized circumstances. He tinkers with and expands the outline to perhaps a hundred pages. Then, with a clear concept of what he is doing and where he is going, he puts it away and sometimes never looks at it again or looks at it only briefly. The process of outlining parallels a process Ludlum followed as an actor: breaking a play into dramatic units (many of his novels follow a three-act play formula) in order to understand its direction, dimensions, and dynamics. As an actor, once he had a handle on the story—its movement, character, and essence—he could then concentrate on his acting performance. As a writer, producing an outline gives him a handle on his fictive creation, so he can concentrate on telling his story. The result is that his novels always have the same thrust as his outline, but not always the same plot specifics.

## THE INFLUENCE OF OTHER WRITERS

As a youth attending a strict Episcopalian preparatory school, Ludlum's earliest readings were the Bible and the *Book of Common Prayer*, as well as the usual childhood stories, like the Hardy Boys and Tom Brown. The adventure stories of Sir Walter Scott were early favorites, replaced as he matured by Leo Tolstoy's *War and Peace*, Fyodor Dostoyevsky's *The Brothers Karamazov*, and the novels of Alexandre Dumas and Charles Dickens, whose works he considered a special pleasure (Bandler 2). Ludlum attributes his ability at juggling numerous characters to the lessons he learned from the masterful plotting of these authors. In prep school, he discovered contemporary writers like Ernest Hemingway, F. Scott Fitzgerald, Robert Penn Warren, John Steinbeck, and John Dos Passos.

As a young Marine, Ludlum used his Pearl Harbor duty assignment as librarian to immerse himself in history: the Greeks, the Romans, the Middle Ages, the Renaissance, and eighteenth-century diarists Samuel Pepys and James Boswell. He read straight through Edward Gibbon's *Decline and Fall of the Roman Empire*, a feat of which he is still proud, and then progressed chronologically to the twentieth century and William Shirer's *Rise and Fall of the Third Reich*, a work that strongly affected his vision of politics.

Later, while in college at Wesleyan, a teacher whom he admired stirred his interest in the poetry and plays of T. S. Eliot; Ludlum went on to read other moderns: Maxwell Anderson, William Saroyan, Lillian Hellman, Sidney Kingsley, Arthur Miller, and George Bernard Shaw. He confided to Bandler that Shaw seized his imagination and that he read everything Shaw had written: "He's fantastic—a man who broke all of his own rules" (2). He quotes Shaw's advice, "if you want to get your point across, give your adversary as swift and as good an argument as you can," and argues that that is exactly what he strives for in his own writing. Ludlum attributes the success of his conflict dialogue to Shaw, and is amused that it has sometimes worked so effectively that critics have erroneously taken the powerful arguments of his right-wing fanatics to reflect Ludlum's deep personal commitment, when in fact he is what he calls a "limousine liberal." He had, he notes, simply tried to present "as fine an argument" as he could (Bandler 2). As an actor and a producer, Ludlum continued to explore the conventions of the theater and to find in stage dialogue the rhythms and patterns he would later use to engage and hold his readers' interest. "Plays help the novelist understand what works in dialogue and what doesn't," he told Bandler, and went on to add that if dialogue doesn't work in the theater, "you close on Saturday and join the unemployment line on Monday!" (2). Shakespearean plays like *Othello, Hamlet,* and *Richard III,* with their conspirators, spies, and complicated stratagems, were also an inevitable part of the theater experience that influenced Ludlum's later novels.

In his fifties, his career as a novelist firmly established, Ludlum continued to read voraciously, particularly history. At the time of the Bandler interview (April 1982), he had just finished *The Memoirs of the Duc de Saint-Simon* about the court of Louis XIV at Versailles, Dean Acheson's *Among Friends*, Carl Schorske's *Fin de Siècle Vienne*, and Henri Troyat's *Catherine the Great*. When he was interviewed by Baxter and Nichols he was reading *The Conspiracy and Death of Lin Baio* (52), and when I spoke to him in 1996 he was reading Colin Powell's *An American Journey*. He finds Barbara Tuchman's *A Distant Mirror* intellectually challenging, and recommends all of Winston Churchill's histories: "Such drama! Such use of words! . . . such magnificent b.s.!'' (Bandler 8). Ludlum's greatest fascination is with the period of the two world wars, the Roosevelt-Churchill relationship, and the peripheral socioeconomic developments. While his canon reflects his deep interest in twentieth-century politics, earlier histories remain influential. For instance, the classical and definitive work on manipulative statecraft, Niccolò Machiavelli's *The Prince* (1513), provides a touchstone for the kind of governance that Ludlum deplores: pragmatic, self-serving, anti-democratic, secretive, manipulative of individuals, willing to use violence to stay in power. Ludlum's agents operate in an updated version of this environment.

As a research tool to assist his writing, Ludlum relies on David Kahn's *The Codebreakers*, a definitive work on cryptology. He takes to heart William Stevenson's argument in *A Man Called Intrepid* that all deep-cover intelligence is just an extension of the imagination under severe stress. Consequently, when his threatened hero must act decisively (in situations Ludlum himself has never experienced), he follows Stevenson's advice and speculates imaginatively about how his hero can respond credibly.

Ludlum finds invention easier if the ideas and plots of those writing in the same genre don't interfere with his own creativity. Consequently, he reads little spy fiction, except for some early John le Carré and Len Deighton. He calls le Carré's books marvelous, but admits he does not rush out to buy them; since he committed himself to writing full-time, he has not kept up with the competition. Instead, his portrayal of paranoia goes back to his literary roots: Dickens, Dostoyevsky, Shakespeare, Tolstoy, Dumas, Hugo.

## LUDLUM TODAY

In 1994, Ludlum entered the Emergency Clinic at Norwalk Hospital, Connecticut, and underwent cardiothoracic surgery (a triple bypass) at the Yale-New Haven Hospital, where his nephew is a surgeon. He thanks a fine team of surgeons, family support, and the overall good humor of his wife and children for his survival; he returned to writing during his convalescence. In 1996 his wife became ill and spent a great deal of time under medical care. As of 1996 his novels have been published in thirty-two languages and forty countries, and worldwide sales have exceeded 100 million copies. Ludlum is presently working on a sequel to *The Matarese Circle*, entitled *The Matarese Countdown*, set twenty-five years later, with lead characters Bray and Antonia once again teaming up with a Russian. Reprising his early role as a commercial spokesman, Ludlum recently was featured in an American Express commercial on board the Orient Express, parodying the settings and heroes of his spy thrillers.

Ludlum now spends his time doing what he loves best: traveling with his wife Mary, visiting his offspring, boating and fishing in the Caribbean, and writing books that carry his warnings to heed history, to beware of tyrants and intolerance, and to not give up on the power of the individual to make a difference. He would like to be remembered for doing the best he could with what he had, entertaining his audiences but also leaving them with lessons about democratic values—particularly tolerance.

# 2

# Robert Ludlum's Literary Roots

We are alone. We are committed to the tenets of individual combat and there is no help for him who fails. Save a life and we save a man who will later watch us through the cross-hairs and squeeze the trigger if he gets the orders or the chance. It's no go.

The car burned and the man screamed and I sat watching.

We are not gentlemen.

Quiller in Adam Hall, *The Quiller Memorandum*

Robert Ludlum attributes his skill as a writer in part to his fascination with reading, and advises young people interested in a writing career to read voraciously. His acting experience provided him with a sense of dialogue, pacing, anticipation, and surprise, as well as facility at creating credible conversational and argumentative give-and-take. In addition to these performance-based technical skills, Ludlum learned from the great novelists of the past two centuries about structuring long novels and controlling a plot that sweeps across broad landscapes. Nonfictive historical works have given him interesting stories and plot lines and have inspired him to think deeply about issues and themes significant in his novels; history lends his work depth, providing past patterns that make present events explored in his novels more credibly menacing. The generic conventions of espionage fiction provide him a particular framework in which to create. A liberal's outrage at the violation of human rights and dignity by big government and multinational conglomerates, a fear of conspiracies, and an empathy with paranoid suspicions add a personal intensity and commitment to his fiction, which appeals to a broad-based readership that shares his worries.

## MODERN LITERARY PRECURSORS

Although Ludlum reads fewer spy stories than histories, his novels of national and international intrigue benefit from a rich American and British literary heritage of detective, crime, and espionage fiction, whose roots may be traced to the nineteenth century. The writers in these traditions have firmly established a set of conventions, attitudes, and themes on which their literary heirs, including Ludlum, build.

### Detective and Crime Fiction

Although they are neither detective nor crime fiction, Ludlum's novels reflect some characteristics of these genres. His protagonists detect evil tenaciously, making rational and intuitive judgments based on experience and observation, and sometimes even solving intellectual puzzles. Like private detectives, they are forced by circumstances to pursue villains when the law cannot or will not. They care about individuals, and help the weak and the innocent. When order and community are disrupted by plots and conspiracies, and the familiar and safe is transformed into the sinister and unfamiliar, decent men and women leading ordinary lives become reluctant heroes, championing the basic values of democracy, justice, individual worth, decency, loyalty, honor, and responsibility. Like detective fiction novelist Ross Macdonald, Ludlum is intrigued by the psychoses and neuroses that drive modern man; his studies of social guilt show the individual being tainted as well, and suffering accordingly.

Ludlum draws from the crime novel an interest in criminal and deviant psychology, a concern for the narrow separation between the investigator or pursuer and the criminal or pursued, and the sense of a menacing, seemingly irrational world in which the innocent is forced into criminal acts in order to survive and prevail. In the Bourne series, for example, amnesia produces a psychological identification with the criminal that leads the protagonist (Bourne) to doubt his own responses and to fear that he is in fact the master criminal whom he believes he is pursuing. Bourne's instinct for violence, his readiness to kill in self-defense, and his empathy with the criminal mind, which allows him to second-guess his prey, seem proof of his complicity. Although ultimately he destroys his nemesis, like so many "innocents" in the crime novel, Bourne has been tainted by guilt and cannot face his past and its implications. As in the crime novel, social and personal guilt intertwine, and shades of gray dominate.

## The Spy Novel

Ludlum merges the formulaic patterns of detective and crime fiction with those of spy thrillers to create a richly textured amalgam that draws on several genres, thus providing variety, suspense, and surprise.

Although one might trace the roots of the spy story back to adventure stories of disguise such as Rudyard Kipling's *Kim* (1901)—in which British officers in local garb spy on potential enemies of the British Raj—the spy fiction genre is a modern invention, a product of World Wars I and II, the Cold War, and, more recently, industrial espionage. Since intelligence operations exist to learn the secrets of and to undermine other nations, particularly ideological opponents, espionage is tightly bound to political and economic theories and commitments.

*Genre Characteristics of the Spy Novel.* The genre characteristics of the spy novel are highly stylized. Common plot patterns are the search for the hidden spy, the hunter-hunted spy chase, the spy who comes in from the cold, the good spy on a secret mission beset by problems, the good spy's discovery that the enemy is one of his superiors, the journey into nightmare, and the countdown to disaster. There may be assassinations, attempted assassinations, or abductions; chase scenes and evasion tactics with close calls and narrow escapes; interrogations involving torture, chemical persuasion, or psychological games of various sorts; captured agents exchanged for other agents or information; disguises, drops (leaving key documents or information in hidden spots to be retrieved by other agents), misinformation, shadowing opponents or tagging them; counterspies, double or even triple agents, defectors, plants or moles, and various forms of turnabouts and betrayals; neutrals (the innocent) who are eliminated or recruited; and female lures, tempting agents to their destruction. These elements are all part of the spy novel's repertoire. Confrontations explode into violence, while a single individual sees the ordered pattern behind the surface chaos and confusion. Le Carré, for example, captures this moment of insight as his rogue agent Smiley, in *Call for the Dead* (1961), maneuvers the characters with whom he has been dealing "like pieces in a puzzle, twisting them this way and that to fit the complex framework of established facts"; the pattern that emerges transforms "an academic exercise" into "a game no more" (128–29). John G. Cawelti and Bruce Rosenberg, who label our century "the Age of Clandestinity," discuss such genre patterns throughout their critical study *The Spy Story* (1976).

In fiction, professional spies rely on forged identity papers, plastic surgery, intense training, and a support network to pass as fictitious persons. A "plant," "sleeper," or "mole" is an agent carefully positioned within a target organization or region with a convincing cover until called upon to demonstrate loyalty to the motherland; of course, too long a residence in a foreign country may produce foreign tastes and changed loyalties. An "insider" or "recruit" is a member of the spied-upon government or organization who—for money, revenge, political ideology, love, excitement, or fear of blackmail—shifts loyalties and provides information on a regular basis. These recruits are often essential to a successful espionage organization, but are unreliable. If bought by one side, they can be bought by another, as double agents.

The most popular spy of modern fiction is the solitary intelligence agent engaged in either espionage or counterespionage. His cunning and skill allow him to penetrate an organization or a region to gather intelligence information to further the cause, the nation, or the political ideology for which he stands. If caught, he might die, but he puts aside the possibility of personal injury to do what he thinks is best. Often the hero agent is assigned a Control, who keeps abreast of his activities, serves as a go-between with the intelligence agency for whom he works, and helps develop and carry through plans at a distance. This Control, however, is traditionally unreliable, and ultimately the agent must depend on his own resources and resilience to survive.

Counterespionage, the thwarting of hostile espionage, may involve actively identifying and pursuing the opposition to recover information, secret weapons, nuclear materials, or kidnapped victims, or to prevent disclosure of secret information; it may also involve less glamorous activities, like turning the spies of a rival nation into double agents who channel misinformation back to their original employers. Whether they work for pay, personal revenge, or loyalty to a country or an idea, spies are almost always lonely outsiders, susceptible to fear, paranoid about betrayal, suspicious of all around them, and forced by necessity to rely on instinct and experience, to act decisively, and to expect the worst. Quite apart from the many real spies who have appeared during the twentieth century as intelligence and technology have become determinants of success or failure in warfare, it is easy to see why the spy story, like detective fiction, has enjoyed such phenomenal popularity in modern times. The spy, alienated and psychologically multifaceted while appearing perfectly conventional on the surface, is a made-to-order figure for the modernist sensibility.

Ludlum creates a world of intelligence gatherers, moles, insiders, and double agents from many nations, all spying on each other, precipitating acts of violence, and endangering the lives of ordinary citizens. His amateurs begin with ideals and commitments, but his professionals have been tainted by their vocations and are more willing to believe that the end justifies the means. Some no longer believe in their cause or simply leave the thinking to their superiors. Others struggle to determine where to draw the line between personal morality/responsibility and national duty. Ludlum's creations reflect the development of the spy story from a simple tale of good combating evil to a complex world of shifting allegiances and moral ambiguity, in which villain and hero share traits and sometimes sensibilities. The change in the spy story simulates and parallels changes in belief in the twentieth century: from patriotic belief when the world was divided sharply into contrasting camps, to confusion, anomie, and loss of faith at the end of the millennium.

Ludlum builds on these past conventions, capturing a world of conflicting loyalties and ideologies, of betrayal and confused moralities, where friends seem foes and longtime foes become trusted allies against younger, more unscrupulous opponents; at the same time, however, he also suggests a solid moral base beneath the morass, a middle-American center where love, loyalty, and right somehow continue to exist.

*The Evolution of the Spy Novel.* The spy novels of World War I and II have a clear-cut enemy, and agents risk imprisonment, torture, and a firing squad to get information vital to the war effort—because it is right to do so. An early spy story, John Buchan's *The Thirty-Nine Steps* (1915) postulates an underground German spy ring out of Scotland by way of a London vaudeville act: the enemy is among us. Geoffrey Household's classic thriller *Rogue Male* (1939) shares the sense of moral right inherent in the spy novels of this period: an English sportsman attempts to shoot a central European dictator (obviously Hitler) to avenge the murder of his fiancée by secret police and is pursued to England, where he literally goes underground. In Helen MacInnes's spy novels World War II moral patterns carry over into the Cold War. MacInnes warned in *Above Suspicion* (1941) about the nightmare building in Nazi Germany—the political thugs who destroyed human beings for expediency, ambition, or ideology—and continued to pit ordinary, decent men and women against the faceless agents of totalitarian regimes throughout her canon. The realties of the time infused her novels with a moral integrity impossible in today's spy stories. Despite her post–World War II shift to Communist villians, MacInnes, like Ludlum, argues compellingly that Americans cannot ignore politics, but must defend their received values in the crucible of conflict. Her basic pattern of hunter and hunted, her chases through exotic locations with time-tables and countdowns to disaster, and her overriding sense of worldwide conspiracy clearly laid the groundwork for Ludlum's thrillers.

In the main, however, the morality of most Cold War stories is more ambiguous than that of MacInnes's fiction. In an interview with MacInnes in *Counterpoint*, Roy Newquist argues that the progression of the suspense story has come to assume "a character its early practitioners would scarcely associate with the metièr," for the "arts of sleuthing" and the "rambunctiousness of derring-do" have been joined with a "studied, realistic approach to the temper and pace of the vast world of international relations" (458). Usually, as Soviet, British, and American agents compete for scientific secrets, war game strategies, and insider knowledge, the moral stances shade into gray. Eric Ambler and Graham Greene create shadowy worlds in which the black-and-white morality of earlier spy novels is replaced by ambiguity. Ambler's teams of spies are interchangeable and not very likable; the acts they engage in and the services they render are of dubious value. Greene's spies inhabit a world of moral doubt and guilt, with moral certainty becoming a sure sign of extremism or fanaticism. Modern ambivalence about spies is summed up by Ian Fleming's James Bond series which features a ruthless, cultured daredevil. Suave, debonair, and on the side of right, Bond is nonetheless ready to maim and kill in inventive ways large numbers of villains in order to protect democracies.

John le Carré captures the intellectual challenge of espionage, but also the isolation of agents and the painful confusion of betrayal and divided loyalties. Amid triple agents and double crosses, the Control or Secret Service head in le Carré's novels is unscrupulous and unfeeling; he takes calculated risks that might expose and kill an agent. Le Carré writes of "cold warriors" engaged in "looking-glass wars" presided over by civil servants and corporate managers; in his stories the organization men are outmaneuvered and outwitted by his key protagonist, George Smiley. Smiley is a scholar, a humanist, a detective, and a hunter; his personal life is a shambles, but his skill lies in accumulating information and using his network of loyal former government employees to take the pulse of the opposition and to ferret out the secrets of both sides.

Len Deighton follows in le Carré's footsteps, but adds humor and satire to suspense as he explores the pretensions of "old boy" networks and dilettante civil servants, as well as the interdepartmental competitions that drive espionage. Deighton's novels work against the spy novel tradition, parodying and mocking, providing new perspectives of opposing ideologies, and debunking sacred cows such as Winston Churchill and public-school aristocrats. His works celebrate the competence, professionalism, and humanity of the rank-and-file spy. The protagonist of *The Ipcress File* (1962) is typical: a cunning, adaptable rebel, competent and professional, but with a working-class cheekiness that keeps him an outsider. He is a streetwise loner caught up in internecine competition and double and triple crosses. Witty, irreverent, and deeply distrustful, he is a pawn put in play by scheming superiors.

In the post-perestroika years, the morality of fictional spies has become even more ambiguous. Ken Follett, for example, applies some crime novel conventions to the spy novel, manipulating readers to root for Nazi spies and assassins. The German spy of *Eye of the Needle* (1978) is well-rounded and understandable; contemptuous of the German high command and the National Socialist party, he saves St. Paul's Cathedral from bombing, and, during his escape, proves capable of sudden, deep love, but also of ruthless murder to preserve his mission. Clive Egleton's hard-hitting, cynical tales question the morality of the system and show the good dying for little cause, while the bad are rewarded for murder and mayhem. National security justifies unjustifiable sacrifices, and no one can be trusted. Model citizens prove sleepers and trusted agents with years of honest service prove turncoats. The only question is the degree of guilt, for double-dealing, violence, and treachery are the way of the world. In *The Eisenhower Deception* (1981) the British try to blackmail their American allies, while in *In the Red* (1993) the defection of real-life spies Guy Burgess and Donald Maclean confirms the moral ambiguity of the spy trade, as British intelligence finds justification for distrusting long-trusted agents. Egleton concentrates on professionals who are manipulated and abused, their integrity questioned, their survival simply an accident of the game. Top officials engage in cold, calculating games, in which their pawns are eliminated or endure on the basis of covert stratagems. Yet, Egleton's heroes remain men and women of conviction and courage, who act on conscience even if it means disobeying authority. The wronged central figure of *The Mills Bomb* (1978), Edward Mills, is typical. He hunts an enemy mole, directed by intelligence agents who think of him only as a lethal grenade to be exploded for agency purposes.

Ludlum works in the moral ambiguity of the Cold War and of the post-perestroika period, although at times his heroes and heroines express the values and loyalties enunciated by the clear-sighted and patriotic spies of World War II fiction.

## FILM AND TELEVISION MODELS

Ludlum's theater experience no doubt made him sensitive to the movie and television productions that grew out of spy novels or that built on their conventions. Television spy series were already popular in the fifties, with *I Led Three Lives* (1953), *O.S.S.* (1957), and later *Danger Man* (1961). *The Avengers* (1961), *The Saint* (1962), *The Fugitive* (1963), and *The Man from U.N.C.L.E.* (1964) followed, with *The Fugitive*, a conspiracy/chase story, in particular projecting themes Ludlum exploits: the innocent threatened, the betrayer from within, the individual up against conspiracy, and hard-nosed government agents abusing their powers. The full-length movies that are most in keeping with Ludlum's themes emerged in the sixties and seventies, Ludlum's formative years for generating the concepts and concerns that infuse his canon—although movies depicting the Cold War have remained popular into the nineties.

Films like *The Odessa File* (1974), *Marathon Man* (1976), and *The Boys from Brazil* (1978) bring to the screen the same nightmare possibility that Ludlum envisions: the continuation of the Third Reich underground. In *The Odessa File*, based on Frederick Forsyth's novel of the same title, a curious journalist on the trail of neo-Nazis investigates the paper trail recording the secret exit of Nazi officers and Nazi treasure to Argentina, while *The Boys from Brazil* follows Nazi fanatics to Brazil, where they plot to restore the Third Reich. Their method, the DNA cloning of Hitler, grows out of the official records of real Nazi experiments during the war. In *Marathon Man* an avid jogger is caught in a complex web of intrigue involving villainous Nazis still pursuing their dream of world conquest and a master race. These films are representative of a cinematic convention common since the end of World War II, the notion that the most destructive ideology of the twentieth century could come back to life, phoenix-like, in new environments. Although these three films are well made, the convention they rely on for their thrill of horror has been widely exploited.

The seventies, eighties, and nineties have seen a series of films based on conspiracy theories or the concept of secret realities behind public facades. Steven Johnson, in "Paranoid's Delight," calls the 1970s in particular a banner decade for paranoid films and names four films as the best of the period: *Klute* (1971), *The Conversation* (1974), *The Parallax View* (1974), and *Three Days of the Condor* (1975). These films all offer the paranoid as hero, with the seemingly unlikely fear turning out to be true. The heroes, far more perceptive than the average viewer, can spot the microphone hidden in a lamp shade and the click on the tapped phone: their heightened sensitivity to threat allows them a vision denied the rest of us. Often the plots of these films have confusing narratives (especially *The Parallax View*) and occasionally they are impenetrable; the tangle of hidden motive and agenda becomes impossible to sort out. Johnson argues that this is one of the pleasures of conspiracy stories: "all exits are false ones, and no single map accounts for the entire terrain."

In *The Parallax View* (1974) an investigative reporter probes a senator's death and discovers an assassination agency composed of political conservatives determined to control the political arena. The film suggests a conspiracy of generals, senators, and industrialists as the powers behind the assassination of John F. Kennedy. *Three Days of the Condor* captures the paranoid nightmare come to life of a CIA researcher whose investigation of a minor Arabic novel threatens a secret organization within the CIA. As a result his coworkers are murdered by unknown assassins, his own life is on the line, threatened not by foreign agents but by his own wary colleagues, and even the "free" press is revealed to be under the thumb of government agents. *All the President's Men* (1976) brings the Watergate conspiracy to the screen by focusing on *Washington Post* reporters Woodward and Bernstein.

Oliver Stone's films are typical of this filmic concern with conspiracy. *J.F.K.* (1991), for example, renews speculation about who really killed John F. Kennedy, explores New Orleans District Attorney Jim Garrison's investigation into the assassination, and, like *The Parallax View*, postulates a right-wing group of important conservatives disapproving of Kennedy's liberal stance on issues and using their power, wealth, and influence to dominate American politics. Like the rebirth of Nazism, the conspiracy by a rogue group in an established agency or by a cabal of the powerful has become a cliché of our times. The science-fiction thriller *Invasion of the Body Snatchers* (1956, remade in 1978, and remade for television in 1994) is the ultimate paranoid vision: small-town America being taken over by alien pod creatures that absorb body and mind when a human being sleeps and that replace the infinitely varied and unique human mind with a cold, emotionless, group mind that functions in an orderly, controlled way. Suddenly there is no juvenile delinquency, no crime, and no social conflicts, but there is also no love, no human emotion, and no uniqueness. This nightmare is a double fear: of an all-pervasive conspiracy perpetrated on unaware individuals and of the group-think mentality carried to the furthermost extreme of conformity. The fact that this film continues to be remade suggests that it and the novel on which it is based—Jack Finney's *The Body Snatchers*—touch a deep reservoir of fear in American culture.

Films portraying the secret world of spies and political betrayals seem countless and continue to multiply. The James Bond thrillers are popular both on video and as television reruns, and new films are regularly added to the series. In spite of the disappearance of the Soviet Union, Cold War films remain popular, with the best based on spy novels. High points in the genre include a mid-period Cold War film, *The Manchurian Candidate* (1962). Based on Richard Condon's riveting political espionage thriller of the same title, it established the possibilities of brainwashing and of the enemy within. A decorated Korean War hero returns home to find his stepfather running for U.S. president, and his monstrous mother a committed Communist dedicated to the overthrow of America; the young war hero has been programmed for an assassination that will guarantee his stepfather the presidency. Another psychological study of programming, *The Ipcress File* (1964), from the Len Deighton novel of the same title, stars Michael Caine as a cheeky young intelligence officer who resists brainwashing and destroys the mole in his own agency. This exciting film spawned the sequels *Funeral in Berlin* (1966) and *Billion Dollar Brain* (1967). In *The Spy Who Came in From the Cold* (1966), Richard Burton, a cynical and aging Cold War agent, helplessly observes his world disintegrating. *The Looking-Glass War* (1969), based on le Carré's best-seller, pits British intelligence against East German and Russian spies as the British try to recruit an AWOL Polish seaman to photograph East German missiles. The British miniseries of Deighton's *Game, Match, Set* and of le Carré's novels *Smiley's People; Tinker, Tailor, Soldier, Spy; The*

*Honourable School Boy;* and *The Perfect Spy*, were popular on the American Public Broadcasting System in the 1980s. Such thrillers emphasize action, chases, traps, and narrow escapes in pursuit of the spy, as well as duplicitous moles, amoral double agents, and murderous interdepartmental rivalries—all mainstays of Ludlum's novels.

## INDIVIDUALISM: THE PRIMACY OF THE DISCRETE SELF

At the heart of the detective or crime thriller is the idea that one person, the criminal, can challenge conventional morality and bring civilization to a halt, but also that one person of integrity, intelligence, instinct, and bravery can discover and surgically remove the cancer at the heart of a social structure, thus restoring health to the social body. In spy and conspiracy stories the individual dominates in opposition to what le Carré repeatedly calls the "soulless bureaucracies" that have gained power in the modern world. At the core of the spy story is the idea of large national or international organizations manipulating and controlling the fates of thousands, even millions, and of a lone spy or spy-detector neutralizing or damaging those threats to the little people of the world. Even when the conflict is between one spy organization and another, it is the lone wolf, the eccentric individualist like le Carré's Smiley who has the dogged determination to persist and prevail. Le Carré enunciates this conflict between the individual and the organization man while explaining why the protagonist of *Call for the Dead* struggles against the enemy whom the characters Dieter and Mundt epitomize:

> Everything he admired or loved had been the product of intense individualism. That was why he hated Dieter now, hated what he stood for more strongly than ever before: it was the fabulous impertinence of renouncing the individual in favor of the mass. When had mass philosophies ever brought benefit or wisdom? Dieter cared nothing for human life: dreamed only of armies of faceless men bound by their lowest common denominators; he wanted to shape the world as if it were a tree, cutting off what did not fit the regular image; for this he fashioned blank, soulless, automatons like Mundt. Mundt was faceless like Dieter's army, a trained killer born of the finest killer breed. (147–48)

The conflicting philosophies are "intense individualism" and "the mass"—"blank, soulless, automatons" of "faceless men." Ironically, even an organization whose end goal is good, by its very nature takes on an institutional behavior, requiring individuals to submit their talents to the will and the decisions of the institution. The institution offers security and belonging; in return, it demands sacrifice of self.

Ludlum, like le Carré, firmly believes in the power of the individual to shape, change, and save his nation, and perhaps the world: he calls the individual "paramount." His heroes not only uncover corruption; they root it out. An interesting cultural phenomenon is that Russian critics—reflecting the assumption of their culture that individual action is usually fruitless—dismiss Ludlum's plots as incredible and complain about his unrealistic portrait of strong individuals forced by circumstances to take action that immobilizes powerful, threatening organizations. For Western readers, however, this is a strength, not a weakness, because Ludlum argues a position vital to our concept of democracy and our social selves: individuals can make a difference; they can stand up to threatening, amoral, or immoral groups and, in cooperation with a few like-minded fellow individualists, can bring them down. Doing so might be at great personal cost, but doing so is right. Identity is found in discrete individuals, not in their connections to others.

Ludlum believes that a good hero is reluctant, forced by circumstances to overcome his own fear and to discover the best within himself. Typically, he is an educated, competent professional caught up in momentous events that anger and outrage him. Whether an academic, historian, accountant, or soldier, once thrust into action, he behaves heroically. Ludlum's definition is realistic: he portrays decent human beings who are pushed to the edge and find within themselves the determination and courage to successfully, even triumphantly, oppose tyranny. Having been made the unwilling tools of governments and corporations, such heroes fight back and, in doing so, sum up the hope and strength of a democracy: stubborn individuals who resist group pressure to conform, to ignore the deceptions around them, or to be bribed by position or wealth.

Sometimes Ludlum's heroes strike out blindly, but often their instincts are good. As the lone individual pits his intelligence and wit against a giant conspiracy, personal loyalties take precedence over national ones and an instinct for survival helps him stay one step ahead of his pursuers. Past events must be reinterpreted in the light of new understanding, past relationships reevaluated, and motives questioned. In other words, the seemingly distant schemes of a nebulous national or international organization make the hero vulnerable and force him to see his world with far more cynical eyes as the events become personal. Ludlum's innocents are doomed to repeat this movement from ignorance to knowledge, from naiveté to painful awareness, from innocence to culpability—and gain strength from it.

## THE PSYCHOLOGICAL FOCUS OF LUDLUM'S FICTION

Ludlum's novels, rooted in the Western cult of the individual, often analyze individual psychology. Ludlum draws on medical studies of neuroses and of psychopathic or disturbed personalities to demonstrate three recurring ideas:

1. the way organizations adopt the terminology of psychoanalysis—terms like *schizophrenia, divided or multiple personalities, paranoia*, and *personality disintegration*—to separate and alienate the individual from the group;

2. the way in which the individual is traumatized and disturbed by physical and emotional suffering;

3. the profound psychological effects of engaging in secret activities—psychological tension and a double, almost schizophrenic, vision of reality.

Ludlum shows organizations labeling individuals with authoritative, scientific-sounding psychoanalytical terms to make others question the sanity and credibility of those so labeled. (An extreme real-life example of this phenomenon, of course, was the Soviet government consigning dissidents to "treatment" in mental hospitals.) This method hits the individuals where they are most vulnerable: in their sense of self, their relationships with other individuals, and their understanding of reality. Oftentimes the battering of the individual involves the use of chemicals to try to brainwash or debrief them and the use of traumatic loss (the kidnapping or death of a loved one) to weaken their resolve.

Ludlum also shows how easy it is even for a strong individual to be led to doubt himself or herself, when all they have trusted and everyone they have believed in proves false, their "normality" becoming a false mask that hides a twisted inner reality. His heroes and heroines, how-

ever, are able to draw on the secret wells of human resilience, an inner
strength and will that allows individuals to battle their own neuroses
and psychoses and overcome their internal doubts and fears. Strengthened by their inner confrontation, they go on to battle and defeat the
ogres outside themselves: the megaorganizations that deny human values, undercut individuals, and accrue power and wealth for their own
sake. These are Ludlum's villains, who are overcome by his heroes and
heroines within the conventions of the spy genre.


## LUDLUM'S PARANOID HEROES

   Along with heightening the perfectly rational fear of strangers, complex urban civilization brings specialization of trade and craft, distinctions of social class, unique roles for some individuals, and government
in layered and hierarchical structures. This division inevitably alienates
groups from each other, making it harder for people with little shared
experience to understand the motives and agendas of others; just as inevitably, it arouses suspicions about some groups taking special advantage, exploiting others, or even mounting coups against the government.
In urban areas simple numbers allow potential enemies to be unseen and
diffuse: the alleged Powers Behind the Throne, the secret priesthood of
believers, the hermetic lodge of disciples, the arcane group of zealots
who meet in the forest by moonlight. Paranoia of this kind, however, is
as old as civilization itself, and, in moderation, performs the useful task
of alerting us to the potentially nefarious doings of others. This version
of psychological awareness, updated for civilized life, triggers the fight-
or-flight reflex under circumstances of physical violence. Citizens in a
society where no one suspects anyone else would be vulnerable to exploitation or takeover. Paranoia is a brake on the undisciplined self-
interest of powerful groups, a warning of trouble ahead: possible
miscreants should not go too far and should provide clear signals of
benign intention. (Reputedly, the handshake developed as a demonstra-
tion that no weapon was being held.) Degrees of fearfulness and trust,
nervousness and confidence are distributed along a wide range with var-
ying dimensions in different cultures and groups. Middle Eastern political life, for example, is notoriously paranoid, while Scandinavian politics
is not. The distinction between what is *extreme* and *irrational*—the medical definition of paranoia as delusion and sickness—and what is per-

ceptive and sophisticated depends on competing visions of how the world truly works, and here Ludlum offers much food for thought.

## KEY PATTERNS IN LUDLUM'S FICTION

Ludlum's novels rely on a repertoire of patterns that make the confrontation between individuals and organizations exciting. The first pattern is the hunt: the individual fleeing as the minions of the organization pursue in exciting urban and cross-country chases, with near misses and unexpected encounters that keep the reader on edge and confirm the power and organization of the enemy. The protagonist might enter a bank, for example, knowing that several supposed patrons are assigned to capture or kill him: how can he exit without injury and how can he recognize the faces of evil that surround him in the innocent landscape of ordinary folk pursuing ordinary concerns? Threatened on every side, he no longer knows whom to trust. Colleagues and friends may be part of the invisible web. Midway, the hunted stops running, analyzes the strategies and patterns of the opposition, turns the tables, and, in an exciting reversal of roles, becomes himself the hunter. As he pursues his prey to their lair, he develops effective strategies to defeat the seemingly undefeatable.

A second pattern teams the hero with a strong, supportive heroine who at first doubts his honesty, motives, and even sanity, but with time and proximity comes to recognize and appreciate his integrity and to commit herself to justice and to the exposure of whatever forces threaten. A third Ludlum pattern sets up a collision course early in the action, shifting scenes back and forth from hero to adversary, crosscutting as in a film. The action quickens; the scenes shorten; readers hurtle from villains to hero and back again, until the inevitable confrontation and denouement.

Another standard pattern starts with the hero's psychological disintegration, followed by his gradual healing and his final return to health. Psychological assessment is used as a weapon by the enemy, who labels the hero *schizophrenic* or *paranoid*—labels that make potential allies interpret his genuine fears as paranoid fantasies. In some cases, the hero doubts his own sanity, but confirmation of conspiracy proves the solid basis of his distrust. The Bourne series in particular studies personality disintegration and a divided self, amnesia, post-traumatic stress syndrome, and the confusion that results from chemical debriefings.

## LUDLUM'S EARLY NOVELS

Ludlum's early novels were learning experiences through which Ludlum discovered his personal style and message. Despite their driving tension and pacing, these first novels are somewhat sketchy and very much products of their period; their stories are now somewhat dated for readers more blasé about drug use, pervasive crime, and political chicanery than Ludlum's early readers.

In *The Osterman Weekend* (1972) news director John Tanner finds his suburban home staked out, his wife and children threatened, and his long-time neighbors and friends suspected of being Communist conspirators. A Communist traitor in the CIA has set up a sting operation to deflect suspicion onto vulnerable private citizens. No one is who he appears to be, and no one can be trusted. The vision of the paranoid hero established here has become Ludlum's signature theme: an innocent caught up in a nebulous, threatening conspiracy, protecting those he loves from nameless aggressors, some of whom may well be old friends leading double lives of infamy. "They," the enemy, are everywhere, storming private homes, whispering secret messages or threats, invading private lives, and pushing psychological buttons that make people dance to their tune. The difficulty of distinguishing between friend and enemy, government agent and foreign infiltrator suggests the potential for core groups of fanatics using secret surveillance, blackmail, and police and government agencies to sway our nation from within, determine its policies, direct its activities, destroy its institutions, and threaten its citizens.

In *The Matlock Paper* (1973) Ludlum's portrait of universities brings to life parents' fears, as government failure to promote and subsidize higher education drives the New England Ivy League universities to join forces with an evil organization that enslaves the brightest students, blackmails their influential families, and—by infiltrating campuses, placing their cohorts among the faculty and administrators, and buying high-level support by endowments—controls the education of future leaders in order to brainwash and control the nation. The world has been turned upside down when those entrusted with educating young people betray that trust and exploit vulnerability and innocence. Matlock's personal sense of betrayal makes him paranoid, "involuntarily turning around, trying to find the unseen, observing eyes," yet finding "none that he could distinguish" (228). *The Matlock Paper* also raises the following question:

when Nazi-like behavior produces Nazi-like retaliation, have the ends justified the means?

Ludlum's curiosity about the absence of an autopsy on J. Edgar Hoover (whom the author has called "a political first cousin to Adolf Hitler") and about the secret Hoover files, rumored to be filled with blackmail information, produced *The Chancellor Manuscript* (1977). Therein prominent Americans, fearing how damaging Hoover's legendary secret files might be in the wrong hands, conspire to assassinate the controversial FBI director and destroy the files, only to discover that half of the files have already been stolen on behalf of a corrupt, power-hungry, Richard Nixon–like president who wants to secure an authoritarian grip on the country and to crush dissenters and opponents. Novelist Peter Chancellor investigates. What we see is a dramatized version of Ludlum himself at work, writing about Chancellor writing about Hoover: Chancellor's writing habits and approaches parallel those of his creator. The novel offers good examples of the two kinds of paranoia Ludlum exploits: the "bump in the night" jump-out-of-your-seat kind, when Chancellor is trapped by enemy killers in an old house in Washington, D.C., with all exits blocked and bullets from silenced weapons thumping into the woodwork and the plaster, terrifying in their randomness; and the more "civilized" kind, which leads the hero to the reality of hidden forces behind the obvious exterior when he escapes to ask help of the FBI. The scenes are powerful and involving; the reader, caught up in the situation, feels like ducking for cover in the first case and distrusting everyone in the second.

Ludlum's early works are, to some degree, like Peter Chancellor's sketchy outlines: interesting, provocative, but lacking the specific details that could breathe life into character and place. Occasional flashes of realistic detail, however, suddenly infuse the stories with energy and strong emotion: the pathetic body of the family dog tossed carelessly into a child's bedroom (innocence violated); the Tanner basement transformed into a bunker with heavy incoming fire (the home as castle, assaulted); an abandoned depot as an eerie, half-lit battleground (the familiar as alien); the horrifyingly graphic description of Patricia Ballantyne, her head shaved, her lips bruised and split, her eyes blackened, her blood-soaked body a welter of bruises and gashes (again innocence violated). These details capture our fears and live in the memory long after character and plot are forgotten.

# 3

# Monolithic Corporations Threaten

## *Trevayne* (1973) and *The Cry of the Halidon* (1974)

Eternal vigilance is the price of liberty.

Thomas Jefferson

*Trevayne* and *The Cry of the Halidon* reflect Ludlum's commitment to social and political issues. In these two novels Ludlum defined these issues as the conflict between the military and/or government agencies and the citizenry; the growing power of monopolistic corporations, behind-the-scenes manipulators, and power brokers; elitist attitudes leading to the disenfranchisement of the less privileged, racism, discrimination, poverty, and broadening gaps between social classes; personal greed; and a complacent acceptance of corruption and collusion that ends in wasted tax dollars and the undermining of democratic values. Ludlum initially published *Trevayne* and *The Cry of the Halidon* under the pseudonym Jonathan Ryder, but both novels have since been reissued under his real name. Although they include exciting chase scenes, graphic violence that is convincingly realistic, and intriguing arguments between men with very different worldviews, they depart enough from the style and themes of his other works to be recognizably distinct.

Both books deal with the overweening power of monolithic corporations that (octopus-like) have sent out tentacles to grasp power and envelop their prey. In *Trevayne*, Genessee Industries, with subsidiaries nationwide, has a stranglehold on the American Department of Defense and the defense industry, controls defense industry management and labor, buys the votes and influence of powerful senators and judges, employs the Mafia as enforcers and executioners, and affects White House strategy through the President's right-hand man; its next goal is to broker the presidency. In *The Cry of the Halidon* a multinational corporation plans to escape the legal restrictions of first-world nations by taking over Jamaica economically and politically and making that island its power base. In other words, *Trevayne* explores how secret cartels influence defense contracts and threaten decent citizens who might publicly decry their hidden power, while *The Cry of the Halidon* raises the possibility of financiers freed from national loyalties, a law and a power unto themselves.

Both novels reflect America's fears in the sixties and seventies of big business unleashed, and voice the social and political concerns of the time. Both blend the novel of ideas and the investigative thriller. *The Cry of the Halidon*, however, adds the ingredients of the adventure travel story, with its encounters with native peoples and strange customs in alien environments, and of utopian literature, with its description of a successful, hidden Jamaican community envisioned and implemented by the offspring of former slaves.

## *TREVAYNE*

*Trevayne* is a parable of democracy, a study of the competing voices of American values and politics. In it Ludlum asserts the value of a clash of opinions and of American dissonance and distrust. *Trevayne* demonstrates the ease with which decent citizens can be led, in the name of compromise, consistency, "the good of the nation," order, and continuity, to betray the basic principles of a working democracy: freedom of information and choice. The novel takes its title from protagonist Andrew Trevayne, a good citizen, a hard-working individualist, and a family man, who enjoys doing a job well and deeply respects democratic principles.

### Plot Development and Structure

In the process of being appointed to head a bipartisan Senate subcommittee to investigate improprieties in U.S. Defense Department spending,

Trevayne finds his college-age son accused of a hit-and-run murder while intoxicated, his teenage daughter and her friends suspected of trafficking in heroin, and his wife drugged, sexually compromised, and left in a hotel bedroom, her body marked with lewd symbols. At first Trevayne fails to connect these bizarre incidents with his appointment; once he makes the connection, he plans to drop out of the running. A private talk with the president of the United States, however, convinces him that his principles demand that he oppose such blatant attempts to undermine democratic processes. If this nightmare can happen to him, what could these anonymous villains do to ordinary citizens? Thus, he has strong personal and patriotic motives for staying the course of the investigation.

The appointment hearings confirm the strength of the opposition and their unscrupulous strategies, including falsely accusing Trevayne of underhanded dealings with Mafia chieftain Mario De Spadante. Spadante converses with Trevayne on a plane trip, gives him a ride from the airport, and provokes him into calling De Spadante's home, all acts later twisted to question Trevayne's integrity. A lone-wolf investigator, at odds with most of Washington and beset by those who would thwart him, Trevayne, once confirmed, chooses a competent team to investigate defense industry spending. When they fix on Genessee Industries as deserving the most intense study, Trevayne has them track down key personnel for clues to nefarious activities. The investigation ranges nationwide, exposing Genessee's numerous subsidiaries and illegal influences that extend to the White House. Genessee representatives undermine the subcommittee's search for information wherever possible, and De Spadante, a Genessee employee, tries to kill Trevayne. Trevayne and his team nonetheless persist and prevail.

The final battle for democracy and for democratic controls is not against conspirators but against Trevayne's own ego and ambitions. Genessee spokesmen seem to concede his victory, and their top officials promise to retire from public life. They appeal to Trevayne's ego, however, by arguing that, with the president of the United States dying of cancer, only he can unite the nation, and they vow to support his bid for presidency. Convinced of his duty, despite his wife's skepticism, Trevayne turns in a watered-down report that downplays Genessee's illegal activities. Only afterwards does he grasp the full picture: he has been duped, and, if elected, will be easily blackmailed into acting as a Genessee pawn. These revelations come from James Goddard, a Genessee accountant in charge of computer records, who turns over the annual report in exchange for clemency, and from Paul Bonner, a military officer who saved Trevayne's life and now contemptuously rejects Trevayne for becoming Genessee's hired hand and for accepting block votes from the military and from other Genessee backers.

In other words, the novel asks how much pressure big business exerts on government, who really runs the country, and how much say Americans really have in their "democratic" government. In doing so, it reflects the questions asked by many Americans during the Nixon presidency, the time in which it was written.

Each of the novel's five parts marks a stage in Trevayne's movement toward political enlightenment and self-knowledge. The first part (Chapters 1–12) focuses on the loving husband and caring father, who listens seriously to his children's arguments, tries to understand their points of view, and guides them to consider other perspectives. It also shows the development of the political man, who comes to understand he is being manipulated and learns to manipulate in turn. The second and longest part (Chapters 13–34) follows the investigative steps: the gathering of a team, the plotting of a strategy, the implementation of an investigative plan, the moves and countermoves to confuse the opposition and ward off their attacks. Eventually the hunters are hunted, as De Spadante tracks down and attacks Trevayne, an action that spurs the team to pursue Genessee more aggressively.

Part III (Chapters 35–41) shows Genessee fighting back: overtly through the press, with the vitriolic newspaper reporter Roderick Bruce as their main tool, and covertly through appeals to Trevayne's ego, ambition, and self-righteousness. Uncovering the secret demons that drive Bruce (a homosexual lover killed in action in Vietnam under Bonner's command) stops the public defamation of Bonner and the potential defamation of Trevayne.

In Part IV (Chapters 42–53) Trevayne gradually realizes he has been a fool, blind to his own weaknesses; he faces the president, discharges his commission, and demands that the full report be published. The president, however, teaches him a lesson in political expediency: the destruction of Genessee would deeply injure the nation, but the Trevayne team information can be a check on Genessee and restore a balance almost lost. Part IV ends with a presidential assassination and with the elevation of an amoral lunatic to dominance at Genessee. Part V (Chapter 54) is the aftermath, a brief record of Trevayne's presidency through the eyes of distinctly different observers.

In addition to this external division into five parts, there is an internal division based on competing perspectives, with Trevayne meeting and countering opposing political and social arguments in a series of one-on-one debates continued throughout the novel.

## Genre Conventions

Ludlum draws on the conventions of literature and drama to structure debates between characters representing different political views. The literary debate or trial by argument is the ancient Hellenic means of finding truth, employed by Socrates in his dialogues, Plato in *The Gorgias*, and Sophocles in his tragedies. Traditionally, two characters, representing distinct political, philosophical, or religious perspectives, were set in opposition. For example, in Sophocles' play *Antigone*, Creon, the voice of authority and the status quo, argues for the powers of his office, while Antigone argues for higher values than those of the state and for the individual's right to place family and religious obligations above the arbitrary laws of dictators. Pitting polar opposites against each other provides insights into the more muddled issues that lie behind real historical events, issues that lose their clarity offstage.

Ludlum employs dramatic opposites for similar reasons. The debates between Trevayne and his son Steve reveal political differences inherent in the generation gap of the sixties and seventies, with the father defending the system and the son calling for change. In an interesting turnabout, the youthful Paul Bonner defends the status quo and conservative military values while Trevayne argues the liberal position, the necessity of challenging officialdom, of guarding against the guardians, and of tearing down in order to ensure strength. Each encounter between Trevayne and a Genessee representative becomes a debate of political theories, with, for instance, the Jewish survivor of the Nazi death camps, Alan Green, asserting a morality based on his Holocaust experiences, and the aristocratic Ian Hamilton, a fixture of the east-coast establishment, claiming privilege as his right and elitism as necessary to counter the idiocies of the unwashed masses. The final debate between Trevayne and the president of the United States sets the idealistic view that there should be no secrets in a democracy and that wrongs should be immediately righted, no matter what the economic cost, against the pragmatic view that sometimes secrets are necessary and that costs must be considered and compromises made.

In making his novel a forum for political debate, Ludlum works in the theater tradition of provoking controversy through dramatized debates.

He also builds on the television experience of his audience, particularly such popular modern forums as *Firing Line, Meet the Press*, and *Face the Nation*, where issues are scrutinized through verbal combat. The strength of debate as a narrative device is that the readers, as in drama, must decide for themselves the weaknesses and strengths of the arguments and the degree to which they are convincing or satisfying. Ludlum's goal is as much to provoke thought on a subject as to change opinions, an always unpredictable and uncertain objective of debate.

## Character Development

Except for the protagonist, Andrew Trevayne, and his nemesis, Paul Bonner, the characters in *Trevayne* are static. Trevayne's wife Phyllis is like Odysseus' Penelope, a model of loyalty and steadfastness: a faithful wife, a nurturer who stands by her man, even when she doubts his motives. Most of the other characters represent opposing points of view that together compose a cross section of American opinion. Trevayne's son Steve speaks for the younger generation, a generation of high ideals and high expectations but cynical about the status quo's representatives and impatient for change. Steve regards an aggressive, open, Ralph Nader-style confrontation as a viable way of dealing with vested interests, monopolies, and abuses of various sorts. Trevayne's right-hand man, Sam Vicarson, is an older version of Steve, an idealist committed to exposing fraud and restoring power to ordinary people. He is decent, hard-working, energetic, and committed to community values and socially conscious good works; a lawyer during work hours, he spends his free time doing pro bono work in the ghetto. His name suggests his righteousness: Samuel—the Old Testament judge and prophet—Vicarson—the vicar's son.

Paul Bonner, a Vietnam hero and one of the Pentagon's "Young Turks" (101), is a worthy opponent, critical of Trevayne's quest and very much like a younger Trevayne in his honesty and bluntness. The two men are similar in their self-righteous indignation, loyalty, and tactical skills. Bonner's physical prowess and specialized skills as a stalker-hunter fuel his arrogant belief in the superiority of his perceptions, an arrogance paralleled in Trevayne. Bonner is Trevayne's opposing voice: a conservative and a hawk, convinced that Trevayne's investigation will rip the nation apart. He believes in a military hierarchy and in competence, and he acts out of high ideals to thwart the subcommittee report, only to be shocked and horrified when he finds that his military superiors have been corrupted. Although Trevayne distrusts Bonner's soldierly skills, these skills save Trevayne's life and Bonner's contempt for Trevayne's momentary yielding to ambition forces Trevayne to reevaluate his own motives. Bonner's discovery that his heroes have feet of clay confirms Ludlum's argument against a ruling elite. Bonner is impetus and nemesis, a convincing summation of conservative values worth protecting but also a warning about their excesses.

In contrast to Bonner's high-minded conservatism are the rationalizations of the defenders of Genessee Industries. On the fringes is Brigadier General Lester Cooper, an old soldier who has had to deal with the contempt of civilians for the military personnel they need to defend them. He compromises to make sure the military gets its budget, bending democratic interests to promote stability; his trust in the military hierarchy of rank makes him vulnerable to the elitist arguments of fellow conservatives. Also on the fringes are Walter Madison, Trevayne's personal lawyer, a man who can be bought cheaply and who willingly betrays friends and values for powerful contacts, and the vindictive newspaperman Roderick Bruce, who uses his position of trust to slander and defame opponents. The core defenders of Genessee include Senator Alan Knapp and Senator Norton, who let regional needs and the pressures to perform inherent in their office sway their judgment; Robert Webster, who betrays his position as a White House officer and confidant of the president to be the power behind the throne; and Senator Armbruster, who defends accommodation as inherent in a system dependent on checks and balances and considers Genessee a benevolent contributor to the social and national welfare. Aaron Green has more personal motives; a death-camp survivor, he relies on Genessee to protect against future horrors and to exorcise his Holocaust nightmares. Ian Hamilton, in turn, is a New England aristocrat, a representative of the landed gentry dedicated to the belief that the elite must show the way for the unenlightened. Mario De Spadante, a stereotypical Mafia member, does the dirty work for these prominent men: blackmail, intimidation, violence, and murder.

In contrast to these stereotypical, one-note figures is Andrew Trevayne. After preparing us to expect a conquering hero, Ludlum instead shows us a potentially tragic man, whose strengths become his weaknesses and whose blindness is born of personal pride and arrogance. Trevayne is an overachiever, successful in his endeavors and devoted to justice. He is a good father and a loving husband, but when he devotes himself to a task, he becomes caught up in it to the exclusion of all else. Thus, his transformation from private man to public servant is made more credible. When he accepts the presidential challenge to take on Genessee, he commits himself fully and pursues the truth steadfastly, developing strategies to deceive and mislead those who would interfere with his goals. His pride in performing such a seemingly impossible task and in taking on such a monolithic corporation, however, makes him vulnerable to flattery and to the suggestion that his country needs only him and that he should rise to the occasion. His wife's cynicism has little effect on him, but his male counterpart, Bonner, holds the mirror to his face and forces him to see himself as another Ian Hamilton or Alan Green, blinded by personal experiences into betraying democratic principles. His admission of his limitations and his return to a true course prove his inner fortitude, courage, and principles. Later, when his country does need his services as president, he seems transformed: he is empowered by experience and the weight of office to bear on his shoulders the continuing battle against Genessee—to preserve the values and principles he once taught as a private citizen within his own family.

## Themes

The themes of *Trevayne* are related to the protagonist's character, the struggle to find the truth and make it public, the debate sequences, and the concluding misrepresentations.

First, Ludlum argues that a single committed individual can make a major impact. Trevayne relies on intelligence, wit, hard work, personal sacrifice, and stubborn diligence to perform a seemingly impossible task. By gathering convincing documentation of Genessee's methods and interlocking activities, he helps stave off a silent takeover of the government by the representatives of a private power. He truly does help make America safe for democracy.

Second, Ludlum captures the incredulity and anger of ordinary citizens faced with the behind-the-scenes conspiracies Trevayne and his team uncover. Various characters call it "Madness! Insanity!" and ask a question repeated throughout Ludlum's canon, "What kind of world do they/these people/you live in?" The fact that Bonner, the much-decorated war hero, is so angry at the easy use of murder to eliminate political opposition reiterates the question in dramatic form. Bonner argues the obvious truth that hiring killers and supporting Mafia bosses with brass knuckles is different from trying to outsmart a congressional committee.

Third, Ludlum's thesis is a political parable of democracy. The author argues that the strength of a democracy lies in competing voices battling for public acceptance, that this battle for truth is a defining element of our heritage and a mainstay of our system, and that, without it, liberty is lost. By having some very good men argue an elitist stance, Ludlum illustrates the ease with which decent citizens can be swayed to do the wrong thing in the name of right. Senator Mitchell Armbruster, arguing that utilitarian pragmatism means compromising principles, points to the drug clinics, rehabilitation centers, day-care centers, cancer research labs, and mobile medical units in poor neighborhoods supported by Genessee; Trevayne concludes Armbruster "traded the voting strength of millions for tax-deductible marbles" (233). The Jewish benefactor Alan Green argues that "every viewpoint has its own visual frame" (286) and that a small elite can control and limit the excesses of the ignorant masses; Trevayne counters that Green's view is not really different from that of the Nazis he deplored and that the country has the right to know how its money is spent and to expect companies and industries to be responsible to the people.

The wealthy aristocrat Ian Hamilton sums up the Hamiltonian Republican stance his last name suggests. He argues that the American government, a "grotesque, awkward, fumbling giant," is no longer manageable and that democratization has lowered standards and led to chaos: "an inscrutable, totally unreliable economy; terrible recessions, inflation, mass unemployment . . . urban crises which threaten revolution . . . uncontrolled strikes; utility services lost for weeks; a dissolute military, rife with incompetency and inadequate command" (312). For him, the need for order justifies intervention in the democratic process and the transformation of government into "a council of the elite" (313). Noting that American democracy began as a republic, "a state governed by those *entitled* to vote, to shape its policies" (314), he advocates without irony a "benevolent" aristocracy, "The United States of Genessee Industries" (315).

Trevayne, the defender of democracy, rejects any system in which an elite act as "puppeteers" (384), manipulating presidents and voters. He calls instead for a "collective strength," based on openly shared information. He defends the right of the people to know, confirms his trust in an informed citizenry making hard choices, and deplores the tendency to dismiss the opinions of others with categorizing labels. He fears that the growing power of corporations like Genessee is part of a process of de-democratization. In his final telephone conversation with Hamilton, Trevayne asserts that democracies are maintained by a constant battle against forces that would undermine them, that the battle for freedom and truth is never fully won, and that, as Thomas Jefferson said over two hundred years ago, "Eternal vigilance is the price of liberty."

## THE CRY OF THE HALIDON

*The Cry of the Halidon* expresses Ludlum's social conscience and his hope for racial harmony. The story begins with a typical Ludlum situation: a secret meeting of international businessmen plotting immoral acts with global repercussions—in this case, the economic takeover of Jamaica. The idea is to escape national taxes, laws, and controls, and thereby not only increase profits, but also attain power that could lead to international financiers dominating world economies. Ludlum draws on right-wing paranoid distortions of honorable institutions such as the Trilateral Commission, the big think tank supported by Henry Kissinger and Jimmy Carter and feared by the right wing as a stalking-horse for a one-world government.

Ludlum, however, does not explore this idea very far. Once the reader is engaged, the author diverts attention from international conspiracies to focus instead on a local situation. Having visited Jamaica, he knows the flora and fauna, the highways and byways, and brings them to life with detailed description, emphasizing both the beauty and the dangers of the locale. He pits exploitative outsiders against patriotic islanders, and suggests that wisely used funds could solve the island's most significant problems. Only at the end does he return to the international conspiracy, with an incredible tale of an isolated Jamaican community helping the poor worldwide and assassinating corrupt schemers (all members of the conspiracy) in major cities around the globe.

### Plot Development and Structure

The novel moves from London to Jamaica, deeper and deeper into the island's heart of darkness. Part I establishes the outsider's distant view. Part II draws closer to the situation, with the views of locals who have been away and, near the end, of locals who are very much immersed in the conflicts and problems of their island home. Part III enters the heartland, with revelations about exploitation and island defenses. Part IV presents a Jamaican utopia, a secret world created by natural wealth as a defense against outsiders. The four parts correspond to the secret symbolism of the worshipers of the Halidon (the tribe of Acquaba), for whom four is a mystic number, signifying death and power. This symbolism is based on ancient Arawak (an American Indian religion) symbols for a warrior's death march, "in units of four, always to the right of the setting sun" (174).

Part I (Chapters 1–6) alternates between Port Antonio, Jamaica, and London to set a scene of puzzling menace: an international company that is conducting a geological survey in Jamaica is believed by British intelligence to be setting the stage for an economic takeover of the island. The company has disturbingly wide-ranging surveillance and investigative powers, as well as access to private information about the lives of individuals it plans to deal with. The protagonist, Alexander Tarquin McAuliff, a successful geologist with an international reputation for innovative, high-quality work, accepts a million dollars to lead a team of experts to conduct the Jamaican survey. It soon becomes clear, however, that more than a survey is at stake, as McAuliff is caught in the crossfire of British Intelligence (represented by MI-5 agent R. C. Holcroft), the corporation that hired him (Dunstone, Inc., headed by Julian Warfield), and various underground Jamaican factions, both left- and right-wing, with visions of revolutionary coups. The previous survey team members were killed under peculiar circumstances, and, by the end of Part I, before the team McAuliff has chosen has even left London, he feels threatened by sinister, unknown forces.

Part II (Chapters 7–16), set in Kingston and nearby rural areas, depicts McAuliff playing double agent—on the one hand, moving forward with his team of experts to conduct their survey, on the other hand, meeting secretly with Holcroft and his local agent, Westmore Tallon, to share information. Part II exposes the secrets behind the facades, as McAuliff plays detective and investigates each team member in turn. The attractive Alison Brook has just divorced a man deeply involved in narcotics trafficking and has collected incriminating evidence for Interpol, evidence that will send him and his associates to prison. James Ferguson, who is short of cash, has agreed to spy on McAuliff for the exploitative Craft corporation, an island monopoly and his former employer, in return for ample payment and possible reemployment. Charles Whitehall is open about his motivations; a former Jamaican politician who believes fascism is "the only hope" for his island (92), he has returned not only to demonstrate how far he has come since his fellow islanders last saw him, but also to encourage an extreme right-wing local party of elite and highly educated blacks, the descendants of former slaves, to place him in power. Ruth and Peter Jensen are left-wing academics who, while working on a U.S. government project, were caught giving the Communists American secrets, and who have been blackmailed into acting for Dunstone, Inc., ever since. McAuliff's only old friend on the team, Samuel Tucker, a soil analyst, fails to appear on time, having been seized by members of a radical native political faction (led by Barak Moore) seeking information about the mysterious Halidon. The only link to the Halidon, Dr. Walter Piersall, is killed in a hit-and-run accident before he can divulge his secrets. Part II also sees the flowering of the relationship between Brook and McAuliff, and of Warfield's suspicions that McAuliff has been compromised.

Part III (Chapters 17–22), set on Jamaica's north coast, concentrates on a search for Piersall's buried documents, which contain clues to the secret of the Halidon. The search is followed by violence and death: Barak Moore is killed, and Warfield demands that Peter Jensen kill McAuliff. The arrival of the drug lord Marquis, a major investor in Dunstone, Inc., necessitates protectors for Alison: Floyd, Lawrence, and later Malcolm. Whitehall draws on local support for assistance. The information provided by the buried documents suggests a Jamaican conspiracy of silence going back to the nineteenth century.

Part IV (Chapters 23–35) is set in the "cock pit," the primitive area where the Halidonites live. Led by local "runners" who turn out to be Halidonites, McAuliff and his associates face "seemingly impenetrable walls of jungle" and "strange, contradictory forests" (232). They are taken prisoner and shown the secrets of the Halidon: educated, healthy, well-fed descendants of slaves, now in charge of their own destiny, committed to community and dedicated to improving the condition of the world's poor, hungry, oppressed, and dispossessed. The Halidonites, however, are also bound by a sacred oath of secrecy and service, by autosuggestion and group hypnosis, and by the mummified body of Acquaba. Acquaba, symbolic of his modern-day descendants, is imprisoned in a golden cage, but sometimes his body begs for release when the magical wind sends forth his cry. This magical, mythological, utopian interlude is interrupted by intruders. While McAuliff and Holcroft battle Dunstone employees who have infiltrated MI-5, the Halidon warriors kill key heads of the Dunstone financial empire, including Warfield and the

Marquis. The novel comes full circle with McAuliff and the survivors of his small band staying at the same local hotel where the original global conspirators hatched their plan.

## Character Development

Ludlum spends little time on character development in this novel, since a fast-moving plot and a utopian vision dominate his interest. As in *Trevayne*, the plot develops through clashes of perspectives, with key figures representing different political philosophies: Charles Whitehall is a fascist; Barak Moore, Floyd, and Lawrence are radical leftists and would-be revolutionaries engaged in guerrilla warfare; Ruth and Peter Jensen are basically hypocrites, Communist sympathizers compelled to work for ruthless capitalists, but ultimately unwilling to kill for them; Samuel Tucker is a would-be revolutionary looking for a worthy cause; Julian Warfield, as his name implies, sees the world as a racial battlefield and himself as a successful conqueror, an Alexander the Great defending the status quo of the wealthy and the aristocratic. Brook and McAuliff are outside of politics, recognizing the weaknesses in the commitments of others but taking a stand only on the basis of personal loyalties and an internal sense of justice for the underdog. Only these two characters are developed with any depth—mainly with background information about their previous experiences and personality traits that make their actions more credible.

A tall, light-haired American geologist, with high cheekbones and probing, inquisitive gray eyes, McAuliff served in the infantry in Korea, and the survivalist lessons learned on the battlefield serve him well in Jamaica. Doing geological surveys has brought him profits (twenty-three bank accounts around the world, from Moscow to Buenos Aires). He has a reputation as an individualist, a skilled professional, and a trustworthy keeper of secrets. He demonstrates intuitive human skills in his selection of a team and in his ability to play a double role as professional geologist and government spy. He nevertheless finds the traumatic events that envelop him a greater madness than he has ever encountered before, and is initially bewildered and unsure how to respond.

Brook is a foil to McAuliff, a brave, decent woman, intelligent and capable in her field. She has the courage to spy on narcotics dealers and to help bring an indictment against them. Compassionate and intuitive, she quickly appraises situations and knows the best response instinctively. She is immediately attracted to McAuliff, as he is to her, and her growing love for him guides her actions. Her easy alliance and friendship with the islanders provides a positive standard for black-white racial relationships, and her ready empathy wins trust and friendship.

## Themes

The broad theme of global conspiracy, of narcotics dealers and international financiers operating mainly out of major cities in Europe and the Americas, frames the book and motivates the action. Ludlum deplores the amorality and even immorality of those who seek to escape the confinements of laws and of national boundaries; his Mr. Warfield is a stereotypical businessman out of control, focused greedily on increased profits, no matter the human cost. Ludlum finds the idea of a government based solely on economic trade factors appalling.

As in *The Matlock Paper* (see Chapter 2), Ludlum is also contemptuous of the willingness of universities to accept donated money without investigating the commitments involved in such government and industrial grants. Their support and blessing of a clearly bogus operation suggests the ease with which academic cooperation, with its aura of respectability, can be bought.

More important to *The Cry of the Halidon*, however, is the theme of economic and racial exploitation. Ludlum depicts Jamaica as an impoverished island with wide divisions between blacks and whites. Deepseated hatreds and anger derive from the cruelties of the slave trade, from continued exploitation of the island's natural resources and cheap labor, and from the overtly racist speech and behavior of Americans and British alike. The issue is one of treatment, for, when dealt with fairly, the islanders return trust for trust and friendship for friendship. Ludlum's local black patriots are united in their hatred of white exploiters, but disagree about what type of government led by whom would best confront the serious economic problems that have produced shanty-towns, ill-fed children, and widespread illiteracy. Ludlum's description of Old Kingston is graphic:

> the corrugated tin shacks across from the abandoned, filthy barges, peopled by outcasts, the emaciated dogs, the bone-thin cats, the eyes of numbed futility on the young-old women.

The men with no teeth praying for the price of a pint of wine,
defecating in the shadows of dark alleys. (264)

Characters complain about "the simple hardship and the agonizing pointlessness of the coastal towns" (264), and Malcolm, a Halidonite, argues, "It
is the pointlessness that erodes the people most rapidly" (265).

The utopian society Ludlum provides as a counter to Kingston is a
rural community protected by natural defenses and dependent on its
isolation from the outside world. It is neat, clean, and orderly. Its citizens
are comfortably clad in simple, well-washed clothing, and everyone has
books to read, as well as the ability and leisure to do so. Bodies are
healthy, eyes clear, diets properly balanced, intellects sharp. Unlike many
isolated hill peoples ("wornout" races of "poverty-stricken primitives
scratching a bare subsistence from the land" [267]), the Halidonites have
managed to get the best of both worlds. Their ancestors discovered a
core of gold in the heart of the jungle and made sure that treaties and
records left that land intact and unquestionably theirs. They then set
about creating a contradiction, an isolated society with sophisticated
forms of communication with the outside world, a community dedicated
to secrecy and privacy but willing to bring in select outsiders to maintain
the gene pool and to send out their best and brightest to bring back
knowledge. The community promotes political balance and thus supports both conservative and radical Jamaican leaders (the moderating
effect of competing voices advocated in *Trevayne*). The combination of a
community to take pride in and sufficient funds to maintain it is what
the real Kingston lacks. In effect, Ludlum argues that wealth generated
from the homeland would bring the pride of spirit that, together with
funding, could transform Jamaica and Jamaicans. By emphasizing Halidonite charity abroad, he also suggests that the solution for Jamaica
might be the solution for many other impoverished and exploited former
colonies.

## Genre Conventions

Ludlum mixes genres in this novel. *The Cry of the Halidon* begins as an
adventure thriller, following the literary pattern often used for the tale
of a major robbery or a secret mission into enemy territory. This pattern
requires the selection of a team, a mixed bag of unknowns, all experts,
but with some secret in their past that affects present action. Team mem-

bers then engage in suspicious activities that make them distrust each other. There might be a search for a secret document, during which individual team members go missing. There are chases, pursuits, and evasive actions. Wounded team members must be evacuated, while villains use attack dogs, hired killers, and various other forms of violence to thwart the mission. Knowledge acquired on the spot sometimes changes the protagonist's understanding of events and affects the final outcome.

Part IV introduces a totally different genre: the utopian vision. In accordance with the literal meaning of the word "utopia"—"no place"—utopian literature describes a hypothetical locale meant to be either a model for our age to imitate or a satiric criticism of the corruption or inadequacies of present times projected into a foreign or alien location. Utopian literature has its roots in mythological stories of paradise and of a golden age. The first work with this name was written in Latin by Sir Thomas More (*Utopia*, 1516; Eng. trans., 1551); it criticized economic and social conditions in contemporary Europe—especially war, oppression of the poor, taxation, and unjust laws—and then described an ideal community, its religion, government, education system, economics, wars, laws, and customs. In the eighteenth century Jonathan Swift's caustic social satire *Gulliver's Travels* postulated a land where rational horses, the Houyhnhyms, ruled irrational human creatures, the Yahoos. The horrified responses of these intelligent horses to human wars, law courts, and so forth, and their own logical and refined way of life provided the utopian standard against which Swift judged his own age. In the nineteenth century, utopias often appeared as hidden lands discovered on voyages of adventure, with their entrances covered over by landslides or in some other way lost to future travelers. More recently, utopian literature has often taken the form of science fiction, with a projection of a future world superior to our own. Drawing on these traditions, Ludlum's utopian society calls attention to the inadequate living conditions of Jamaica's poor and postulates ideal measures that would rectify present wrongs.

## ALTERNATE READING: JUNGIAN CRITICISM

Ludlum's *Trevayne* and *Cry of the Halidon* lend themselves easily to Jungian analysis, for Ludlum purposefully seeks to depict a physical, spiritual, and intellectual journey human beings make to achieve knowledge, understanding, and power.

Carl Jung (1875–1961), the founder of modern analytical psychology, believed that symbol creation is central to understanding human nature and that there are direct correspondences between the symbolic images of world religions, mythologies, and magical systems and the dream symbols of individuals. He postulated that the unconscious psyche consists of two parts, one personal and the other collective, and that the collective unconscious is an inherited structure common to all human beings. He built his theory of archetypes, universal symbols, and a collective unconscious on the findings of anthropological research. By archetypes he meant a series of innate predispositions that shape the perception of individual experience in ways reflective of universal human situations; thus, archetypal patterns or recurring universals reflect both the individual and the collective human experience from birth to death. Jung went one step further before his death, to postulate that the deepest layers of the unconscious could produce paranormal phenomena like clairvoyance and precognition. His book *Man and His Symbols* (1964) applies his theories to the literary and mythological world heritage, and argues that the hero figure is an archetype that has existed "since time immemorial" (73).

Canadian Northrup Frye, one of the most highly regarded literary critics of his generation, made Jungian criticism, which is rooted in psychology, a respectable literary approach. His book *Anatomy of Criticism: Four Essays* (1957) explores the role of Jungian archetypes in world literature, focusing most particularly on the Judeo-Christian myths of quest, redemption, and fall. Frye's system has provided an analytical base for later literary critics. Another distinguished scholar known for his Jungian interpretations of folklore, dreams, and the role of myth in the human imagination is Joseph Campbell, who studied the archetypes inherent in comparative mythology. In *The Hero with a Thousand Faces* (1949) he describes the Jungian pattern of the mythological journey or quest, the stages of the hero's journey. He names the following elements: the call to adventure, the aid of mentors, the crossing of the threshold, the road of trials, the supreme ordeal and the battle for the elixir of life, returning across the threshold, and benefiting the community with the elixir or boon. The aid of mentors may involve the choosing of worthy companions, while crossing the threshold may involve overcoming a physical or intellectual barrier or journeying to a new and alien place. The trials by combat may be tests of strength and prowess, tests of endurance, or tests of wit. As Campbell says in *The Power of Myth* (1988), the hero may perform a courageous act, save a life, or undergo a spiritual or intellectual experience that leads to knowledge valuable to the community at large (123). The hero goes beyond ordinary experiences and seeks to recover something missing, whether something physical or something as nebulous as lost values. In modern literature the journey into a dark netherworld may be a journey into the darkness of the human soul, and the secret treasure may be the self-knowledge that illuminates understanding.

Both *The Cry of the Halidon* and *Trevayne* employ this universal archetype of the heroic journey or quest to lend depth to parables about democracy and community. The parallels are covert in *The Cry of the Halidon*, and overt in *Trevayne*.

In *The Cry of the Halidon* the mythic journey begins when Alexander McAuliff accepts his call to adventure by signing on as geological surveyor for Dunstone, Inc., and the violence that follows (the bayoneting of Holcroft and the hit-and-run murder of a stranger) impels him over the threshold of ordinary experience. His journey to the strange, exotic world of Jamaica completes the crossing. McAuliff is mentored by an experienced MI-5 operative, Holcroft, and by Alison Brook, whose experiences with Interpol help McAuliff change from a mild-mannered geologist to a heroic opponent of moneyed monsters. He is assisted by capable experts, first from his own world and later from the alien world he has entered. His road of trials takes him into the Jamaican heartland and involves violence and the injury and deaths of companions; it also involves a search for clues and secrets centered on mystical numbers and an understanding of the symbolism of several African and American Indian religions and mythologies. The supreme ordeal is a journey into a hidden world that is alien and mystic and that compels a heroic response. McAuliff traverses the Maze of Acquaba, a trip through so dense and cruel a jungle that natives call it "the odyssey of death" (265); it is a journey through darkness to a valley of light. The experience in this new realm is one of discovery, amazement, and enlightenment, for the Halidonites teach McAuliff how they have wrought their changes, and they share their religious insights with him.

The return across the threshold involves shedding blood to destroy the trail that would allow dangerous predators to discover the sacred, hidden world of the Halidonites. McAuliff must battle for his life, but also for the life of a secret African-Indian society, the descendants of slaves. His contribution is to protect the Halidonite community; by so doing, he benefits the world community, ensuring the continuation of charitable acts to assist the poor worldwide. The emphasis on Ashanti (African), Arawak

(Caribbean Indian), and Coromanteen (African) symbols and hieroglyphs throughout adds to the sense of convergent mythologies. The title plays on the phonetic connections between Halidon and "holy," "holly," "dawn," and "halidom"—which means "holiness," "sanctity," or "a sanctuary for holy relics."

The hero of *Trevayne* does not choose his quest for himself, but has it offered to him by his president and his nation. The call to adventure is a call to service, a call to travel new information highways in search of monsters that threaten the land. It is an intellectual journey to unlock the secrets of the nation and a physical journey throughout the land in search of facts and details that will reveal a community truth. The confrontation with the president and the president's challenge to Trevayne to act for the good of the nation rather than yield to harassment and intimidation is a crossing of a threshold from family duties to public duties, from security to danger, from curiosity to commitment. When Trevayne says, "I won't quit" (55), there is no turning back.

The aid of mentors includes not only the advice and support of the president, but also the public statement of the support of the Senate bipartisan committee and the private assistance some supporters guarantee. It also includes Trevayne's team. In Chapter 13 Trevayne chooses a crew of worthy companions with highly specialized knowledge and skills to assist him in his voyage of discovery: Sam Vicarson (an innovative attorney with a social conscience), Alan Martin (a comptroller and statistics analyst), Michael Ryan (an aeronautical engineer), and John Larch (a construction engineer). He is also assisted by Paul Bonner, a Vietnam hero, tested in battle on Southeast Asia's Plain of Jars, a worthy opponent who is critical of Trevayne's quest but wards off physical attacks on Trevayne and his family.

The road of trials follows. The senators who interview Trevayne fear he will go on a "holy crusade" (85), and the obstacles placed in his way produce that effect: they make him see his cause as righteous, and they steel his determination to expose the truth. Ludlum describes the task in mythic terms. It is "gargantuan" and involves a tangled web, each strand of which must be followed through myriad patterns to its source (166). Ludlum equates "the partially unraveled threads of the web" with "a small clearing inside a labyrinth of very warped mirrors" (170), and only the most clever can use those threads to discover the Minotaur Genessee at the heart of the labyrinth and not be destroyed. Like Odysseus, Trevayne is a man of schemes, a clever trickster who can mislead pursuers. He and his team become masters of misdirection, and counter manipulation with manipulation. He tells his wife that necessity has compelled him to lies and illusions.

As Trevayne and his team search for meaningful patterns and clues that reveal the realities hidden beneath surface documentation, Genessee's representatives engage in "a ritual dance of deceit" (180). The hydra-headed "industrial monster" (287), Genessee, probes, tests, and challenges, but the team separates each head (Manolo, Jamison, Studebaker, Armbruster, Green, Hamilton, Bruce, and Spadante) to attack it separately. Spadante, in particular, requires a trial by combat from the heroic Bonner, who suffers terrible physical injuries, but who kills two of the villainous attackers, immobilizes a third, and badly injures Spadante. The president and his close advisor William Hill later describe two members of Genessee as "Scylla and Charybdis" (432), double destroyers from Greek myth, the first a monster who cannibalizes humans passing too close to her cliffs, and the second a whirlpool that pulls ships and men down to their deaths beneath the sea. The Genessee notebooks are "a labyrinth of very warped mirrors" (170). Trevayne, indignant, sees himself as an angel "raising his sword of wrath" to smite an "emissary from Lucifer" (232)—Genessee Industries in particular and monolithic corporations in general. When the report is finally compiled, Trevayne equates his search for the truth about Genessee Industries with a journey into a netherworld. He thinks to himself, "He'd traveled to and from his River Styx. Like Charon, he'd carried the souls of the dead across the turbulent waters, and now he needed rest, peace. He had to get out from the lower world for a while. And Genessee Industries was the lower world" (363).

The supreme ordeal and the battle for the elixir of life initially seems to be a battle against external forces, the power and might of Genessee Industries, but ultimately it proves a battle against the protagonist's own self. Like Oedipus the King in Sophocles' *Oedipus Rex*, Pentheus in Euripides' *Dionysus*, and many other tragic heroes of Greek legend, Trevayne is blind to his own arrogance. He takes pleasure in routing the forces of evil and in being the conquering hero who restores order and right. But this vanity almost destroys him. When intimidation and force fail to work against him, Genessee resorts to more subtle ploys, feigning submission, flattering his ego, and encouraging him to do what is supposedly best for the nation by offering his countrymen himself as leader and president. Only when he confronts his own blindness, elitism, and will to power, sees the enemy within, admits his ambitions and rejects them, has he truly survived the supreme ordeal and is ready to ensure the ongoing life of a democracy.

Ultimately, Trevayne becomes one of "the guardians of tomorrow" (132), and uses the secret truths uncovered during his journey-quest to safeguard the community and ensure democratic freedoms. Thus, the knowledge gained on his quest meets the final criterion in Campbell's archetypal pattern: the hero benefits his community.

*Trevayne* would probably have been a much better novel if it had ended with the hero's discovery of his own feet of clay. Dramatically, the movement is that of a competent man discovering within himself the seeds of pride and arrogance that would make him deny his democratic values and decide that the rule of the elite would be acceptable if he personally were the benevolent, ruling elite. The discovery of this personal flaw would make an effective final argument that the price of freedom is indeed "eternal vigilance," not simply against the enemy without but also against the enemy within, the secret voice that says, "Because I'm extraordinary, it is all right for me to bypass the ordinary barriers to power inherent in a democracy."

Ludlum, however, passes beyond the negative dramatic moment to focus instead on the positive archetypal pattern: despite a moment of weakness, the hero rediscovers within himself the principles and values of democracy and community. This discovery and the humility it evokes in him mark his return across the threshold.

On the assassination of a good president, he accepts the challenge of Genessee, runs an aggressive campaign, and takes up the mantle of the presidency. Thereafter, he is transmogrified from simple family man into a president whose motto is a "Mark of Excellence." He is marked by his sense of obligation, his "swift grace," his kindness, his "self-effacing irony," and his commitment to continuing vigilance to protect dissident voices and individual choice (459).

Jung, Frye, and Campbell, however, would all note that our mythological patterns envision an ongoing battle between creative and destructive forces, between preservers/nurturers and destroyers. Thus, Ludlum concludes the novel with the battle ongoing, Genessee still struggling for dominance, and Trevayne still countering their every move. Trevayne asserts that there will come a day when Genessee will be expendable, but the Genessee representative replies that it will not be in "our time" (469). By placing *Trevayne* in the context of myth, Ludlum elevates the conflict between Jeffersonian Democrats and Hamiltonian elitists to the level of a world pattern, and confirms that freedom and democracy are not won by a single battle once and for all, but that there is an ongoing struggle, that indeed the price of liberty is "eternal vigilance."

# 4

# The Early Nazi and Neo-Nazi Novels

## *The Scarlatti Inheritance* (1971), *The Rhinemann Exchange* (1974), *The Gemini Contenders* (1976), and *The Holcroft Covenant* (1978)

> The Nazi is among us and we don't see him. He is cloaked in respectability and a pressed suit of clothes.
>
> Robert Ludlum, *The Holcroft Covenant*

In Ludlum's novels the Nazis (an abbreviation of the German word *national-sozialistische* or National Socialist) are quintessentially villainous. In Ludlum's view, one essentially confirmed by virtually all legitimate historians, the Third Reich is dominated by racial primacy, bigotry, greed, and a will to power, and their leaders are psychotics—so obsessive in their hatreds that ordinary people fear not to follow them. They are shorthand for evil: racist murderers, sexual perverts, and supreme egotists dedicated to perpetuating their personal genetics and their personal authority at whatever cost—all in the name of efficiency, order, right, and might. Their unquestioning belief in their leadership's superiority and their robotical adherence to the chain of command prove weaknesses, and their extreme nationalism, their glorification of strength and discipline, and their belief in Aryan racial superiority confirm their villainy. Ludlum shows how the warped mentality that idolized youth and paramilitary prowess, that disguised the concentration camps and the Holocaust behind a massive propaganda machine, and that arrogantly declared Hitler's rule the fulfillment of a millennium of German national history, tainted the utopian dreams of future generations, converting them into neo-Nazis. Ludlum fears the dangers of the "Nazi mentality" in modern governments and organizations and believes compromise with Nazis or neo-Nazis impossible for people of decency and morality.

Nazis dominate three main novels (*The Scarlatti Inheritance, The Rhinemann Exchange,* and *The Gemini Contenders*), and neo-Nazis dominate two others (*The Holcroft Covenant* and *The Apocalypse Watch*). Nazis are secondary villains in other works—a stereotyped neo-Nazi Southerner in *The Road to Omaha, Der Nachrichtendienst* Prussian nationalists in *The Scorpio Illusion,* an escaped Nazi war criminal (a doddering, marginal villain) in *The Parsifal Mosaic,* and a demented Nazi general bent on world conquest in *The Aquitaine Progression.* The term "Nazi" becomes Ludlum's shorthand for a whole set of political attitudes and acts; in general he uses the Nazi like a stock stage figure to elicit a powerful negative emotional response. Thus J. Edgar Hoover behaves like a Nazi; military hawks are Nazis at heart; giant international business conglomerates employ Nazi tactics; the Scorpio network of the international elite looks back to the Nazis (the *Schutzstaffel*) as their model; and the threat of a small core of fanatics seizing a nation and controlling its governmental policies, the essence of Germany's bitter experience with the Nazis, drives his plots.

Throughout his canon and most particularly his Nazi and neo-Nazi stories, Ludlum repeatedly raises the question of responsibility. His favorite words for villainy are "madness" and "insanity." This word choice would seem to suggest diminished responsibility: madmen are not held responsible for their deeds. Clearly, however, Ludlum does not intend to provide loopholes for culpability. He holds his villains directly and personally responsible for their acts and takes authorial pleasure in their punishment and death. Instead, his terms "madness" and "insanity" mean "unbelievable" or "not within the experience of ordinary people." When his heroes also declare themselves "mad" and the events enveloping them "insane," they are not speaking literally of their loss of reason and responsibility, but of events beyond comprehension and experience, so stunningly horrifying that they are unsure how to respond.

## GENRE CONVENTIONS

Ludlum provides his own special twist to World War II and postwar spy thriller convention. In his wartime spy stories, the protagonist flees, evading capture in violent encounters, and the opposition is always close to triumphing. Thus, a Ludlum hero races along nighttime streets, the headlights of an unknown pursuer glaring in his rearview mirror; a dark vehicle passes, and shots ring out. Action moves about internationally from sophisticated metropolises to sleepy villages, with the narrator providing a sketchy description of the highways and byways traveled. Supposed "accidents" take innocent lives, but the hero always confuses the conspirators and paves the way for their defeat. An identifying pack of cigarettes that not only tags an agent for strangers but also throws him psychologically off balance, or a human hair, carefully placed to indicate whether or not a secret search has occurred, are standard tradecraft Ludlum's agents use. *The Scarlatti Inheritance* includes secret color codes (the red and black stripes of the Scarlatti alliance) and mysterious seals for secret organizations. In the tradition of double agents, unclear loyalties, and traitors among those closest to the protagonists, Ludlum makes everyone suspect—a brother, a sister, even a mother. Competing agents include Nazis, neo-Nazis, members of the CIA or the British MI-5 and MI-6, the hired personnel of greedy entrepreneurs, and sometimes members of special factions—like pro- or anti-Zionist groups, with the pro-Zionists usually death camp survivors zealously dedicated to undermining Nazis and annihilating any movement toward a Fourth Reich.

Like his literary predecessors, Ludlum pits quietly heroic, competent men of integrity against the amoral schemes and terrible machinery of vicious, evil men, and provides empathetic, self-sacrificing women with keen perceptions, strong loyalties, and a deep inner strength to assist the heroes. The heroes of traditional anti-Nazi war stories—such as Alistair MacLean's *Where Eagles Dare* and *The Guns of Navarone* and Jack Higgins's *The Eagle Has Landed*, and *Cold Harbor*—are tough, confident, and closemouthed. They act to save Churchill from kidnapping, to destroy impregnable Nazi strongholds, to expose traitors, to infiltrate enemy territory, and to stop Nazi villains from taking innocent lives. Even when tested to the limits of physical and mental endurance, secrets, lives, and the fate of nations are safe with them.

In this tradition, Ludlum's key protagonists—Matthew Canfield (*The

*Scarlatti Inheritance*), David Spaulding ("the man from Lisbon" in *The Rhinemann Exchange*), Adrian Fontine (in *The Gemini Contenders*), and Noel Holcroft (*The Holcroft Covenant*)—are driven men, responsible for others. To meet that responsibility, they may endure a loss of public reputation, of friends, of relatives, and perhaps of love. Spaulding must put humanity before love and Fontine must destroy his own brother. They face difficult odds and prevail. Spaulding's toughness is typical. He sneaks aboard a trawler where industrial diamonds vital to the Nazi war effort are guarded, immobilizes or kills the guards, and fulfills his mission; a deep wound, however, slows his escape and attracts a writhing mass of conger eels. He escapes—barely—but after a long sleep is ready to assault the Nazi stronghold and settle affairs with a gunfight. Fontine scales a wall of jagged rock to face a deranged killer at its top, while Holcroft survives a plunge over a mountain cliff. Like the action heroes of modern blockbuster films, Ludlum's protagonists are capable of superhuman feats.

Despite the staggering number of deaths in a Ludlum novel, Ludlum does not personally approve of weapons or violence. He knows from first-hand observation while in the military, confirmed by discussions with experts, that a person shot or stabbed cannot just spring up and fight on as if nothing happened. Instead, a victim's mind and body are affected and recovery is often slow and unpleasant. Consequently, although Ludlum is opposed to violence, he uses the savagery necessitated by the suspense/adventure/espionage genre: the injured in his books are really hurt, their pain inescapably clear. In fact, he is quite proud of one critic's comment that the last thing anyone would want to do after reading a violent Ludlum scene is to get in a fight.

This approach to violence is in keeping with a wartime spy genre convention which runs counter to the superhero norm: to temper superhero toughness by describing the physical pain, suffering, and psychological trauma he must endure—sleeplessness, cramped muscles, torn ligaments, knife and gunshot wounds, and fear for personal safety and for the safety of assistants and of those dependent on him. Ludlum captures the psychological toll such strain takes on the hero's humanity as killing comes too easily and his bloody deeds no longer repulse him. This loss of feeling makes Spaulding seek retirement and transforms Andrew Fontine from a good soldier into a crazed killer. Ludlum extends the conventional pattern of humanizing heroes to reveal insecurities and weaknesses, distaste for what necessity compels, loneliness and need for love, confusion, panic, and disbelief. But a drawback of these humanizing touches is that the final conversion of a hero like the disoriented, easily driven Holcroft to hardened killer may seem contrived.

Like his contemporaries (Ken Follett, John le Carré, Len Deighton), Ludlum tackles moral questions. His Nazis are evil, their leaders paranoid madmen driven by private demons, but the Allies too have their share of culpability and must be on guard against corruption within. In *The Scarlatti Inheritance*, Ludlum's villain is an American war hero in league with the Nazis, but the international financiers who place personal profit above humanistic commitments and join with the villain to help bring the Nazis to power are even more to blame. In *The Rhinemann Exchange* an American company that underbids the competition and claims it can produce a high-altitude guidance system in time for a planned military invasion is the real enemy, its motive profit; that company's failure to fulfill its commitments forces the United States to secretly negotiate with the Nazis to win the war. In *The Gemini Contenders* a Vietnam hero decides that an elite military team should rightfully rule and judge the weak, the untrained, the inferior. Spaulding voices the ultimate moral problem of the modern hero/spy: "we don't know our enemies any longer" (*The Rhinemann Exchange*, 376).

The use of a *doppelgänger* (a ghostly double, an almost exact counterpart) calls attention to this fear. In *The Rhinemann Exchange* the first *doppelgänger* is simply a substitute for Spaulding, a stranger of his height, build, and coloring, in identical clothes, selected to lead enemy agents away from a secret rendezvous. The second *doppelgänger*, A. S., however, is more sinister. A. S. are the initials for both Albert Speer (Hitler's architect and minister of armaments and planner of the war economy) and Alan Swanson (of the State Department), a fact Spaulding uses to suggest a conspiracy even more sinister than the one actually occurring, a conspiracy his Nazi opponents readily believe. In *The Gemini Contenders* one brother is the reverse image of the other: while both are well-educated and successful in their fields, one is a defender of democratic principles and the other a would-be despot, one a creator and the other a destroyer. In *The Holcroft Covenant* the duality lies in the two faces of the *Wolfsschanze*: one is an upright, moral group of German officers who tried to save their country by assassinating Hitler, the other an immoral group of would-be tyrants offended at Hitler's incompetence and determined to assassinate him and to bring the world to its knees through outrageous acts of brutality and terrorism. Agents of the second group regularly pretend to be agents of the first to access secrets. As in virtually all modern high-quality spy fiction, moral absolutes are few and shades of gray common, with confusion between good and evil a central theme.

Double-dealing, violence, and treachery are the way of this modern world. A recurrent role in Ludlum's fiction is that of the "reverse conduit," an operative who is left in place and fed disinformation to mislead the enemy. The innocent are duped into acting against their own interests and morality; Holcroft, for example, is set up as a conduit for Nazi funds and for the rise of the Fourth Reich under the guise of humanitarian restitution for war crimes. Questionable loyalties keep plots moving. Leslie Jenner of *The Rhinemann Exchange*, an Israeli agent with humanistic motives and a record of self-sacrifices for a good cause, initially seems a Nazi agent, as does Yakov Ben-Gadîz in *The Holcroft Covenant*, a survivor of the concentration camps desperate to prevent a Fourth Reich. In *The Rhinemann Exchange* both the U.S. government and the German Reichstag must rely on go-betweens they find distasteful or whom they distrust, but they soothe their consciences by assassinating key players at mission's end. Spaulding, chosen for his double expertise as engineer and killer, is also designated for death. In *The Gemini Contenders* zealots eliminate anybody who could betray their secret, a priest kills his devout brother and then turns his weapon on himself, and death after death follows to protect a secret.

So many popular fiction novels focus on World War II and Nazi Germany that they almost form a minigenre of their own: what critics have called the Nazi or neo-Nazi spy/adventure story. Despite their limited historical focus, the content of such "Nazi novels" is wide-ranging. They tell of secret operations to assassinate Hitler, to steal war plans, to rescue important prisoners, to sabotage technological advances, to buy or steal technological or scientific secrets, to detect and expose double agents, or to pave the way for invasion. They also claim to tell the "true" story of how high-placed Nazis escaped imprisonment or death and fled to South America, how German scientists were rescued from the Russian zone of Berlin, or how the Nazi hunters ferreted out war criminals (particularly in Argentina, Brazil, and Paraguay) and brought them to justice. These writers, including Ludlum, assume a readership familiar with the conflicts of World War II, knowledgeable about Hitler, Speer, and others whose roles in the Third Reich have become infamous. They sometimes show German officers of honor and integrity undermining, standing up to, or actively battling the Gestapo and the SS; a common trait of all these novels, however, is the unquestioning assumption that the dedicated Nazi was a traitor to humanity, deserving defiance, defeat, punishment, and death. *The Valhalla Exchange* (1976) by Harry Patterson (alias Jack Higgins/Hugh Marlowe) is typical: VIP American and French prisoners of war become endangered pawns in the schemes of the notorious Nazi Martin Bormann; seeing that defeat is inevitable, Bormann tries to save himself, offering to trade the freedom of his hostages for a new life in South America. His self-serving, cowardly use of the innocent to escape his just deserts epitomizes the cowardly Nazi of popular fiction convention.

The neo-Nazi tales focus on modern-day villains: would-be Hitlers and Bormanns. They deal with the search for Nazi treasure and with plots to restore the Reich; stories include the cloning of Hitler, the smuggling out of the country of children of "pure blood" as the hope of the Reich's future, and the maintenance of a worldwide network of Nazi conspirators. Ira Levin's well-known neo-Nazi novel *The Boys from Brazil* (1976) focuses on the real-life Nazi doctor Josef Mengele, safely hidden away in the jungles of Brazil, continuing his inhumane genetic experiments to produce a superrace of Nazi soldiers. Frederick Forsyth's *The Odessa File* (1972) postulates an obsessively dedicated Mafia-like organization of former S.S. members, the ODESSA, formed to reestablish SS power worldwide, to fight Jewish opponents, and to carry out a "Final Solution" of mass murder twenty years after Hitler's death.

*The Scarlatti Inheritance, The Rhinemann Exchange, The Gemini Contenders*, and *The Holcroft Covenant* are very much in this Nazi novel tradition. *The Scarlatti Inheritance* traces the evolution of a Nazi supporter. *The Rhinemann Exchange* explores the extremes to which both Nazis and anti-Nazis will go to obtain vital technological materials or weapons' plans. *The Gemini Contenders* exposes Hitler's scheme to discredit Christianity, a scheme still in place after the war. *The Holcroft Covenant* envisions a Fourth Reich, established by the children of the Third Reich, planted at the war's end in strategic American families and bankrolled by $780 million in Swiss banks. Whether in Nazi or neo-Nazi novels, Ludlum's heroes question their own sanity, but also ask, like the German hero Schellenberg in Harry Patterson's *To Catch a King* (1979), "Am I really the only sane man in a world gone mad?" (316).

## NARRATIVE PERSPECTIVE

To some degree in all these works, a third-person omniscient narrator (one who is distanced from the action but who can enter the minds of characters) allows Ludlum to alternate between conspirators and opponents and to see through the eyes of key figures, recording doubts, fears, and private reactions. The narrative perspective of all four novels, however, centers on the main male lead, who is caught up in a nightmare situation and must unravel its myriad threads to fulfill his sense of justice, undermine a frightening conspiracy, save his own life and those of numerous others, and protect the woman he loves or innocents for whom he feels responsible. Particularly in moments of stress, sudden action, panic, or exhaustion, Ludlum's protagonists have dual voices: their spoken words are juxtaposed to internal responses set in italics, reflecting their physical, emotional, and moral states. In *The Rhinemann Exchange*, when Spaulding sees the tableau of death around him and the sheet-white Eugene Lyons (mathematical genius and human wreck), Ludlum writes:

> *The man's dying*, thought Spaulding.
> *Death.*
> *He had to concentrate.*
> *Oh, Christ!* He had to *think*. Start *somewhere. Think.*
> *Concentrate.*
> Or he would go out of his mind.
> He turned to Feld. The Jew's eyes were compassionate.
> And yet, they were the eyes of a man who killed in calm deliberation. (362–63)

Thus, readers share in multiple perspectives: (1) the calm exterior of the professional agent, (2) his internal response to shock, confusion, and horror, combined in (3) the protagonist's ability to operate on two levels, both as a shocked human being and as a competent professional weighing options and deciding strategy.

## *THE SCARLATTI INHERITANCE*

Ludlum's first novel, *The Scarlatti Inheritance*, initiates patterns used throughout his canon. The novel grew out of two magazine photographs showing the economic collapse in Germany following World War I: a shopper pushing a wheelbarrow filled with valueless currency that illustrated the country's hyperinflation; and a group of jack-booted Nazi precursors. Mentally comparing the photographs, Ludlum wondered where the money for the boots came from if a wheelbarrow full of Reichsmarks could not buy a loaf of bread, and hypothesized secret financiers bankrolling the Nazis (Baxter and Nichols 51–52).

The novel resulting from this premise begins with four fictional *New York Times* clippings: the 1926 disappearance of a war hero, the son of a wealthy American industrial family; the 1937 disruption of reciprocal trade agreement negotiations between I. G. Farben, Germany's largest munitions manufacturer, and U.S. firms, with an unidentified member of Hitler's War Ministry using English invectives to brand the slow progress as unacceptable; a 1948 report of the secret 1944 defection of a high-ranking Nazi, code-named "Saxon"; and a 1951 discovery, in Kreuszlingen, Switzerland, of an oilcloth packet, imprinted with the word "Saxon" and containing wartime Berlin armament installations maps. These clippings prepare readers for an exposé of the behind-the-scenes realities that interrelate these skimpy news clips—a conspiracy by the German and the American governments. This movement from a seemingly factual base, often established through news reports, to a fictional explanation involving conspiracy has become a Ludlum trademark. As the protagonist Matthew Canfield tells his son the truth, he reports the extreme secrecy of his information: "no more than ten people have ever seen it in full, and most of them are dead" (18). The information, typed by a rotating pool of vetted military typists, is in a secret file, out of sequence, with the key to the code in a separate folder protected by lead seals. Even the British agents who assisted the Americans have been kept in the dark. As the narrative progresses, readers learn that these clippings are but the tip of the iceberg.

## Character Development: Ulster Scarlett

The missing American is the war hero of the first clipping, Ulster Stewart Scarlett, the son of wealthy industrialist Giovanni Scarlatti, an Italian immigrant whose rags-to-riches success resulted in a financial empire, strengthened by his marriage to Elizabeth Wyckham of the wealthy and aristocratic Chicago Wyckhams. Scarlett is a bully and a coward, a man with little talent, frightened of competing with ordinary people and of

not living up to the promises of his birth. His mother fears him capable
of the worst she can imagine, but protects him to protect the family. His
prized World War I decorations, supposedly for fearlessly destroying
three enemy machine gun nests to rescue what remained of his platoon,
are a sham. The German withdrawal lets the opportunistic Scarlett set
the stage to seem as if he had single-handedly routed the enemy: he
shoots a wounded German, Heinrich Kroeger, and kills two fellow
Americans to create the illusion of continued fighting. Then, confronted
by an armed German officer (Gregor Strasser, an amoral man much like
Scarlett), he cuts a deal to mutual benefit. Strasser is an anti-Semite who
believes in the German right to *lebensraum* (living space) and is committed to rooting out the traitors that he believes lost the Germans World
War I and to establishing a firmer political, industrial, and financial base
for the next war. He wins Scarlett's allegiance to the Nazi cause and
becomes his secret friend and coconspirator. A long correspondence en-
sues, with Scarlett assuming the code name Heinrich Kroeger as a re-
minder of their meeting.

Back home, Scarlett works with gangsters during prohibition and au-
thorizes violence and murder, including the attempted murder of undercover government agent Matthew Canfield. Scarlett's marriage to the
eminently acceptable, aristocratic Janet Saxon and his attention to the
family business promise reform. A long honeymoon in Europe, however,
is part of his scheme to raid the family fortune; playing on the foolishness
of the family financial advisor and using the financial strategies learned
from the financier's tutelage, Scarlett secretly withdraws family securities
worth over $270 million, then uses his requests for trust account funds,
through months of European travel, to squirrel away another $800,000.
The disappearance of the fictitious *New York Times* article marks Scarlett's
new life as Nazi financier and advisor.

After failing twice to murder his own mother, Scarlett confronts her
directly, requesting silence in return for the lives of their extended family. Plastic surgery and brainwashing by Strasser's Nazi propaganda
make him see himself as a "weapon of power" helping major industrial
players from America, Britain, France, Sweden, and Germany sweep the
National Socialists and Hitler to power. His stolen funds help hide a
Nazi training compound on fourteen adjoining estates in Switzerland
and produce thousands of elite troops safely "beyond the scrutiny of the
Versailles inspection teams" (272). The second clipping, then, reveals
Scarlett's role in ridding the world of misfits, leading a new order, con-
solidating foreign support, and scheming alongside Rudolf Hess, the

deputy leader of the Nazi party, and Joseph Goebbels, the Nazi propaganda minister, in matters of consequence and power. Although Scarlett/Kroeger was supposedly killed in Zurich when his mother terminated his carefully constructed scheme, the third clipping supports Matthew Canfield's conjecture about a cover-up, and his suspicion that Scarlett/Kroeger was wounded but not killed.

## Plot Development and Structure

Beginning his story with World War I and the thirties, Ludlum delineates the personal insecurities and ambitions that led individuals to support the Nazi rise to power, and the potential for the unscrupulous to find financial backing, through blackmail and a promise of profit, for building a war machine, in spite of international regulations and limits. The novel's action begins in October 1944, when a brigadier general and the wartime Secretary of State Cordell Hull are faced with Canfield's revelations about Scarlett's survival and its implications for hastening the war's end. The story ends with Canfield and Andrew Scarlett Canfield (whom he adopted after marrying Scarlett's ex-wife) facing a semi-invalid, hate-ridden Scarlett, still determined to wield power, this time through his son. Scarlett has tantalized American officialdom with promises to betray the Reich, but dreams of passing on to his son the "power to change the world" (352). This power is in the form of millions of dollars in Swiss bank accounts, whose release is contingent on his son agreeing to his plans. He offers the Nazi fortification plans to the Allies in exchange for his son's commitment to his scheme for power, unaware that the Nazi High Command has betrayed him, the plans had been obtained weeks before, and he is expendable. There is no honor among thieves, implies Ludlum.

The fourth clipping (about the "Saxon" packet of maps) is ironic, a forgotten piece of history, a bargaining chip that did not work out. Canfield shoots Scarlett in the heart, his death confirmed beyond dispute. Janet, Andrew, and Matthew are finally freed of this madman, whose dreams of power depended on the deaths and betrayal of so many innocents. Scarlett is an American, but his madness is in tune with the madness of the top-ranking Nazis responsible for the death camps.

Against such lunacy, ordinary people placed in extraordinary situations must suppress their best instincts and kill in order to survive, to protect the weak and innocent, or to serve a higher good affecting many lives. In contrast to Ludlum's villains, decent people like Canfield recognize the insanity of what they are forced to do; and they seek human contact and engage in acts of expiation to regain normality and sanity.

## Themes and Patterns

In addition to fleshing out the realities behind the headlines and exploring the insanities of history, Ludlum delineates the deep loyalties between men and women that inspire self-sacrifice and valor, and depicts decent, upright family men drawn into world conflicts that could engulf them and destroy their families unless they are very courageous and clever. His protagonists often fall in love at first sight, and his heroines generally have little to do except inspire and provide a solid base of sanity and security for his beleaguered heroes. Canfield, on government assignment to cultivate Janet Saxon Scarlett's friendship, falls in love and eventually marries her. Theirs is a true romance, and the birth of Janet's son by Ulster draws them even closer. That commitment brings responsibility, a key word in Ludlum's novels: decent human beings assume responsibility for their acts and accept the obligations imposed on them by friends, family, and nation. Canfield is a good father and a protective husband; he bears responsibility for his wife's and adopted child's lives, as well as those of their relatives. To protect his family, he fabricates testimony that hides Scarlett's damning role as traitor. Later, he must face the consequences of that act—both for his family and for his government. Ludlum makes this feeling for family and rectitude in the face of sanctioned madness part of his standard repertoire.

Ludlum's villains often employ blackmail against decent people who have a sense of shame and guilt. Blackmail, however, also shames wrongdoers into acting properly to avoid public exposure. Elizabeth Scarlatti threatens to spread sordid rumors of drugs and promiscuity about her daughter-in-law, unless she agrees to silence about Scarlett's true nature and his peculiar behavior on their honeymoon. Later, Elizabeth faces the evil consequences of her cover-up. The trusted bank advisor, Jefferson Cartwright, whose ineptitude allowed Scarlett to steal so much so easily, in turn, blackmails Elizabeth, threatening exposure of the family's financial loss unless she buys his silence with money and position. Scarlett, however, has a more effective way to silence him: murder. In fact, Scarlett used his time with the Mafia to compile files on key figures he could later blackmail; his power over the Zurich alliance is based on blackmail. He blackmails his own mother to protect the Zurich list of international financiers supporting the rise of the Third Reich. Elizabeth yields to his requests until she understands the horrifying implications of his scheme. She then puts her life on the line to stop him by sending cablegrams threatening those financiers with public exposure and financial ruin (even at the cost of her personal ruin) if they do not turn the tables on her son.

Elizabeth Scarlatti embodies Ludlum's theme of power gone awry. First, she assumes responsibility for her son's acts: "I'll destroy my son. I shall expose Ulster Scarlett for what he is. . . . I implanted an idea. An idea which has become warped in the process of maturing" (262). Then she elucidates the root of the trouble: the stimulating, all-consuming "game" of building an industrial empire, doubling earnings in the marketplace, and acquiring possessions and wealth, which gave her husband and her joy in the acquisition of power. She says that she sincerely believed herself equipped for the responsibility: "The more convinced I became, it had to follow that others were not equipped. . . . Whether he understood it or not, that's what my son saw happening" (263). As a consequence, her son has become "a madman" in alliance with "psychopathic malcontents," and she vows to "stop at nothing" to prevent the "final madness" of a Nazi conspiracy to seize world power (264), even if it means destroying everything she and her husband once built together. These themes of misused power, of well-meaning citizens arrogantly presuming that they are infallible and that others are less capable of choosing for themselves, of parents who are blind to the defects of their offspring, and of power-plays theoretically for the greater good echo throughout Ludlum's canon. Ludlum ties misused power to class snobbery, greed, schizophrenia, and megalomania. Even the government agency for which Canfield works thinks of him as "a pawn who trapped himself" (126). This idea of expediency and of dedicated, loyal civil servants as pawns recurs.

Mixing historical figures with fictional settings, a recurrent part of Ludlum's technique since this first novel, creates the illusion of historical "truth" and of peeking in on the secret realities of public figures. Mini-portraits of historical personalities serve the same function as a *roman à clef* (a novel about real people, thinly disguised by slight changes to names and minor characteristics): they reduce larger-than-life historical figures to understandable men and women with feet of clay. In this case Ludlum undercuts the myth of Hitler and Goebbels as supermen and reduces them to petty criminals and thugs—racist, paranoid, and dangerous. In *The Road to Omaha* and the Bourne series, Ludlum will again use news clippings to provide verisimilitude.

## THE RHINEMANN EXCHANGE

*The Rhinemann Exchange* (originally titled *Cable Tortugas*) is the only one of Ludlum's novels that he did not invent in full; instead the idea came from a conversation with fellow boaters on a beach in St. Thomas ("Ludlum on Ludlum") about the possibility of international liaisons in Buenos Aires in World War II.

### Plot Development and Structure

Typically, Ludlum begins with action or events that establish the integrity and competence of the hero, and then describes a situation requiring the hero to act. Sometimes he alternates between representatives of two opposing governments or factions. Sometimes he simply tosses the hero into the midst of the action, followed by a hunter-hunted pattern: the protagonist pursued and threatened, not knowing why but gathering information and insights, making allies, and then turning the tables on his pursuers. The denouement reveals dark, hidden secrets of betrayal and conspiracy, while the end is always positive—order restored, evil defeated (at least temporarily), the hero vindicated, the heroine safe in his arms, and his allies, though injured, stronger for their participation in the contest.

The Preface of *The Rhinemann Exchange* is actually the end of the story: David Spaulding and Jean Cameron are in Washington, D.C., where he is to deliver his testimony and explain his deeds. The rest of the book reports the events that brought them to this place. The Prologue tells how a gentle, educated man of good breeding, peacetime engineer David Spaulding through military training in guerrilla warfare tactics and field experience organizing and operating a spy network in Portugal, became the "Man from Lisbon," a cold, efficient, uncompromising agent, who pretends to be a playboy attached to the Lisbon embassy but who secretly smuggles people and secrets out of Germany. He is a man apart, burdened by responsibilities, intuiting treachery. Part I establishes his well-rounded competence, his nose for conspiracy and double-dealing, and his worries about becoming a stone-killer for whom empathy, anger, and involvement no longer exist (Chapters 3, 6, 8).

After establishing Spaulding's humanity, skill, and competence, Ludlum turns to the world situation, alternating between German and American leaders, each group trapped in secret war plans halted by circumstances (Chapters 1, 2, 4–7). The Germans have been unable to acquire the quantity of industrial diamonds necessary to make their rocket project at Peenemünde viable. The Americans have been unable to produce the high-altitude gyroscope necessary to prevent midair collisions and keep their bombers on course at altitudes high enough to avoid heavy flak (ground-to-air fire) during the invasion of Germany. The solution is worked out through a Swiss go-between: the Germans will trade gyroscope plans for diamonds—a secret, incredible deal between warring nations. The trade will be made in Argentina, with Erich Rhinemann—a seemingly neutral German–Jewish industrialist—overseeing arrangements.

The choice of Spaulding soothes the leadership's conscience: he is a knowledgeable engineer who can verify the authenticity and workability of the gyroscope blueprints, but also an assassin who can ruthlessly destroy any who might betray this deal. The plot is complicated by a Jewish group, the Haganah, which tries to kill him before his mission begins and which shadows him in New York; the Haganah only know that they must stop Americans from dealing with Nazis. Spaulding is ignorant of his real function and the real nature of a deal called "The Rhinemann Exchange." He becomes increasingly suspicious as he is spied on and threatened, his every action anticipated. Chapters 20 and 21 end Part I with a traitor at the American center at Fairfax, the death of a key American participant (Ed Pace), the introduction of key American players, and Spaulding's decision to act alone at the center of action.

Part II takes place in Buenos Aires. Chapters 22–25 introduce the female lead, the mysterious opposition, and Spaulding as hunter. Spaulding contacts the Germans in Chapter 27 and the Haganah in Chapter 28, muddies the waters in Chapters 29–35, faces the truth of his mission in Chapters 36 and 37, risks his life to gain information in Chapter 38, and then exploits that information to redefine his mission and defeat the enemy in Chapters 39–42. When Haganah agents finally confront him with their knowledge of his mission, he is shocked. He is determined to get the vital plans, but redefines his main mission: preventing the Germans from escaping with the diamonds. An alliance with the Haganah results in much bloodshed, but Spaulding does fulfill his assigned mission— and more. Chapter 43 sums up the repercussions and the final successes.

## Character Development

In his early works Ludlum draws well-rounded, complicated protagonists, with explicit motives and values, but his remaining characters serve the plot as stereotyped villains and one-dimensional figures.

Among the latter, Brigadier General Alan Swanson of the War Department, the American motivator of the Rhinemann exchange, will do whatever it takes to get the gyroscope plans, even consort with the devil. Although he is humanized by guilt, he differs little from his German counterparts. Accountant Walter Kendall, who has planned the exchange, is a self-serving sadist: he is described as "ferret-like" (151), an "animal," a "sewer-rat," a "predator," an "invader," "filthy," and "sick" (130). A coward, he enjoys the misery of others, but flees when his life is endangered. His counterpart is the Jewish financial wizard, Erich Rhinemann, who betrays his own people out of greed and commitment to a Nazi vision of power. His fellow Jews call him "pig," a damning insult for those for whom pork is an abhorrent meat forbidden by God, and they happily assist any who oppose him.

Asher Feld, the leader of the Haganah faction, hates Nazis for their butchery of fellow Jews and concentrates on "priorities." Leslie Jenner, who sets Spaulding up, has sacrificed her reputation and safety for the Jewish cause. Spaulding assumes she has prostituted herself for the Germans, but she is really working for a higher cause: defeating the Nazis and helping Jewish refugees.

Jean Cameron, the love interest, appears late in the book (in Part II) and has few lines, but clearly motivates Spaulding and helps delineate his character. He needs to love someone as wholesome, competent, and loyal as Jean, and his ability to function well and complete his final mission depends on her background presence: getting a doctor, finding a safehouse, influencing allies to trust him, and providing hope for a sane future.

Eugene Lyons, who helps Spaulding with his final mission, is developed more fully than Jean and wins greater sympathy. Initially he seems a ruined man, unable or unwilling to speak, physically depleted, but with an agile, active mind. He is a genius in aerophysics and an expert on gyroscopes. A failed marriage, heavy drinking, and bad debts, however, resulted in imprisonment for murder and, later, skid row. Rescued from this self-punishment by a government in need, his life has become numbers, equations, and diagrams. He has not talked in ten years, and spends all his time between laboratory and hospital. His two hired companions, though loyal, think him unreclaimable. His immediate rapport with Spaulding, however, helps him find within himself the strength to support him when need be, to pull him from the waters of the River Plate, tend his wounds, drive him to safety, and lend moral support. At the book's end, Lyons has overcome his fears and weaknesses and regained self-worth and purpose. His transformation confirms Spaulding as more creator than destroyer.

Spaulding is defined in part through his responses to other characters. His gut reaction against Kendall and Rhinemann suggests his good instincts; his immediate love of Cameron and friendship with Lyons are equally defining. An architectural engineer by training, he is a builder, a romantic who takes pride in form and function. But the demands of war and patriotism have forced him into a role at odds with his true nature. As an agent provocateur, he can be independent and creative, and establish a network of agents based on loyalty and checks and balances, but he must also be ruthless, murderous, and destructive in the name of right. He is, nonetheless, unhappy with such compromises, which is why he is so important to the Rhinemann mission. A competent civilian professional with military skills, he is also a man of vision and integrity, who can evaluate the consequences of his deeds and who is independent enough to do what is right—even against orders. Ludlum sees this rebellious independence that results from a strong sense of values and loyalties as the hope of democracies.

## Themes

*The Rhinemann Exchange* depicts war's dehumanizing effects and personal devastations. It shows how war transforms people, requiring them to act against their nature and to learn deadly skills that run counter to civilized training but that become easier to practice with constant use. Thus, the mild-mannered Spaulding becomes an efficient, deadly killer who easily garrotes a traitor, tortures a prisoner to elicit vital information, and cunningly traps traitors. He plunges his bayonet into a Nazi's stomach, "ripping it downward, killing the man instantly," while blocking the start of a scream with "rigid fingers thrust into the dead man's

mouth" (103). When his closest friend in the region, Bergeron, is captured, tortured, broken, and killed by the Nazis, his associates expect an
explosion of emotion, but Spaulding feels empty—his humanity reduced.
Governments use the crisis of war to justify orders and assignments that
must be followed without question, although they violate both national
principles and the deeply felt values of individual citizens. War justifies
the manipulation of lives, the exploitation of many, and the sacrifice of
the few for the many. Thus, Alan Swanson participates in a plan that
negates his deepest sense of right; Asher Feld concentrates on "priorities" to live with murder; and Spaulding becomes a tool to be manipulated, used, and discarded. Indeed, the final betrayal is that, after
Spaulding has served his nation well, Washington orders his execution.

Greed creates and perpetuates wars, says Ludlum. Greed makes individuals sell secrets and assist their nation's enemies. As in Arthur Miller's *All My Sons*, the greed of dishonest plane manufacturers will
condemn thousands of young Americans to fiery deaths. Industrialists
make fortunes by feeding the war machines of opposing nations; Rhinemann's greed and lust for power lead him to support and validate a
system based on "might makes right," to place possessions above people,
and to work hand in hand with a nation determined to annihilate his
own people.

Especially during wartime, men who betray their country out of personal greed and ambition are unspeakable, argues Ludlum. He complicates this theme, however, with a question of priorities: which loyalties
take precedence? Jean Cameron asks for his personal loyalty, but Spaulding forces her to see that national loyalty to save thousands of lives
has priority, and that only when he fulfills his national obligations can
they consider their private lives. American Lieutenant Ira Burdock, however, has chosen his Jewish identity over his American identity, and
betrays his American office to revenge himself on the Nazis and punish
the perpetrators of the death camps. Ludlum uses the Shakespearean
technique of foils to explore different facets of a single theme through
varied situations and varied characters. Walter Kendall and Erich
Rhinemann, for example, have no loyalties, except to themselves. Others have loyalties to an ideal or an organization that represents those
ideals, but not to individuals, while for some of the nicest people
in the book, personal loyalties to individuals take precedence. Some
demonstrate loyalty only by adherence to the commands of authority;
others understand that the deepest loyalty involves commitment to
values that must be defended, even if their defense means violating

orders and breaking rules. At the close of the novel, those survivors for whom "words of conscience" have lost meaning have penance imposed: forced service as government clerks (445–46).

Other thematic ideas are more commonplace: the strong should help the weak and the vulnerable; respect for competence can promote competence; love can overcome seemingly insurmountable obstacles; and with time villains will get their comeuppance.

Ludlum's most significant theme throughout his canon is that the lone individual can make a difference. Most historians agree that a key distinction between World War II German and American soldiers was that the Germans were not innovative; decisions came from above and, in times of crisis, superiors had to be consulted before action was taken. In contrast, the American soldiers seized the moment in times of crisis and acted as they thought necessary or effective—for example, charging ahead on D-Day despite landing miles from where the plans indicated. This willingness to take responsibility and to act on their own authority, innovatively and even creatively, helped win the war. Ludlum's heroes have this sense of self-reliance and personal decision-making.

When Jean Cameron speaks hypothetically and disbelievingly of a David who believes "that he'll influence the outcome of the whole war" when he's "only one among millions and millions" (203), the irony is that in fact only Spaulding can influence the outcome of the whole war, for he is the only one among millions who is in the right place at the right time and has the skills necessary to prevent the Nazis from getting diamonds for their rockets and to seize the blueprints needed for American guidance systems. Her question, "Haven't you done enough?" (292), turns on the integrity of the hero: he has not yet done all that he can and must do to fulfill his obligations not simply to a nation, but also to individuals whose lives would be lost if he failed to act. Dachau, Auschwitz, and Belsen compel individual commitment (367). When Spaulding's individual effort meets up with those of a committed cryptographer, a committed physicist, and committed death camp survivors, they are a force to be reckoned with.

## THE GEMINI CONTENDERS

Long at the top of the best-sellers charts when it first came out, *The Gemini Contenders* pushed Ludlum's total hardcover and paperback sales past the ten million mark (*World Authors* 555). Criticized as "implausi-

ble," "improbable," "florid," "unbelievable," and "inaccurate about details," it is nonetheless not only a very engaging story about significant
issues, but also one of Ludlum's finest creations. It is well-written, its
characters well-developed, its plot complex, its action breathtaking, and
its ideas innovatively carried out. Ludlum's exploration of the Nazi mentality—both in Hitler's Germany and thirty years later in the America of
the Vietnam War years—and his probing of faith, loyalty, historical
truth, and responsibility provide depth of meaning. Like Robert Duncan's *The Q Document* (1964), whose biblical scholar hero gets entangled
in conspiracy while investigating documents purporting to show that
Christianity is based on fraud and false prophets, *The Gemini Contenders*
applies to a thriller plot New Testament studies and scholarship on the
deciphering of ancient manuscripts. While Duncan concentrates on the
scholarship and documents, Ludlum uses them to explore particular
questions of values and loyalties.

## Plot Development and Structure

The novel is divided into two books. Book One concentrates on Vittorio Fontini-Cristi/Victor Fontine and Book Two on his two sons, Andrew and Adrian. Book One begins on December 9, 1939, about three
months after World War II began, and moves forward chronologically
to sometime in 1945, after Hitler's suicide on April 30 and the German
surrender on May 7, possibly as late as the Japanese surrender in September. Book Two begins in June 1973, after Watergate and a period of
antiwar protest marches, draft-card burnings, and the flight of American
Vietnam War draftees to Canada. Its swift action races through a period
of days or weeks.

Book One consists of a Prologue and three parts, with Part III the
longest section. The novel's opening Prologue may puzzle readers: it
focuses on armed priests from the Greek Order of Xenope guarding a
load of produce and fearing sabotage, behaving like commandos one
instant and kneeling in awe to pray before a large, square box the next.
Though marked as produce, this box is clearly of great value; it is loaded
aboard a secretly arranged night train to be shipped far beyond the reach
of the Nazis. The engineer, a Greek named Annaxas the Strong, is the
devout brother of the priest in charge, Father Petride Mikhailovic. Annaxas has arranged the special documents, including German ones, that
allow the train to pass through enemy territory unchallenged. Yet, at the

end of an anxious ride across Swiss borders into the Italian Alps, when the box has been delivered to Savarone Fontini-Cristi at a secret rendezvous and the train has moved on to Milan, Petride kills his brother, and then himself. Murder and suicide are the ultimate security, for no torturer can force secrets from lips sealed by death. What has required such sacrifice are religious documents entombed for over fifteen hundred years, documents that both confirm and undermine Christian beliefs. Ironically, the Nazis who desperately seek these documents kill the only man who knows their resting place, Savarone Fontini-Cristi. His power, wealth, and industrial might wield influence in Northern Italy and support an underground network of anti-German partisans. Using these activities as their excuse, German officers massacre the Fontini-Cristi family during a family gathering.

Part I (Chapters 1–5) ends with a naive and spoiled Vittorio Fontini-Cristi, the profligate son who has been carousing and womanizing, being shocked into responsibility. Vittorio witnesses the massacre from a distance. Aided by a faithful retainer, his father's underground network, and British agents, who assume he shares his father's secret, he flees the country, but not before his naiveté and squeamishness cost British agent Stone his hand. As 1940 begins, Vittorio leaves behind his prolonged adolescence and assumes adult responsibilities.

Part II (Chapter 6) describes the British interrogation of Vittorio and their decision to continue to investigate him. Part III (Chapters 7–17) is the heart of Vittorio's story. In London, Vittorio meets Mrs. Jane Holcroft, who is initially antagonistic but soon falls in love with him, as he does with her. She is with the Air Ministry, and British Intelligence encourages their relationship, hoping to elicit information from Vittorio; instead, they marry. MI-6 sends Vittorio to Scotland for commando training under the direction of Alec Teague. Vittorio sets up a network of foreign undercover specialists trained in intentional mismanagement, who return to occupied territory with documented proof of skills vital in industry, transportation, and so forth, to do incalculable damage that will seem the result of incompetence rather than sabotage. The idea works brilliantly and allows Vittorio, who has had his name Anglicized to Victor Fontine, to go in and out of occupied territory. He finds himself threatened and pursued, however, by Nazis, by Greek Catholic and Roman Catholic priests, and by the agents of various governments—all desperate for the secret they think he keeps hidden for his own ends. In England, his wife is targeted, but as German bombs obliterate their home, she gives birth in the nearby woods to twin sons, Andrew and

Adrian. (Ludlum intends resonances with another pair of Italian twins, Romulus and Remus, the mythic founders of Rome, to suggest the potential power of charismatic individuals.)

The war over, Victor, who has been tortured and crippled by fanatical priests, revisits the family mansion to speak with a priest from Xenope, only to be betrayed by the vengeful agent Stone. The fanatical cardinal who led the Nazi raid on his family tortures him and leaves him for dead, but Victor does not reveal the clue to the resting place of the missing documents. Physically unable to pursue this clue, he takes his family to America to save them from torture and worse.

Book Two contains four parts, with Part IV the shortest section. In Part I (Chapters 18–21) Victor Fontine learns what has been lost from the priest who originated the pact between the Order of Xenope and Savarone Fontini-Cristi and is once more attacked and nearly killed; this section also introduces the deeply rooted conflict between the two Fontine brothers. The plot jumps forward to June 1973, when Victor's pampered, wealthy twin sons compete for the Fontini-Cristi documents—for very different ends. Part II (Chapters 22–28) contrasts the values of the two brothers and their very different reactions to their father's revelations. Andrew is committed to violence, chaos, and self-aggrandizement, while Adrian is committed to community, integrity, and democratic freedoms. Part III records the battle between the two brothers—the destroyer and the protector. In the final cross-country chase, the soldier, Andrew, leaves death and havoc in his wake, while the human rights advocate, Adrian, races to stop his brother before it is too late. The secrets lie in three tubes in the wartime grave of a Jewish child killed by the Nazi-influenced children of Italian Alpiners. One tube contains the Filioque Denials prepared by Constantine scholars to question the Trinity and the deification of a holy man (Jesus); in the second, an Aramaic scroll reports a first-century investigation questioning the existence of Jesus; the third holds the parchment confession of St. Peter, claiming that the resurrection was a hoax (a common criminal substituted for Jesus on Calvary) and that Christ committed suicide three days later. In Part IV Adrian entrusts these documents to a reputable scholar. The question of what happens once their dates and possible validity are confirmed scientifically remains unanswered; the novel provides no pat answers, only conflict and dilemma.

## Character Development

Ludlum's villains in *The Gemini Contenders* are one-dimensional mad-men, mainly rabid Catholic priests murderously protective of their faith and committed to a holy war. The most extreme fanatic, Cardinal Guil-lamo Donatti, hand in hand with the Nazi SS, murders the Fontini-Cristis, tortures Victor Fontine to near death, and then commits suicide when his quest proves impossible. He passes on his mantle to Enrici Gaetamo, another sadistic priest, who epitomizes the anti-Jewish preju-dices of European Catholics of the time, and who also tries to kill Victor Fontine. The less malicious priests of Xenope are driven to terrible acts (Mikhailovic kills himself and the kindly, devout older brother whose sacrifices supported his education, training, and novitiate). The Nazis are terrible, but somehow less frightening than these priests run amuck. Drunken Nazi officers make a young woman from the death camps a drug addict and a sex slave, and assault her in turns on the floor of a plane in sight of all. Fontine calls them *animale* (beasts). Our other view of this Nazi elite is through the eyes of a blackmailer, whose knowledge of their sexual perversions forces them to betray their national cause.

The main villain of Book Two is West Point graduate Andrew Fontine, a committed Vietnam hawk proud of his high body count. Andrew's belief that personal superiority entitles one to rule and destroy suggests that the Nazi mentality was not limited to wartime Germany. Believing his honorable service insulted by military corruption and by antiwar protests at home, he and fellow officers form a military elite, the Eye Corps, to uncover corruption in the service, punish offenders, and some-day seize the Pentagon. He sees his cause as righteous, but his brother questions the Eye Corps's methods and motives and suggests Andrew has chosen evil means to institute reforms. The threat of legal retaliation and congressional hearings produces paranoid delusions and insanity. Trained for murder, he kills indiscriminately.

His twin brother Adrian is his diametrical opposite: a peacenik who has opposed the draft and the war and used his legal skills to change the system from within. Responsible and humane, he has been at odds with his brother since childhood. When he understands how irrational and dangerous his brother has become, he assumes personal responsi-bility to stop him. These twins embody the conflicts that split America (mainly by generations) in the 1960s and 1970s.

*The Gemini Contenders* has several finely sketched minor characters.

One is the homosexual courier who accompanies Victor on his European mission, Anton Lübok. A blonde Jew, the son of a Czechoslovakian ballet-master, he is a multilingual translator for the Wehrmacht, a powerful, intelligent man, with an "acid tongue," a "withering stare," and a hot temper (143), as well as the lover of numerous officers in the Nazi inner circle. His sexual predilection is his weapon for blackmail, opening doors and providing him documents and privileges. Though paid to arrange Victor's death, his quick wit and clever contrivances save his life. Another sharply drawn minor character is the Scottish Brigadier General Alec Teague, a member of MI-6 who is quick to recognize Victor's worth. He helps Victor discover his inner strengths, protects his family, and devises an ingenious sabotage plan for creating bureaucratic chaos that Victor quickly makes his own. His dependability and commitment help make the Loch Torridon secret training project the success it proves to be.

Victor Fontine is the driving force behind the novel. Ludlum convincingly traces Victor's maturation from pampered Italian playboy, accustomed to fast cars, fast women, and little responsibility, to professional saboteur and saboteur-trainer. The author contrasts the hardened, experienced agents who rescue him with the naive, sentimental Victor, and shows him learning harsh lessons at great cost to others. But these lessons stick. The first sign of change is his serious commitment to Jane Holcroft; the second is his enthusiastic participation in the military training and the competitive spirit these "games" awaken in him. That his knowledge of accounting and finance can contribute to the Loch Torridon mission gives him purpose and meaning, and he becomes a professional, secure in his abilities and with a sense of duty and responsibility that makes him volunteer for and survive dangerous missions. The skills that helped him survive and thrive during wartime bring him great wealth and respect in peacetime. An impartial, devoted father, he fears his secret knowledge could endanger the next generation, and takes steps to fulfill his obligations to the future.

## Themes

*The Gemini Contenders* explores father-son relationships, family ties to land and place, love at first sight, the demands of wartime service, the difference between professionals and amateurs, and the great value of education and training. Ludlum's key concerns encompass broad philosophical questions of guilt and responsibility, including the nature of evil, the defining characteristics of organizations, and the human propensity for fascism and group-think.

Ludlum distrusts large formal organizations, because they encourage members to think alike and because they often sacrifice individuals for the good of the whole—by policy. Thus, the Catholic Church, as the ultimate in international organizations, is potentially a hotbed of conspiracy, which may nurture characters like Donatti, Gaetamo, Father Petride, and the other militant priests of Rome and Xenope. With the cornerstones of their faith crumbling, Ludlum's fallen priests ally themselves with Nazis and become torturers, murderers, and suicides. Like the Nazis, they take orders without question and justify the means by the ends.

Another major theme concerns why some people are evil while others are not. Using twins allows Ludlum to discount racial, genetic, and even environmental causes. The two Fontine boys are of the same race and genetic makeup. Their parents are good people, intelligent, successful, and decent. They have provided their sons with uplifting experiences, parental support, love, kindness, and generosity. They have taught them values, and have expected the best. The twins have been well educated and well trained and are recognized experts in their fields, knowledgeable and competent. Then why is Andrew so bad and Adrian so good? Why does one become a crazed killer and the other a responsible citizen? Both are in many ways superior to those around them, but for Andrew superiority justifies exploiting others and forcing them to submit to his will, whereas for Adrian it entails an obligation to serve and uplift others. Ludlum provides no answers as to why such contrasts occur, but suggests that the difference is innate rather than the result of training or education: the brothers have been at odds since childhood because of very different natures.

The novel's structure also suggests that the two brothers illustrate questions raised in Book One. The fanatical, obsessive struggle to save the secret religious documents from seizure by the Nazi propaganda machine is understandable, but why does the struggle continue years later? Ludlum's answer is that fanaticism, obsession, power struggles, disdain for life, and many other negatives associated with the Nazi war machine do not characterize only one group, one time, or one place, but are instead part of the human makeup. No matter what their overt political persuasions or national allegiances are, some people are by nature Nazis, just as Andrew is by nature evil. They value allegiances, self-image, power, and personal gratification above human lives. This knowledge explains the fears of Noel Holcroft and paves the way for the neo-Nazis of Ludlum's later books. "The Nazi is among us and we don't see him," warns Holcroft. "He is cloaked in respectability and a pressed suit of clothes" (*The Holcroft Covenant* 381).

## THE HOLCROFT COVENANT

Ludlum's distress at a growing ultraconservatism on both the political left and right—a position he equated with international fascism—fueled *The Holcroft Covenant*, which confirms his interest in the Nazi mentality and the forces that drive it. Writing the novel helped him define his feelings about this movement and come to terms with it fictionally. The book also gave the reader a real-world threat to give urgency to the plot.

### Plot Development

A prologue set in Germany in March 1945 establishes the past; the story then leaps forward to the 1970s and to Noel Holcroft's meeting with the Zurich banker Manfredi, who explains the Holcroft Covenant; it then leaps forward again into a near future in which worldwide assassinations precipitate an international police network financed by Third Reich monies. This police network helps the Fourth Reich take control of Germany and the world. The progression is that of a nightmare past becoming an even more terrifying future, thanks to secret activities in the present.

Ernest Becker, in *Escape from Evil* (1975), makes the provocative claim that "evil rests on the passionate personal motive to perpetuate oneself" (122). In *The Holcroft Covenant* the evil is the Nazi passion to perpetuate the "pure" German genetic line and to create a future world dominated by the specially selected children of the ruling elite of the Third Reich. Thousands of these *Sonnenkinder*, or "children of the sun," chosen for their parentage and potential, are transported by submarine out of Germany at the war's close, set up in comfortable homes around the world with adopted parents who are above suspicion, and financed by stolen wealth that ensures the finest education and that opens doors to future careers in politics, government, police and military forces. In some unexplained way knowledgeable about their special role, they are guided into positions of authority. When the time is right and their maturity and social status are confirmed, plundered wealth (780 million dollars), stolen from the wartime German government's wide resources, will be released through a bank in Zurich to fund a world takeover by committed neo-Nazis.

The story examines an elaborate scheme to launder the money by using as an innocent front Noel Holcroft, whose father (*Reichsführer* Heinrich Clausen) originated the plan. Holcroft's mother, Althene, a firm anti-Nazi, denounced her husband and fled Germany with her son; the neo-Nazis, however, make Holcroft believe his father repented his wickedness and planned restitution for those who suffered at Nazi hands. Holcroft is to join a Von Tiebolt and a Kessler (children of his father's coconspirators) in Zurich to take possession of the funds. Action alternates between Holcroft's search for answers and the opposition's attempts to frighten and mislead him. To keep him off-kilter and noncritical, Erich Von Tiebolt, the true heir to the Nazi plan, arranges multiple murders around Holcroft and provides clues suggesting his pursuit by members of the ODESSA organization, the *Rache*, and the *Nachrichtendienst*, supposedly competing but equally fanatical Nazi groups. The *Nachrichtendienst*, however, is really composed of those who tried to assassinate Hitler for moral reasons, and its few surviving members have joined forces with Jewish survivors of the Nazi death camps to stop the Holcroft covenant from resurrecting the Reich.

Holcroft travels to Brazil, England, France, and Switzerland seeking answers, confronting MI-6 and Interpol agents, and leaving behind corpses murdered by Von Tiebolt and his agents, but attributed to Holcroft. The neo-Nazis plot, Holcroft experiences the results of that plotting, and eventually Helden Von Tiebolt, one of Erich's sisters, provides a third perspective as another innocent betrayed, one with connections that lead quickly to the truth. Erich Von Tiebolt, secretly the international assassin "Tinamou," murders his incestuous sister Gretchen and her husband, Holcroft's stepfather, his mother, and his closest friends, among others, and has a whole Israeli Negev desert settlement annihilated. Holcroft finally learns the truth, but it is too late; upon signing the bank papers releasing the funds, he is marked for death and his reputation is tainted. Despite all their precautions, Jewish death camp survivor Yakov Ben-Gadiz, Holcroft, and his beloved Helden are left for dead by neo-Nazi killers. The Epilogue projects a totalitarian future, whose only hope are Yakov, Holcroft, and Helden—healed, trained, and committed to fight against the neo-Nazis, for justice and democracy. Holcroft's first target is Erich Von Tiebolt, followed by the *Sonnenkinder* on the master list a surviving Jewish *Nachrichtendienst* agent has copied.

Despite the many holes in this plot and the practical questions of feasibility left unanswered, in the midst of the action, with bodies dropping left and right and innocent bystanders thrust into the field of death, credibility is not a central concern of the reader.

## Character Development

Character development in *The Holcroft Covenant* is sketchy and limited. The villains are diabolical, perverse, and sadistic, sacrificing even those close to them for their personal aggrandizement and power. Heinrich Clausen and his co-conspirators, Erich Kessler and Wilhelm Von Tiebolt, are stereotypical Nazi officers, butchers who destroy their world and seek to infect the future with their compulsions and ambitions. The beautiful, promiscuous Gretchen Von Tiebolt, who has married to further her brother's cause, confirms her brother's wickedness. Erich Von Tiebolt, the best-developed villain in the novel, is a handsome, arrogant blond, a model Aryan and the Führer or leader designated to lead the chosen to power. As a journalist, he has a devious cover for his alter ego Tinamou, a ruthless contract killer who assassinates important international figures and then blackmails his behind-the-scenes employers into carrying out his will. His own mother called him "insane" and his work "contemptible"; he put a bullet in her head (469). He deceives British intelligence and kills a fellow assassin to prove himself a brave, honest citizen, but he underestimates the strength, resilience, and humanitarian commitment of Holcroft, Helden, and death-camp Jews like Ben-Gadiz.

The central character, Noel Holcroft, is supposed to be a kind, well-adjusted architect, stable and secure. He has an impressive mother whom he adores, a good-hearted stepfather who has cared for him as his own, and loyal friends to help him (Sam Buonoventura and gay fashion designer William Estes, both killed in ghastly ways). Yet, the shock of learning his father was an infamous Nazi officer and the hope that he repented and planned restitution, sealing his pact with the future with his life's blood, make Holcroft turn his life upside down and race wildly around the globe tracing unsubstantiated rumors and accepting absurd stories of death squads and terrorism as absolute truth. Helden Von Tiebolt is a romantic foil to Holcroft, a capable, honest woman who has befriended an old man (Herr Oberst Klaus Falkenheim), a survivor of the *Wolfsschanze*, the famous group of high-ranking German officers who heroically tried to assassinate Hitler. Helden and Noel's love is a strong positive contrast to Gretchen and Erich's incest.

## Themes

Some themes in *The Holcroft Covenant* respond directly to key statements of Nazi belief. For example, Hitler wrote in *Mein Kampf* that terror produced by force wins an easy victory over reason (Vol. I, Chapter 2: 53). Holcroft's dismayingly irrational behavior demonstrates Hitler's point. Von Tiebolt terrorizes Holcroft into panic, horror, and irrationality; his emotional vulnerability makes him an easily manipulated puppet. Hitler also claimed that the masses are more easily deceived by a great lie than a small one (*Mein Kampf*, Vol. 1, Chapter 10: 313), and it is by a great lie, the promise of massive restitution to victims of the Nazis, that Holcroft is committed to his father's covenant. Furthermore, Hitler's reliance on the power of the spoken word to compel is echoed by the almost mesmerizing quality of Von Tiebolt's speech, a power readers are told of but don't actually experience.

Hannah Arendt, in her book *Eichmann in Jerusalem* (1963), says that Adolph Eichmann and the Nazi high command talked about concentration camps in terms of "administration" and about extermination camps in terms of "economy" and that abstract language to cover atrocities was typical of the S.S. mentality. They labeled this approach "objective," a quality Eichmann at his trial was still very proud of. Ludlum's Nazis also reduce horrible acts to the language of the banal or the ordinary, calling genocide the necessary "weeding out" of the imperfect and unfit and describing the goal of world conquest as "legitimate," murder as "expedient" or "necessary," and the practice of assassinating heads of state as an "exercise."

The infamous Nazi anthem Horst Wessel Lied claimed that "Today all Germany is ours" and added, "Tomorrow the whole world." This is the future possibility Ludlum envisions unless ordinary citizens like Holcroft remain vigilant. In the final lines of the book Holcroft warns, "They were everywhere. It had only begun" (500), which echoes the earlier statement about the hidden Nazis among us, disguised by their respectability and presentability (381). Attractive, rich, well-educated men and women in positions of authority but committed to dominance, power, and control and willing to use any weapons and betray any loyalties except their group commitment to attain such goals—these are the demons Ludlum warns against.

Related is the theme of appearance versus reality and of shifts of perception that transform one's understanding of reality. The Von Tiebolts confirm the cliché that an attractive exterior can hide moral depravity. Gretchen's stunning beauty and Erich's physical perfection hide perversion and evil, while the furtiveness of the agents who steadfastly oppose the Nazis makes them highly suspect. The main questions of perception center on Holcroft. Some assume that his genetic heritage defines who he is and what he will do; others believe that his American upbringing will leave him too soft and muddled to discern a conspiracy and to stand up against it. Holcroft's own misperceptions—his belief in the covenant made by his father and in the sincerity of Erich Von Tiebolt, his acceptance of ODESSA and the *Nachrichtendienst* as the villains—dominate a large part of the novel. Not until Chapter 44, when he faces the Sephardic Jew and *Nachrichtendienst* agent Yakov Ben-Gadiz, does Holcroft reconsider the facts, which assume a different aspect when viewed through Helden's testimony about her brother, through Holcroft's dead mother's farewell letter and her violent death at the hands of Erich Von Tiebolt. With the suspicions of MI-6 confirmed and Von Tiebolt's seminal role in giving birth to the Fourth Reich revealed, the details and events that formed a positive pattern are suddenly realigned and redefined to project an undeniably negative image.

Holcroft asks the supposed friends of the Von Tiebolts, the Cararras, "What kind of world do you live in?" His initial response to terror is incredulity—"It's crazy" (102)—and then the realization that "This was not his world" (221). As the novel progresses, however, Holcroft begins a fragmented, running monologue on the lessons trial and error teach him. He worriedly recites information at odds with what he has been led to believe. When told that the death of his stepfather and of the old man in the car that ran him over was a "freak accident," he thinks, "It was bloody well murder" (196). He begins to verbalize the practical lessons of experience about the distortion and manipulation of truth and to put them into practice. Helden teaches him the survival lessons she has learned, creating hypothetical situations and discussing potential responses: "You have money; buy an extra seat ... and don't let anyone sit next to you; don't get hemmed in" (248). Holcroft brings these lessons to mind as necessity compels him to act on them: "Do the unexpected rapidly, obviously as if confused" (259); "Lie indignantly ... with confidence . . . invent your own variations" (262). When Holcroft finally realizes his image of his father and of Von Tiebolt are false, he resolves "I . . . will . . . kill!" (482). At this point he is ready for the final lessons about aggressive confrontation: "Use your fingers! They're weapons; never forget it"; "Roll out of a fall; don't crouch"; "Escape, escape, escape! Use your surroundings; melt into them!" (498).

## ALTERNATE READING: MARXIST-LENINIST CRITICISM

Ludlum's novels about Nazism lend themselves readily to Marxist-Leninist criticism, which finds in literary works confirmation of the economic and social theories of Marx and Lenin and of socialist values and interpretations. Marxist-Leninist critics view literature as a sociological phenomenon with historically and economically determined components. Their focus is causal: the social, political, and economic conditions which produce certain types of literature and the motivations which drive their authors. Literature is symptomatic of what troubles a society and art is a social servant. Such criticism emphasizes the materialistic over the epistemological; that is, it values the depiction of physical realities over spiritual or emotional concerns or a search for truth. It finds the differences and conflicts within a society fought out in art.

These critics are generally highly negative about popular fiction, belittling it as bourgeois "mass culture" as opposed to the high culture of true literature and finding in the reader-pleasing popularity of a writer like Ludlum proof that the goal of popular fiction is personal profit rather than an improved society. In other words, for Marxist-Leninists, formalist art for art's sake or even art for escapist fun is not true art and therefore not worthy; instead, art should be serious, with a politically correct message to confirm seriousness.

For this reason Soviet critic Tatiana Nekriach, in her 1986 article "Zagadki populiarnosti: Politicheskie romany Roberta Ladlema," tells her audience that, although some of Ludlum's works were published in Russian in the *Literature Gazette* (1985), they should not be taken seriously for they lack the vision of a Mark Twain or a William Faulkner (35). "We don't like our readers to judge American writing by Ludlum," says Nekriach, who adds, "Though he is very popular, popularity is not everything" (35). Furthermore, she is not only offended that Ludlum's protagonists are driven by personal and egoistic motives rather than political ones but also that they may even be antipolitical (33). She deplores works with no clear political ideology, and claims Ludlum's writing "borders on a lack of principles" (33). She calls Holcroft "a professional destructor," and most of Ludlum's characters "not even masks, just representations—like lightly painted cardboard" (34). Most of all she is offended that Ludlum fails to investigate the roots of the events he describes or to explore the effects of capitalism on the dialectic of events, and that, in *The Holcroft Covenant*, he even sympathizes with a "fascist" (35).

Despite such a negative view of popular fiction in general and of Ludlum in particular, Marxist-Leninist critics do share some perceptions with Ludlum. The latter would probably agree with the official definition of fascism established by the 1928 Thirteenth Plenum of the Executive Committee of the Communist International—still the accepted definition for Marxist-Leninist critics: "Open, terrorist dictatorship of the most reactionary, most chauvinist and most imperialist elements of finance capital" (Kernig, *Marxism, Communism and Western Society: A Comparative Encyclopedia* 65). To this definition the *Great Soviet Encyclopedia* adds a summatioon of the Nazi party political stance—"antidemocracy, extreme anticommunism, chauvinism and racism"—and condemns its indulgence in "unrestrained demagogy" (17: 379). Under the subheading "National Socialist Party," in their article on Germany, Gintsberg and Mukhin blame the ruling classes for using the Nazi Party "to terrorize the workers' movement in Germany" and to "unleash a war" to divide up the world for themselves (6: 352). Like the National Socialists described in these Marxist encyclopedias, Ludlum's Nazis are authoritarian, chauvinistic, imperialistic terrorists, proud of their Führer, or, if neo-Nazis, of their new leader.

The term "finance capital" in the 1928 definition of fascism is important to a Marxist interpretation of the wellsprings of National Socialism, for Marxist-Leninist critics blame the German upper class and greedy industrial magnates seeking an expansionist economy for the rise of German fascism. Fritz Klein, for example, does so in a 1953 study ("Vorbereitung") that details the role of big industrialists in forming Hitler's cabinet, while Gintsberg asserts that "the ruling circles brought the fascists to power" (17: 379) and "giant monopolies" influenced government policy (6: 350). Moreover, Gintsberg and Mukhin name the "extensive financial support that Germany received from the Western powers," particularly "American capital" (6: 352). In *The Scarlatti Inheritance* Ludlum postulates ruthless western businesses, international financiers, and industrial magnates financing the rise of the Third Reich out of a greed for greater and greater profits; his neo-Nazis in *The Holcroft Covenant* are obsessed with financing and with controlling key positions in business and industry as vital to world domination. The idea that western capitalists and elite leaders were complicit in the rise of Hitler comes up in *The Chancellor Manuscript*, where the young Chancellor's revisionist view of the causes of World War II is quickly suppressed.

Furthermore, Marxist-Leninist critics describe the National Socialist or Nazi "philosophy" as anti-modern, anti-intellectual, irrational, and inconsistent (Kernig, *Marxism, Communism and Western Society* 68)—adjectives that characterize Ludlum's Nazi villains. Both agree on the terrorist nature of Hitler's regime and see the atrocities committed by the S.S. and the demagoguery of Hitler as intrinsic to the system, not as the acts of deranged individuals. Ludlum emphasizes an elite core dominating the masses as a significant part of the Nazi mentality, and Marxist-Leninist critics agree. "Ideological indoctrination" succeeded in "deluding" a "significant portion of the population," according to Gintsberg and Mukhin (6: 352). Finally, Marxist-Leninist critics also point to the important role played by Communist partisans in defeating the German invaders. They argue that Hitlerites saw the Communists as their key enemies, banned trade unions, and scapegoated German Communists; and that ultimately, "the Soviet people provided the German people the necessary aid to liberate them from fascism" (Gintsberg and Mukhin 353). Ludlum gives the Communist partisans credit in *The Gemini Contenders*, where they help Vittorio Fontini-Cristi flee Nazi pursuers and contact British agents; he suggests the importance of their underground resistance, although he does not credit them with winning the war.

On the question of final responsibility for defeating the Germans, Ludlum and the Marxist-Leninist critics part company. One of Ludlum's strengths as a writer is his ability to provide alternate interpretations of history and current events. In doing so, however, he is always quick to point out in interviews that he is writing speculative fiction, not fact. Marxist-Leninists, in contrast, assert their interpretations of history as indisputable fact. The Communist partisans did help the war effort, the Russians did rush in to help take Berlin, and twenty million Russians did die in World War II, but the implication that the Soviets were almost single-handedly responsible for freeing the German workers from their Nazi oppressors is misleading.

Ludlum and Marxist-Leninists also disagree about the relationship of Nazism to the German character. Russian Communists find the roots of

National Socialism not only in the social, political, and economic dialectics of the time, but also deep in the German psyche; they find the regime's authoritarianism and militarism, its exaltation of the State and of its leader, and its worship of success and force a product of historically demonstrable German national characteristics. In contrast, Ludlum argues that the Nazi mentality is not an anomaly, but transcends nationality and is potentially a part of any culture. He argues his case through Andrew Fontine, a British-born American of Italian ancestry whose madness parallels that of Ludlum's Nazi villains.

Communists have strong opinions about fascists and Nazis, given that the Communist Revolution was in part a reaction against fascism. Both Nazis and Communists, however, turn to group solidarity for guidance and the correct path, whereas Ludlum, as a representative American, finds his hope in the individual. In fact, at heart, this is what bothers Soviet critic Tatiana Nekriach so much. The Nazis placed the survival of the state above the survival of the individual and were committed to a national policy of eliminating individual will. Committed Marxists also think in terms of the masses, not the individual, favoring organized social groups, committees, and group-think. Ludlum finds this attitude the weakness of both the political left and right. He repeatedly shows individuals demonstrating reserves of inner strength, determination, and commitment that enable them to persevere and overcome. Where the Nazi would turn to his superiors for orders and the Communist would debate the issue in a committee, the democratic Ludlum hero decides for himself and acts alone or with a few loyal companions. And he overcomes.

Nekriach claims this is absurd; individuals can't win over large organizations, in her opinion. But Ludlum disagrees. As a firm believer in democracy, he is committed to the principle of the individual and to the belief that each person can indeed make a difference. Spaulding may be "only one among millions and millions," but he is the right one, in the right place at the right time; his vision of morality and his disdain for the enemy guide his hand as he defeats an army and a nation. Adrian Fontine, a single individual, holds in his hand the power to change history. Noel Holcroft, by destroying an elite minority, can stop a scheme to rule the world. In other words, while Marxist-Leninist critics praise committee decisions for the good of the community, Ludlum's protagonists demonstrate how a lone individual can "influence the outcome of the whole war" (*The Holcroft Covenant* 203). Perhaps this is one reason why so many former Soviet Marxists read Ludlum with such enthusiasm. Ludlum reports high book sales throughout the former Soviet Union, and Russian members of the Moscow, St. Petersburg, and Nizhni Novgorod organizations of Teachers of English to Speakers of Other Languages (TESOL, SPELTA, and NNELTA) report Ludlum as a classroom favorite.

# Comic Satire

## *The Road to Gandolfo* (1975) and *The Road to Omaha* (1992)

Personally, I believe questions of ethics are never anything but questions of point of view.

Simon Groom in Eric Ambler, *The Dark Frontier*

*The Road to Gandolfo*, which Ludlum laughingly calls "liturgical drama," could have been a serious book following a "What if . . . ?" formula: a projection based on real events—the kidnapping of important Italians for political or financial gain with the ante raised ("What if the Pope were kidnapped and held for ransom?"). It could also have been an exploration of Vatican conspiracies, a reworking of "the Nazis are among us" theme, a dramatization of German and Arab terrorist threats, and a consideration of the American rejection of Vietnam heroes. In fact, the playwright John Patrick told Ludlum that film producer Ray Stark wanted Ludlum to write a script for a serious thriller about the kidnapping of the Pope. Ludlum, however, thought such a story would degenerate into proselytizing. Later, though, he became intrigued with the idea as comedy—mixing stage comedy techniques with the conventions of the comic/satiric novel. With Watergate in the headlines (a scenario that he argues would not have played in Peoria) and the real politics of the times verging on the absurd, Ludlum wrote a spoof so at odds with his earlier suspense novels that his publisher insisted on a pseudonym (Michael Shepherd). First published in 1975, *The Road to Gandolfo* did not appear under Ludlum's own name until 1982.

Humor in Ludlum's suspense novels is subordinated to plot or lost in the darkness of events. In *The Scarlatti Inheritance*, when the Protestant head of the Scarlatti family is cloistered in a convent for her protection, her quips about Roman Catholic "voodoo mumbo jumbo" (192) are stifled with reminders that silence and contemplation are good for the soul. This low-level humor, however, is a momentary diversion from disaster, the dawn explosion that kills sisters and novices and damages the famous Abbey of York. The film version of *The Rhinemann Exchange* captures the understated, humorous lines of that novel, particularly the dry wit of the self-deprecating Holcroft. But in *The Road to Gandolfo* and *The Road to Omaha* Ludlum unleashes his comic side.

Critics found this unpredictable switch disturbing: in their opinion, these two novels were either not funny enough or not the black humor indictment of the military mind they should have been. Yet black humor is not part of Ludlum's repertoire, and is surely not intended here. Ludlum began as an actor and a stage producer, and his comic strategies are those of the stage: slapstick, exaggeration, caricature, and repartee. The earlier novel has hilarious comic moments, while the later one is clearly a satiric spoof, not a black comedy. Many of the elements of the adventure/conspiracy form are still in place, but without the seriousness of the genre.

## PLOT DEVELOPMENT AND STRUCTURE

Both novels trace the zany exploits of rogue hero General MacKenzie Hawkins and his coerced associate, lawyer Sam Devereaux. They are a traditional comic duo, one wild-eyed and full of schemes, charging into the fray with gusto, the other timidly following, heart in mouth, overwhelmed, a reluctant participant in the mad pranks of his companion. Hawkins, nicknamed "Madman Mac the Hawk," marshals his reluctant troops, including a bevy of voluptuous former wives, and whips them into fighting shape; in *The Road to Omaha* he recruits two would-be muggers and transforms them into elite forward troops. A retired general, he is Ludlum's stage manager, directing events and people in a comic spectacle charged with satiric potential, and leading diverse forces to a confrontation that mocks high pretensions and reduces all to absurdity, even Ludlum's serious themes of conspiracy and paranoia.

## The Road to Gandolfo

*The Road to Gandolfo* follows an extortion scam from conception and planning to financing, trial runs, and failure. Each section quotes Shepherd's *Laws of Economics* to define the progression of the scam as a series of economic strategies: Part I, planning and instigation; Part II, blackmail to ensure investors; Part III, recruitment, training, and deployment of key operatives; Part IV, public demand for the product. Ironically, Part IV shows the Church unconvinced that the Pope's return is essential, although the kidnappers appreciate his value and vision. Action progresses chronologically, except for the Prologue—a tantalizing but puzzling glimpse at the results of the Gandolfo operation: a bemused, bumbling replacement Pope, unsure about how to genuflect but clearly endearing to Catholics.

Geographically, the scenes in Part I move from the celebration of the Feast of Gennaro in St. Peter's Square, Rome, to Washington, D.C., Southern California, and Peking. When Chinese People's Republic Education Vice-Prefect Lin Shoo arrests Hawkins for destroying the oversized male sexual parts of a ten-foot jade statue in Son Tai Square, Hawkins executes a daring escape using a World War II Zippo lighter and a package of Chinese firecrackers, only to be turned away by an embarrassed American Embassy. Hawkins's roaring demands for admission are greeted by a quavering "No one's home, sir" [30]. Sam Devereaux, a bright young military prosecutor who arrested an honest General Heseltine Brokemichael mistaking him for his corrupt cousin General Ethelred Brokemichael, is sent to negotiate Hawkins's release from a Red Chinese prison. His new job is a military punishment for his mistake. Devereaux collects affidavits from Hawkins's lovely former wives, has Hawkins publicly apologize, and extricates him from China, thereby reducing his embarrassment potential. Hawkins's condition for cooperation is access to classified G-2 reports. Hawkins photocopies confidential files on illegal activities and dupes Devereaux into signing their release. Part II begins in the Washington G-2 archives, and moves to the Drake Hotel on Park Avenue in New York, Devereaux's central base of operations.

The confidential papers enable Hawkins to blackmail a Cosa Nostra/

Mafia chieftain, Angelo Dellacroce; a British industrialist, Lord Sidney Danforth; former double agent, blackmailer, and Third Reich supporter Heinrich Koenig; and an Arab chieftain, Azaz-Varek (a Tel Aviv slum-lord who privately subsidized Israeli fuel purchases during the Egyptian war). Hawkins enlists Devereaux in his campaign to extort ten million dollars from each of these four villains, and Devereaux alternates black-mail with an active love life. The action moves from a secret meeting on a North Hampton golf course, to Geneva, Switzerland, the Savoy Hotel in London, and West Berlin. Devereaux rides on a milking stool amid a truckload of chickens for a clandestine meeting in an East German cow field, then catches a hijacked French plane to Algiers and a private hel-icopter to Tiz Ouzou, a stretch of desert traversed only by Bedouin tribes. Devereaux's meeting with the last of the blackmail targets marks the end of Part II, and provides a comic sense of the passage of time by focusing on everything from a terrorist heist to a menu of boiled camel testicles that discourages a ravenous Devereaux from eating.

The game plan is to use the forty million dollar blackmail payoffs gathered under the auspices of the Shepherd Corporation, to kidnap Pope Francesco the First and request one dollar per Catholic world-wide—approximately four hundred million dollars—as ransom. Part III begins at the Vatican, moves to the Chateaux Machenfeld, Switzerland, then along the road to Gandolfo, and finally back to the Chateaux, where the story ends in Part IV. These geographically ordered scenes frame the action and, despite the far-flung shenanigans of Devereaux, concentrate attention on the Pope, his public self at the beginning, his private self at the end, and the hidden conflicts and conspiracies within the Vatican in between.

In the final phase of the kidnapping operation, Hawkins rents a cha-teau and hires seven agent-provocateurs to assist with logistics, timing, and diversionary strategies. Ironically, the aging Pope, a kindly, well-read man of peasant stock, has only three months to live and is troubled by the prospect of a rich, spoiled, Machiavellian aristocrat taking his place. The plan to substitute the Pope's cousin (a failed musician and actor and his cousin's look-alike) for the kidnapped Pope fits the Pope's need to ensure the continuation of his caring papacy. Hawkins ends up helping the Pope regain his health and govern by phone (even planning the reforms of Vatican II). While the cousin handles the debilitating Vat-ican political agenda and its endless processions, the real Pope hones his gourmet cooking skills. Devereaux falls in love with one of Hawkins's former wives, Anne, and anticipates marriage—far from Hawkins.

The sequel (*The Road to Omaha*) reports the Pope's recovery and thwarting of the unscrupulous Cardinal Ignatio Quartze, Anne's imitation of Sister Teresa, and the lovelorn Devereaux embarrassed by his riches and fearful of his mother discovering his deeds.

## The Road to Omaha

*The Road to Omaha* begins with a brief Prologue with skeptical Indians commenting on a white man playing Indian chief, follows with thirty-one chapters on bringing the Indians' case to court against fierce opposition, and closes with an Epilogue that reports the Indians winning the Supreme Court case.

Chapters 1–13 establish the situation, players, and alliances, as Hawkins and Devereaux fight the United States government for land legally belonging to an Indian tribe (old treaties giving the tribe hundreds of acres are buried in inaccessible vaults). Hawkins (self-termed Chief Thunder Head) heads the senile Council of Elders of the little-known Wopotami tribe as honorary chieftain (with feathered headdress, buckskins, and tepee), and employs an 1878 treaty and the tribe's legal counsel (the vulnerable Charlie Sunset Redwing) to claim the state of Nebraska (including the headquarters of the U.S. Strategic Air Command). Hawkins ("the Hawk") makes the thoroughly modernized tribe look ethnic by "reviving ancient tribal ways" (that is, through props based on Hollywood cowboys-and-Indians films) and by recruiting the reluctant Devereaux to represent the tribe before the Supreme Court.

Chapters 14–25 trace plots and counterplots as Hawkins's legal team prepares its case. Participants include: the CIA and the Mafia (CIA head Vincent Mangecavallo acts for the Mafia dons, but later switches sides); the "Filthy Four," a set of assassins recruited by the unscrupulous Secretary of State Warren Pease and directed by former NFL linebacker Hyman Goldfarb; Fawning Hill Country Club members (Bricky, Doozie, Froggie, Moose, and Smythie) anxious to protect their narrow, moneyed interests; the Secretary of State's team of secretaries (the real power behind the government elite); an antiterrorist team of professional actors designated the "Suicidal Six"; and all the legal (and illegal) impediments that prevent a case from reaching the Supreme Court.

In the romantic subplot the attractive Wopotami, Sunrise Jennifer Redwing distracts Devereaux from his obsession with the now saintly and inaccessible Anne; after much comic byplay, a pursuing Hawkins traps these lawyer-lovers in their own logic. Jennifer joins the Hawkins-Devereaux team to aid her brother, her tribe, and her new love.

In Chapters 26–31, Hawkins orchestrates disguises and a strategy for safely penetrating a well-guarded Supreme Court. The final assault begins with the arrival of the cleaning staff and of the Indians at 5:45 A.M.; the court is penetrated at 1:06 P.M., and the justices are enlisted in the Indian cause shortly thereafter. With the case won, the tribe enriched, and various participants happily or unhappily reaping their rewards, Hawkins sets off for Hollywood as Mackintosh Quartermain to make a blockbuster action film with Sir Henry Sutton and the Suicidal Six. The patterns of action are those of a French farce: misalliance, confusion, betrayal, mistaken identity, thwarted love, good humor, and underlying cynicism. The comic sensibility is very much that of the "anything goes" sixties and early seventies.

## CHARACTER DEVELOPMENT

In broad stage comedies, in-depth characterization is rare. Instead, sweeping strokes paint quick, limited portraits of one-dimensional stereotypes dominated by distinctive patterns of speech, gesture, or body language. Frenzied activity, pratfalls, comic encounters, and recurring routines substitute for character development. Here, too, Ludlum draws on his stage background for comic technique.

MacKenzie Lochinvar Hawkins and Samuel Lansing Devereaux are the central figures of both books. Hawkins, twice decorated with the Congressional Medal of Honor for heroism beyond the call of duty in deadly combat, lives up to his nickname "the Hawk." He has a cameo appearance in *The Bourne Identity* (291) as a military consultant for David Abbott, the head of Treadstone; Abbott claims to have worked with him in Burma. At the beginning of *The Road to Gandolfo* Hawkins is an army general, known for his highly successful missions for the CIA in Vietnam and throughout Indochina. Halfway through the novel, however, his forced retirement leads to inventive civilian activities requiring a military flair. Famous for wildly imaginative covert operations and a "hawkish" love of war, conflict, and challenge, he is a master of disguise, who can easily replace his ramrod military stance with the more fluid movements of the moneyed aristocrat or the shambling gait of a rural hayseed. His unconventionality won him medals in war, but earns him labels like "dangerous" and "mad" in peacetime. While in the earlier novel his aim is a comfortable retirement, in *The Road to Omaha* he is a gadfly for justice. The genius behind the scams in both books, he stage-manages his world. Once he planned and orchestrated an attack on Nazi Germany; now he plans and orchestrates the kidnapping of the Pope and an assault on the Supreme Court.

Hawkins's disaffected sidekick, Samuel Devereaux, is a good attorney, but no match for "the Hawk," who blackmails him into reluctant participation in nefarious quasi-legal assignments. Devereaux fears further involvement, exposure, and scandal, but nonetheless gets caught up in Hawkins's mad escapades. Devereaux's brilliant legal work may be the key to Hawkins's triumphs, but he is mainly the butt of comedy.

Recurring minor characters include: Aaron Pinkus, Devereaux's boss, a soft-spoken, highly influential legal giant who is both intrigued and appalled by the legal niceties of Hawkins's schemes; Devereaux's prying, easily scandalized mother, Elizabeth; Hawk's wives, particularly Anne (a prostitute turned saint) in *The Road to Gandolfo* and Madge (Lady Cavendish) in *The Road to Omaha*; Heseltine Brokemichael, an upright, vengeful general wrongly accused by Devereaux; and his dishonest cousin Ethelred Brokemichael. In the first novel fear of Heseltine's revenge spurs Devereaux's alliance with Hawkins. In the second one Heseltine, as Director of Indian Affairs, assists Hawkins. The Fontini family of *The Gemini Contenders* are international financiers in *The Road to Omaha*.

In *The Road to Gandolfo* Pope Francesco the First (formerly Giovanni Bombalini), his cousin Guido Frescobaldi, and the nameless African-American priest who supports the Pope are vital to the plot. Following a theater tradition, readers must suspend disbelief and accept the cousins as physically identical, despite the Pope's ill health and his cousin's sturdy, peasant strength. Both are gentle, thoughtful, virtuous, and kindly, and totally at odds with the scheming cardinals desperate to seize papal power. As a young priest, Ludlum's Pope was well-read, a scholar intrigued by controversy and convinced that the Church found its strength in "honest contradictions" (144). Pope Francesco is a raconteur, jesuitical in his disputations and unorthodox in his views, a wartime opponent of Hitler (but later labeled "Highly Suspect" in the files of J. Edgar Hoover), a man of simple tastes who enjoys good wine and a game of cards. He is a master organizer, whereas his cousin is not; cousin Guido is an opera buff, while the Pope is a gourmet cook. Like Christ, the Pope, with his humility and simple faith, converts a prostitute to a religious life.

Key players in *The Road to Omaha* include: Jennifer Redwing, who is fiercely loyal to family and tribe; her brother Charlie, a younger Devereaux, who is duped into letting Hawkins take over tribal affairs; Johnny Calfnose, the unscrupulously flexible information officer for the Wopotamis; two impoverished Puerto Rican street toughs, Desi Arnaz One and Desi Arnaz Two, Hawkins's point men and, at the novel's close, CIA special operatives; Cyrus M, an intellectual black mercenary with a doctorate in chemistry and Roman Z, a Serbo-Croatian Gypsy who delights in extravagant clothing. Sir Henry Irving Sutton, a real actor to whom Ludlum dedicates the novel, steps onto Ludlum's fictive stage to "play" the Hawk in a diverting attempt to confuse the enemy. When the "Suicidal Six" try to dupe Hawkins with a fake Swedish Nobel Prize for being "Soldier of the Century," Sutton promises them big roles in a Hollywood production for changing allegiances.

The villains in *The Road to Gandolfo* are limited to the greedy, ambitious Cardinal Ignatio Quartze and the rich, hypocritical international villains whom Devereaux blackmails into funding the Gandolfo operation. The more numerous villains in *The Road to Omaha* include the President, the Vice-President, the White House chief of staff Arnold Subagaloo, a clique of East Coast school chums (the behind-the-scenes powers), the former prep school roommate of the President and now secretary of state Warren Pease, and a neo-Nazi Southerner, who is quickly eliminated from the CIA support team.

## THEMES

Ludlum's comedic themes parallel those of his serious books: appearances are deceptive; conspiracies and hypocrisies abound; those in positions of leadership and authority are vulnerable to the criticism, jealousy, ambition, and violence of others and to their own ambitions and preconceptions; justice is undone by private interest groups greedily striving for dominance; most government activities involve cover-ups and depend more on personalities than on ethics; the CIA is bumbling yet dangerous; the military betrays its own; war is hell, but personal loyalties tested under adverse conditions cement friendships; blackmail can work for good or ill; and most of the time the ends do not justify the means, although sometimes they do. Loyalty is important, but betrayals are more common; jargon hides a world of sins; life is absurd; fiction reflects life, and life reflects fiction. The world is a stage, and men and women are merely players, acting out tragedies and farces in equal measure.

Betrayal is the way of the world. In *The Road to Gandolfo* the U.S. government betrays the trust of an effective army officer, Hawkins. His four major blackmail victims have betrayed their countries, allies, and associates, stealing funds and compromising public values. Hawkins's ex-wives betray Devereaux, using their sexuality and ingenuity to manipulate him for Hawkins's purposes. In the Vatican, Cardinal Quartze, with "the compassion of a disturbed cobra" (148), betrays the Papacy; his forced retirement to a villa far from the seat of power is a deserved comeuppance. In *The Road to Omaha*, the U.S. government has reneged on its treaty with the Indians, and the powers behind the scenes willingly sacrifice their own (the CIA director) to serve their cause. The greatest betrayals are those of the American ideals of democracy and diversity: both elected and appointed officials label those different from themselves "dangerous" and "un-American deviates out of the mainstream" (520), and "deniability" dominates most high-level conversations. These betrayals by word and deed are set in opposition to the simple religious piety of the kindly Pope in *The Road to Gandolfo* and to the loyalty shown Hawkins by military personnel who survived because of his strength and his military insights.

Acting and actors dominate both novels, with the "scripts" of both "productions" replete with disguises and role-playing and life depicted as a movie or stage production. *The Road to Omaha* frequently refers to dramatic productions like *Beckett* and *Show Boat*, Broadway parlance, the Stanislavski method, and the community knowledge of actors, including the story of the British Othello who became so immersed in his role that he tried to kill his Desdemona over a pastrami sandwich in a Forty-seventh Street delicatessen (89). The French playwright Jean Anouilh, a stagy, dramatic writer even among the dramatists of the 1930s and 1940s, receives accolades throughout, and his statement about there being times "when there was nothing left but to scream" (153) becomes a running gag. General Ethelred Brokemichael promises Hawkins will be "history" when he finishes with him, then notes that Brian Donlevy used the same line at Zindelneuf in the 1939 movie *Beau Geste* (311). Bits and pieces from Shakespearean productions echo in the speech of all, with references to Rosencrantz at Hamlet's Elsinore castle and borrowings from Holinshed, Shakespeare's main source for his history plays. Sir Henry Sutton spouts a mixture of *Hamlet* and *Richard III* in a stentorian voice; "If you prick me, do I not bleed," roars Devereaux, echoing Shylock in

*The Merchant of Venice* (112). The Stanislavski Warriors of the Suicidal Six team of antiterrorist actors have been trained in acrobatics, swordsmanship, dance, martial arts, double takes, pratfalls, costume, movement, dialects, and voice; as typical actors, they are "the most bled and most misunderstood human beings on the face of the earth—especially when unemployed" (307). Noted actor Sir Henry Sutton, disguised as Hawkins, sets out to meet the Stanislavski Warriors with the cry, "We're going onstage!" (337).

Disguises and role-playing dominate the action. The Pope's cousin convinces the world that he is the real Pope, and subsidizes 163 opera companies while he can. Hawkins shifts roles and disguises to meet his game plans. In *The Road to Omaha* he switches from Indian Chief in full regalia to Hollywood producer with yellow beret, purple ascot, pink silk shirt, bright red trousers, white Gucci loafers, and a Louis Vuitton suitcase. He and his cohorts change wigs and body stance from scene to scene to escape detection and avoid assassins. Hawkins's ex-wife Madge convincingly plays various roles, from reporter for *Viva Gourmet* to Hollywood impresario. The psychobabble of the military psychiatrists is convincing evidence that a disguised role-player is what he claims: if he talks the talk, he must walk the walk.

## GENRE CONVENTIONS AND NARRATIVE STYLE

*The Road to Gandolfo* and *The Road to Omaha* are comic spoofs that mock human pretensions and reduce to the absurd cherished illusions about government, class, gender, race, organized religion, and the military, among other targets. The titles recall the 1940s screwball movies in which Bob Hope, Bing Crosby, and Dorothy Lamour mixed song and dance with vaudeville sight gags and silly dialogue: *Road to Reno* (1938), *Road to Singapore* (1940), *Road to Zanzibar* (1941), and so on.

Ludlum's satiric jests are partly in the tradition of William F. Buckley's "Blackford Oakes" novels, but less serious, less satiric, and more critical of the right-wing establishment. Buckley is conservative politically, while Ludlum is liberal, but both writers insert real people among fictional characters, make betrayal and conspiracy key themes, and indulge in bedroom farce—although Buckley is more specific about sexual high jinks than Ludlum, who prefers innuendo. Blackford Oakes's adventures skate on the edge of reality; the Hawk's adventures skate over the edge and almost into comic-book fantasy. *The Road to Gandolfo* seems a bizarre melding of *The Cardinal* (1963) and *Monsignor* (1982), both serious films about Vatican corruption and the internal power-plays implicit in electing a Pope, Peter Sellers's *Pink Panther* movies—with disguises, chases, and much merriment based on sight gags, funny accents, pratfalls, and gender, national, and class differences—and Peter Sellers's film *Being There* (1979), wherein a simple man's seemingly profound comments change national policy.

Ludlum also builds on a long tradition of heist or scam movies and novels, especially those depicting how the process is carried out. Subjects include robbing a seemingly theft-proof bank (*The Italian Job*, filmed in 1969), armored car (*The Brinks Job*, filmed in 1978), or train (*The Great Train Robbery*, filmed in 1979), and deceiving seeming experts (Jonathan Gash's Lovejoy mystery novels provide excellent models). Ludlum adheres to the standard structural pattern of these films and novels; the tradition is to introduce the key players (often a band of ragtag losers) and their expertise; to establish the significance of their goal and the difficulty of carrying out the scam or heist; to describe the careful preparation of surveillance and planning and the role of each member of the group; and then to record the event step by step as it is carried out, often with a countdown, a description of the inevitable problems that must be dealt with quickly and ingeniously, the final results—total failure, partial success, or full success—and their ramifications. In *The Road to Gandolfo* Devereaux imagines himself in scenes reminiscent of Rex Harrison and Margaret Lockwood in *Night Train to Munich* (1940) or *Murder on the Orient Express* (1974), and recruits experts in "camouflage, demolition, sedative medicines, native orientation, aircraft technology, escape cartography, and electronics" to help carry out his game plan (194).

Ludlum also relies on a number of standard comic stage techniques. In particular, *The Road to Omaha* builds as much on the conventions of the theater as on the resources of the novel. Among the comic and theatrical techniques Ludlum employs are:

- *Caricature*: Richard Nixon, "his pet 150-pound dog, Python, protectively on his lap." (*The Road to Gandolfo* 63).

- *Comic description*: Hawkins, dressed absurdly, hunched over a tiny moped, his large feet repeatedly slipping off the pedals as he alternately curses and threatens (*RG* 26).

- *Comic digression*: In a serious diplomatic discussion between representatives of the United States and of the People's Republic of China, the American lawyer's casual use of the term "hazzerai" ("A trial or a lot of hazzerai") leads to a recurring digression:

"Hazzerai?"
"It means trouble. It's Jewish."
"You don't look Jewish . . ."
"What about this trial?" (*RG* 45)

- *Comic definition*: Overpowering a mugger defined as "Counter-insurgency" (*The Road to Omaha* 86).
- *Comic disguises*: Hit men disguised as a priest, an orthodox rabbi, and a Baptist minister; a polished attorney disguised as an Ozark rube; commandos disguised as hobos; and so on.
- *Comic repetition*: The word "pot" is repeated with various meanings, in the manner of Samuel Beckett (*RO* 485)
- *Comic reversal/the world turned upside down*: Male dominance is reversed by the victories of Madge and Jennifer Redwing at the end of the story.
- *Deflation*: When the imprisoned Hawkins refuses to cooperate, his lawyer resorts to the aggressively obscene language of a stereotypical boot-camp conversation followed by "Incidentally, Regina Greenberg says hello" [deflation from contrastive styles]. Hawkins's lawyer tells the stunned Chinese diplomat that the above statement employs a highly classified military code (*RG* 50).
- *Exaggerated behavior*: Devereaux screams hysterically, "with such uncontrollable frenzy that his mother bolted up from the settee, shot over the oval coffee table, and ended up splayed out on the floor" (*RO* 67).
- *Hyperbole (exaggerated language)*: The Hawk calls his single-handed firecracker attack on his Red Chinese guards "an American counterstrike" with "all weapons on repeat-fire, blazing barrels of thunder and lightning" (*RG* 27–29).
- *Incongruities*: A right-wing, no-nonsense Marine general hums *Mairzy-Doats* ["Mares eat oats, and does eat oats, and little lambs eat ivy"], a popular nonsense song from the forties.

- *Ironic juxtapositioning*: "A . . . teen-age hero at the Battle of the Bulge and West Point football" (*RG* 8).

- *Over-precise description*: "A long coffee table on which there were four MAC-10 machine pistols, twenty magazine clips, sixteen grenades, four miniaturized radios, two flamethrowers, four infrared binoculars, and a dismantled egg-shaped bomb that could blow up at least a quarter of the state of New Hampshire—the lesser southeastern part" (*RO* 280).

- *Parody*: "This is 'Scratch Your Assets,' you lucky, *lucky* person you!" shrieked the voice over the line. "All you have to do is tell me what tall, bearded President gave the Gettysburg Address and you win a Watashitti clothes dryer from the Mitashovitzu Company, who just happens to own this *great* station! What's your answer, you *terrific* person?" (*RO* 147).

- *Reductio ad Absurdum*: Hawkins's former wife Regina Greenberg defines her sexual need for Devereaux as "a national emergency" (*RG* 41); *The Road to Omaha* reduces conspiracy theories to absurdity.

- *Reversal of expectation*: After soundly beating his two muggers, the Hawk analyzes the pros and cons of their tactics and execution, and offers them a position as his "support adjutants" (*RO* 87); "We do things differently in civilian life, General. Dereliction and incompetence are necessary components in the lower ranks of the work force. Otherwise, their superiors, who are frequently less competent but speak better, could never justify their salaries" (*RO* 109).

- *Serious conversations about religion, philosophy, or history in unexpected situations*: Amid comic chaos, an enthusiastic discussion of a fourteenth-century ruler, Casimir the Third, also known as Charles the Great of Poland, his treaties with Silesia and Pomorze, and his legal temperance. This technique is after the manner of Spanish film director Luis Buñuel (*RG* 488).

- *Situation Comedy*: An American Marine escapes imprisonment by Red Chinese and battles his way to the American Embassy in macho fashion only to hear, in response to his shouts and heavy knock, "No one's home, sir." The "sir" is the final comic touch (*RG* 30).

- *Vaudeville comedy routines*:
  - *Fake translation*: A Puerto Rican with superior English skills "translates" the thick accents and street diction of fellow Puerto Ricans from their English to standard English (*RO* 204).
  - *Slapstick*: Throughout both novels there is much running about, characters bumping into each other and falling down, feigned fighting, and sight gags of all sorts; half a dozen red-wigged characters of various sizes and shapes are mistaken for each other; the Hawk rides the "rolling swells" of his waterbed, loses his balance, falls backward, thrashes about atop rough waters, and tries to reach the ringing cellular telephone inside his beaded tribal tunic (*RO* 73).
- *Word play*:
  - Samuel *Lansing* is a courtly *Lance*lot who "tilts at windmills"
  - *Alliteration (repetition of sounds)*: "Passive possum"; "big . . . blazing barrels"; "Nanny's Naughty Follies"; "Stanislavski Suicide Six"; "Hymie the Hurricane"; "the Hebrew Hercules"; "Wopotami Welcome Wagon Wigwam" (*RG*; *RO*).
  - *Bawdy double entendre*: "Several items came up, one in particular—" "It usually does" (*RG* 41).
  - *Comic accents*: The two Desis speak a comic Spanglish: "We din' want to wake chu all up" (*RO* 280) or "Hey, Comandante, wad chu tink?" (192); the Japanese use "r" for "l" as in "my rovery friends in Horrywood" (461).
  - *Comic jargon (a form of fake erudition)*: "Stress collapse," "schizoid progression," and "conflictive objectives" are offered as psychiatric explanations of Hawkins's urinating on the Embassy roof (*RG* 54–55).
  - *Comic misunderstandings*: A question about prison term length, "What could he draw?" is answered with, "How so? Draw? The sculpture?" (*RG* 45–46); the mission code name WOPTACK creates puzzlement—"Wop . . . attack?" (*RO* 60).

- *Comic names and titles*: Python, the name for Nixon's dog, sums up Ludlum's view of Nixon squeezing the life out of the country; Warren Pease's name is a pun on war and peace; Vincent Francis Assisi—"Vinny the Bam-bam"— Mangecavallo's last name suggests a mangy horse or "horse eater," while the mistaken use of Mangecuvulo suggests "ass-eater"; Calfnose; Subagaloo; "Meat" D'Ambrosia; the filmscript *Mutant Homicidal Lesbian Worms*.

- *Comic name-calling*: "You bellowing relic from a fifth-rate war movie" (*RO* 232).

- *Comic rhyme*: "I really thought you had the right *stuff*, but I can see now that I can't bring you up to *snuff* [author's emphasis]" (*RO* 46).

- *Contrasting levels of diction*: The working-class language of the Vice-President and his wife contrasts with the elevated diction of Aaron Pinkus ("crumb-bum buddies" and "scumball friends" versus "Hysterical recriminations will get us nowhere") (*RO* 128); financial wizards swear with "great green gobs of greasy, grimy gopher guts" (*RO* 222).

- *Incongruous verbal combinations*: "a gaggle" of executives (*RO* 50).

- *Metaphor*: a character is shown "sinking down to the curb like an overripe, overdone baked potato punctured by a fork" (*RO* 195).

- *Mispronunciation*: Lin Shoo continually mispronounces words, calling Lincoln *Lin-Kolon*, Alcatraz *Holcotaz*, Spiro Agnew *Speeroo Agaroo* (*RG*).

- *Puns*: Suite/sweeties (*RO* 201); batman (someone who performs minor tasks for someone else)/Batman (the comic book hero) (*RO* 270).

- *Put-downs*: Hawkins calls civilian males "fancy pants" and "lace-panties," and defines diplomacy as "lace-pants fol-de-rol" (*RG; RO*).

- *Silly nonsense words*: "Golly gosh and zing darn" (*RO* 18).

- *Understatement*: When the general shouts nasty insults a Chinese diplomat remarks, "He is not always the essence of courtesy" (*RG*: 49).

In sum, Ludlum draws on a variety of genres and conventions, but in the main combines the comic techniques of the stage with the action of the thriller to create a slapstick parody of the scam/heist novel.

## ALTERNATE READING: FEMINIST CRITICISM

A fundamental and valuable service of feminist criticism is to recover, reprint, reread, and reevaluate the works of women writers, who have often been left out of the literary canon. In doing so, feminist critics are in effect revising literary history to provide a worthwhile correction to the imbalance of historical perspective. Another direction feminist criticism has taken is to attack "patriarchal" interpretations and treatments of literature and characters, and to provide a balance through either a "matriarchal" interpretation or an attempt at gender-free discourse. One assumption of such criticism is that patriarchal culture relies on linguistic strategies to "subsume 'otherness,' " as Robert Fowler's *Dictionary of Modern Critical Terms* phrases it (93). Mary Jacobus in *Women Writing and Writing about Women* (1979) argues that feminist writing thus challenges the "themes and representations of female oppression" (12). Luce Irigaray believes that it scrutinizes texts for signs of "heterogeneity," that is, diversity, and for space for "the feminine imaginary" (Fowler 93–94). Feminist criticism has also brought pressure to bear on the analysis of texts, advocating "politically correct" diction and denouncing sexist language and attitudes.

Feminist critics would find Ludlum's two road novels, in their diction, humor, and characterization, sexist representations of male hegemony or dominance. At the heart of these novels is a male military cadre assembled around a patriarchal figure, whose wartime prowess has avowedly earned him the right to direct the lives of subordinate males. His female companions respect his superiority and help him keep the lesser males in line. Hawkins is the alpha wolf of the male pack, a football hero, a West Pointer, and a warrior, who can live in the forests "better than most animals" (*RG* 25), who attacks the Red Chinese with phallic firecracker rockets, and who urinates on the Stars and Stripes when his country betrays him. Devereaux calls him "a walking military-industrial complex," a "military fruitcake" (*RG* 241). The Hawk bends the more intellectually oriented beta males like Sam Devereaux to his will by the sheer aggressive force of his dominating personality. His Arab competitors may consume the boiled testicles of camels, but the Hawk has shot the enormous "jade balls" off the statue of an enshrined Chinese dictator. The adventures revolve around male power plays, where violence is the answer to conflict and oneupmanship is vital to personal identity.

The humor is sexist, with sophomoric jokes about breaking wind and having erections, and about the size of sexual parts, from the phallus of a Chinese statue to the length of General Hawkins's Havana cigars and the bust size of his former wives. The general's favorite derogatory put-down is "lace-pants," and he delights in whipping the weaklings around him into manly shape. Plays on the word "ass" recur, as in "This is 'Scratch Your Assets'" (*RG* 147). In *The Road to Gandolfo*, Devereaux's rationality is held hostage by the sexual attentions of the Hawk's "Harem," whose purpose is to ensure that passion and sexual high jinks distract Devereaux from the ethical impropriety and the dangers of his nefarious activities. Much of Devereaux's time is spent praising and ap-praising breasts, each pair "magnificent in its individual style. Full and Round. Narrow and Pointed. Sloping yet Argumentative" (35). The attire of these seductive and manipulative *houris* is provocative and sheer, ex-posing the "extraordinary endowments" (117) they use as weapons in the service of their master, the Hawk. Despite being divorced from him, these women fawn over Hawkins, extolling his masculine virtues and expressing their gratitude to him for helping them discover their inner power. Yet, no matter how high they climb on the social scale or what feats they accomplish, they remain, in Hawkins's words, "my fillies" (389). The characterization goes beyond a James Bond sexual fantasy to become a sexual caricature.

In *The Road to Omaha* the humor is even more sophomoric. Devereaux repeatedly spills drinks on his pants and is chided for urinating on him-self by his mother and his would-be lover. The female lead (a successful lawyer) is forced to wear a blonde wig that denies her ethnicity and to dress in a bodysuit that exaggerates her hips and breasts and that makes her look like a streetwalker's parody of Marilyn Monroe. The joking nickname "Pocahontas" reduces her to a stereotyped "squaw," whose function is similar to that of the Harem in *The Road to Gandolfo*: to keep Devereaux involved in the action and to distract him from the question-able ethics of his contribution. Other ethnic jokes include the Hollywood cowboy and Indian stereotypes the Hawk imposes on his adopted tribe of modernized Wopotamis, and the Spanglish and comic misunderstand-ings of the two Puerto Rican thugs, Desi Arnaz I and II, whose specialties are hot-wiring cars and picking pockets and locks.

Despite humor based on sexist and ethnic assumptions, Ludlum credits his women characters and his ethnic minorities with intelligence and competence. Jennifer Redwing can keep pace with and perhaps even outdazzle Devereaux in the legal arena. The women in the Hawk's Harem control their own lives and do what most of the men in the novels are unable to do—transform themselves into what they want to be. Anne chooses self-fulfillment in a celibate religious vocation over marriage to Devereaux; Madge has made herself an expert on antiques and a Hollywood organizer and mover: she knows how to make things happen. At the novel's close Madge orchestrates the dreams of a number of the male figures, and Jennifer Redwing ensures a better life and an improved future for her tribe.

Eleanor Devereaux, however, seems a much more likely spokesperson for Ludlum than Redwing or Madge. She attacks "those Janie-come-lately liberated females" for their failure to understand that "the man still has to go keep the lion from invading the cave" (*RO* 29); she concludes that "when a man gets broiled because the pressures become too much, it's a reasonable petcock to let off steam" (29). Feminists would not be impressed by Ludlum's gamesmanship, and would argue that he tries to have it both ways: he espouses a male patriarchal system and engages in sexist humor based on a male perspective, yet claims to be "enlightened" by providing a final reversal. One might argue that his female victories are simply part of a comic strategy going back to the Greek comic writer Aristophanes's *Lysistrata*—with the successes of the heroines a comic reverse and the world turned upside down—and that Ludlum in *The Road to Omaha* is to some extent thumbing his nose at such feminist critics. Sexist and ethnic humor that may have been generally acceptable in 1975 in *The Road to Gandolfo* was not at all politically correct in 1992, when *The Road to Omaha* was published, but Ludlum revels in defying politically correctness.

# The Bourne Series

## *The Bourne Identity* (1980), *The Bourne Supremacy* (1986), and *The Bourne Ultimatum* (1990)

Today, all I know is that I have learned to interpret the whole of life
in terms of conspiracy. That is the sword I have lived by, and as I
look round me now I see it is the sword I shall die by as well. These
people terrify me, but I am one of them.

John le Carré, *The Honourable Schoolboy*

The Bourne series is one of Ludlum's finest creations, and *The Bourne
Identity* is Ludlum at his very best. His writing is more detailed, graphic,
and concrete than in his earlier novels, his syntax is more sophisticated,
his descriptions of location and action are more convincing. Ludlum creates a strong, credible heroine, a vulnerable but capable, complex hero,
integrated images suggestive of myth, and recurring themes bound to
essential concerns of the human psyche. *Time* critic Michael Demarest
praises *The Bourne Identity* as "absorbing . . . a Bourne from which no
traveler returns unsatisfied" (101). Every piece of a complex puzzle carefully fits together; the plot is tightly directed, without subplots to distract
from a compelling human story. Ludlum builds on fears that all can
share: What if I lost my memory? How could I find my way? Whom
could I trust? And if, with such a loss, I found myself the center of an

international hunt with every clue suggesting that I had been a murderous, evil gun for hire, how would I cope?

The epic and mythic motifs are writ large in these three volumes. Like his mythological namesake, the Greek Jason, Jason Bourne must make an odyssey of discovery, journey through strange lands and amid strange peoples to find his Golden Fleece. The Golden Fleece this modern Jason seeks, however, is the treasure stored in his own damaged mind, a treasure that can open the doors to lost friendships, lost family, and lost self-knowledge. The financial treasure that he finds in a Swiss bank, guarded by villains as deadly as any multiheaded monster, is merely the means to finding that greater treasure. Like the questing heroes of myth, along the way he is aided and supported by beings with extraordinary powers. His first assistant/companion is a figure of reason and logic, Dr. Geoffrey Washburn, who provides Bourne a methodology for discovering clues to his identity; his second enduring companion and aide is Marie St. Jacques, whose specialized knowledge of business and economics furthers his progress and whose intuitive feminine powers cut through false conclusions and despair. A third companion, Philippe d'Anjou, teaches him about his past, who he was and what he did, so he can shape his future. During his quest for knowledge and self-understanding, he must battle monsters, which are either the product of his own fears or men transformed into demons or would-be gods. Like Odysseus in the land of the Lotus Eaters, he must also battle an inner lassitude that would have him yield to fate.

Ludlum repeatedly invokes images of labyrinths, a reference to the complex maze of Greek myth that Daedalus constructed for Minos, King of Crete, and which had at its center a monstrous bull-man, the Minotaur (with which the terrorist Carlos the Jackal is associated). Bourne wanders labyrinthian streets from Europe to Asia, and his course inevitably leads to his nemesis, Carlos, and to death and destruction. Bourne also wanders the corridors of his amnesiac mind, and the monsters that await him are phantoms of his own imagining or monstrous projections of the self he was or could have been. In *The Bourne Supremacy* a mirror in his mind shatters as he sees the creature he could become without his beloved and her healing sanity.

In his search for self, Jason crosses continents only to circle back, like Oedipus, to his place of origin only to be accused of murdering his father-figure, David Abbott, the creator of his alternate personality. On his journey he must face his potential for evil and reject his alter-ego, Cain—a blood-thirsty mythical creation of the CIA—who could murder his own brother (or even father) and destroy a world to satisfy his lust for power. The biblical Cain was the first to commit fratricide, and CIA agents like Alexander Conklin fear that the mythical name has triggered the modern Cain's actions. Jason must also come to terms with his own vengeful id, the "Delta" personality in him, released by the strafing of his wife and children and by the betrayal implicit therein. Only when he finds the David within himself, the biblical slayer of giants but also his youthful lost self, can he truly be reborn, plan for the future, and make strides toward wholeness and sanity. Thus, the name "Bourne" suggests his birth and rebirth—"You're Bourne." "Obviously, born again, you might say" (*BU* 137); the name also suggests the burden of responsibility he has borne for so long. Its archaic meanings suggest his temper and temperament when under attack (Latin "to seethe or boil"), the destination that compels him to a particular place ("a terminal point"), and the limits ("boundaries") imposed on his quest. Bourne mourns his loss of identity, and fearful possibilities haunt him.

Accused of being a defrocked Jesuit, Bourne avenges the sacrificed "Abbott" or "Monk" and battles the false priest (Carlos), his dark angels, and unholy minions, including nuns in the Magdalen Sisters of Charity. Bourne is the Christian knight, baptized in the sea and reborn a new man; he battles the forces of darkness and evil that sow dissension and hatred, foment wars, and pave the way for Armaggedon, the end of time.

## GENRE CONVENTIONS

The Bourne series builds on the literary tradition of the *doppelgänger* (a German term meaning "double who accompanies someone"). The *doppelgänger* refers to a psychological mirror image or to a split personality. Although the twin images may simply reflect the divided nature of human beings (the public side versus the private, the active versus the passive, the conformist versus the rebel), most often they reflect good and evil. The concept was used in Edgar Allan Poe's "William Wilson" (1840), Robert Louis Stevenson's "Dr. Jekyll and Mr. Hyde" (1886), Fyodor Dostoyevsky's *The Double* (1846), Joseph Conrad's *The Secret Sharer* (1912), and Vladimir Nabakov's *Despair* (1936).

In more recent fiction, Elleston Trevor, writing as Adam Hall in the Quiller series (1985–present), has fused the espionage thriller with psychoanalysis, as Ludlum does, to explain motivating behavior, obsessions, and psychoses through Freudian psychoanalysis and to depict war-induced stress syndrome. Using the jargon of psychoanalysis—"alpha waves," "guilt-transference," "isolation factors," "retrogressive amnesia"—and stream-of-consciousness internal dialogues between a divided self, he explores the psychology of a mind under pressure, of humans forced to the edge physically, emotionally, and intellectually, yet responding to trauma. Trevor's Quiller engages in interior dialogue that reflects his divided self: a chilling, clinically detached "I" records, computer-like, his efficient, practical, and daring responses to danger while a more cautious, fearful self comments on the stupidity of his heroic assaults. Quiller's duality, his internal dialogue, and his clinical detachment provide a pattern for Ludlum's Jason Bourne.

However, Ludlum complicates the duality. There is a split between the real and treacherous Jason Bourne of the Vietnam days and the Jason Bourne who replaces him for agency purposes. The divided self of the replacement David Webb/Jason Bourne is multiplied by his Delta and Cain personalities. There is also an unidentified Jason Bourne in the Far East whose description matches exactly the original passport of Webb/Bourne. This double, a creation of Philippe d'Anjou, signs "Jason Bourne" in the blood of his victims to call world attention to his assassinations. His activities occur while the Webb/Bourne protagonist is quietly recuperating from his traumatic experiences by teaching at a private university in Maine. Thus the *doppelgänger* makes for interesting plot twists, complex characterization, and deep psychological resonances.

Throughout *The Bourne Supremacy* in particular, the Webb/Bourne personalities of the divided self engage in an internal dialogue; St. Jacques notes that the two personalities even sound different, the one warm and scholarly, the other cold and commanding. Webb sees through bemused, untrained eyes, while Bourne views the same scene in survivalist terms: the kind and degree of response required, the weapons needed. Webb wryly muses that a terrifyingly alien scene in a dangerous Hong Kong alley is not Disneyland; Bourne, in contrast, studies the same alley as he would a "combat zone behind enemy lines" (*BS* 153). As the pace quickens, Bourne commands and Webb obeys, purposely yielding to his Bourne identity to achieve goals requiring skills in martial arts, weaponry, espionage, and sabotage Webb denies having. A final issue is whether the Webb personality is strong enough to seize control when the Bourne identity has completed his difficult tasks. At the end of *The Bourne Supremacy*, Webb expresses his deep loathing for his alternate personality, but his wife argues that "we all have a dark side" (646) and that survival frequently depends on that dark side.

Ludlum's description of the Hong Kong pretender trained by Philippe d'Anjou alludes to Mary Shelley's *Frankenstein* (1818), in which a scientist exceeds human limits by creating life, but the creature produced in his laboratory haunts him until it finally destroys him. D'Anjou (code-named Echo), through plastic surgery, conditioning, and training, has brought to life a monster, who breaks free of his creator, then hunts and kills him. D'Anjou describes him as "Frankenstein's monster" with "none of that creature's torment" (*BS* 249). Bourne feels equally responsible for this soulless killer, describing him as "a stalker of death that came from a lethal virus," birthed and perfected "in the laboratory of his [Bourne's] mind and body" (*BS* 196). The Frankenstein allusions resonate with questions of guilt and responsibility.

Ludlum also employs a detective fiction device from the forties: the amnesiac (usually a murder suspect) who seeks clues to his past but fears himself a villain, and whose conscious attempts to recover his memory simply heighten the stress that represses it. A number of *cinema noir* films were pegged on this exciting device, including Alfred Hitchcock's *Spellbound* (1945) and *Mirage* (1965). The roots of this recurrent popular mystery convention go back to Sophocles' tragedy *Oedipus Rex*, in which Oedipus searches for the murderer of the former king, finds all clues pointing to himself, and pieces together the jigsawed memories of his past to understand his present.

A more common genre convention employed here is the hunter/hunted chase: pursuit through exotic regions, with excitement and fear generated by constant movement and danger. Suspense mounts as deadly antagonists narrow the fields of contact for a final confrontation: the Jackal stalks Bourne, and Bourne lures the Jackal to a deadly trap. The protagonist, hunted like an animal, flees for his life, but then the hunted becomes the hunter, a pattern repeated in all three Bourne novels. The action spans continents: in *The Bourne Identity* it moves from France to Switzerland, back to France, and to America; *The Bourne Supremacy* leaps quickly from Maine to Hong Kong and Red China; *The Bourne Ultimatum* moves from Maine to Washington, Montserrat, Paris, Moscow, and points south in the former Soviet Union.

## STYLE

Ludlum's writing style is at its best here. His early novels were like abstract scripts or stage directions, whose particulars had to be imagined.

The sign on the door said FBI, but the specifics behind that door were missing. The Bourne series breaks that pattern of abstraction, and is better for it. Ludlum lucidly tracks St. Jacques and Bourne's race through Zurich streets:

> They circled the block, emerging on the Falkenstrasse, then turned right on the Limmat Quai toward the cathedral of Grossmünster. The Lowenstrasse was across the river, on the west side of the city. The quickest way to reach it was to cross the Münster Bridge to the Bahnhofstrasse, then to the Nüschelerstrasse; the streets intersected. (*BI* 93)

Processes are simple, precise. Ludlum names times ("ten minutes past noon") and describes relevant materials ("a dark, lightweight raincoat and a dark canvas hat, a pair of gray tennis sneakers, black trousers and a sweater, also black . . . a spool of 75-pound-test fishing line with two palm-sized eyehooks through which a three-foot section of line would be looped and secured at both ends, a 20-ounce paperweight in the shape of a miniature brass barbell, one ice pick, and a sheathed, highly sharpened, double-edged hunting knife with a narrow 4-inch blade") and function ("these were the clothes he would wear at night . . . These were the silent weapons he would carry both night and day") (*BS* 120–21). Later he explains exactly how the fishing line and barbell are used, and describes the ice pick and knife in action. This concrete, particularized style provides a full visual scene, as in a film rather than an abstract stage set.

Battle scenes are graphic. The encounter between Carlos and Bourne at Treadstone is representative. Ludlum's sentences are longer than before, with detail piled on detail and parallel participles and absolutes hurtling the action along:

> Bourne whipped his head back as the razorlike edge of the blade sliced the flesh under his chin, *the eruption of blood streaming across the hand that held the knife.* He lashed his right foot out, *catching his unseen attacker in the kneecap,* then pivoted and plunged his left heel into the man's groin. . . . Jason sprang back off the ground, *crossing his wrists, slashing downward, blocking the dark arm that was an extension of the handle.* . . . Bourne spiraled the arm downward, *twisting the wrist now in his grip, crashing his shoulder into the assassin's body, yanking*

*again as Carlos plunged sideways off balance, his arm pulled half
out of its socket.* [emphasis added] (*BI* 521)

Don Campbell of the *Los Angeles Times Book Review* reports being "caught
up irretrievably" in this "pulse-tingling style" and argues that Ludlum's
writing throughout the Bourne series exemplifies "how it should be
done" (8).

Ludlum's descriptions of place are richly detailed, even in dream sequences. Jason sees in his mind's eye a vision of a Hong Kong he once
knew: "the crowded hotel lobbies and lounges with their softly lit chan-
deliers of gold filigree where the well-dressed remnants of the empire
reluctantly mingled with the emerging Chinese and entrepreneurs" (*BS*
118). Grammatical absolutes compact descriptive details ("Their confrontation would be brief, *the impact of the message startling, the threat inherent*"
[*BI* 390]), while strings of parallel participial phrases extend images:
"Men and women of all ages, from children to ancients, were dressed in
rags, and pungent, heavy smoke curled slowly upward, *filling the space*
between the decaying buildings, *diffusing the light, heightening the gloom*
of the dark stone walls blackened by use and misuse" [emphasis added]
(*BS* 118).

Imagery heightens the mythological connections. Jason Bourne is a
chameleon, a master of metamorphosis—like the Greek seagod Proteus
capable of changing colors and shapes—or else is a spider scurrying
across a web, both traditional images of tricksters. His self-assuring internal mantras are like the magic chants of a shaman: "I am a chameleon
. . . I can change my color to accommodate any backdrop in the forest, I
can shift with the wind by smelling it. I can find my way through the
natural and the manmade jungles" (*BI* 312). Sometimes he is a cat "stalking silent" through forests (*BS* 235). These images are appropriate, since
Bourne must fade into the background, yet attract his prey to pouncing
range. He skillfully weaves a "tapestry of lies" to serve his ends (*BI* 272).
His enemies call him "a snake pulled out of Medusa's head, groomed
for a mythical title" (*BI* 303), an image Ludlum plays on in his choice of
a Hong Kong seller of snakes as Bourne's contact. In *The Bourne Ultimatum*, when confronted with opposition code names like "Cobra" and
"Snake Lady," Jason jokes that he "snaked" his way in (*BU* 138). Other
images suggest his precarious situation: he balances on taut parallel
wires, above a deep, dark abyss into which he could plunge at any moment; he feels "like a caged animal" studied by a vicious horde of beasts
from some very different species (*BS* 127); a surprise attack comes with

"the impact of a single furious wave against a shoal of rock" (*BU* 572). The descriptions of China build on the mythology of that culture, with the Hong Kong skyscrapers like "alabaster giants, reaching up through the mists," holding aloft the sky as China's fables say their mountains do (*BU* 112).

## PLOT DEVELOPMENT AND STRUCTURE

The three Bourne novels interlock, sharing a common protagonist (Jason Bourne) and other characters and repeating patterns of hunter/hunted, *doppelgänger*, loss, and separation, which lead to long journeys and a reunion at the end. Action moves forward chronologically, except for flashes of memory as the step-by-step movements and discoveries of Webb/Bourne in *The Bourne Identity* repeat and elucidate the past. Ludlum sets up a collision course early in the action. The shifting of scenes back and forth from hero to adversary, with the action quickening and the scenes shortening until the inevitable confrontation and denouement heightens suspense, hurtles the action forward, and suggests a hidden pattern governing apparently random events; Ludlum adds to this pattern the suggestion that individual psychologies are bound to repeat past patterns as subsurface memories, finely developed instincts, and subconscious wishes kick in.

As the story progresses chronologically, it moves full circle spatially. Webb/Bourne began his journey at Treadstone, where he and Abbott devised the deception and the mission that sent him world wide in competition with Carlos. The first of the three novels records half the circle of action, beginning in midaction with the sinking of the Marseilles's trawler that costs Webb/Bourne his memory and the slow physical recovery that follows. After returning to Marseilles and proceeding to Zurich, Bourne hides out in the small towns around Zurich before heading for Paris, where most of the remaining action occurs (Chapters 11–34). The final chapter occurs in New York, mainly at the Treadstone headquarters, where Jason Bourne was "born," and the epilogue is set on a nameless beach, where St. Jacques and Webb begin the return to normality.

### The Bourne Identity

The Preface provides fictional news clippings about the real international terrorist Carlos. Part I (Chapters 1–9) begins with an injured man washed ashore in stormy Northern Mediterranean seas, awakening from a coma with amnesia and bullet wounds to his head, and ends with Marie St. Jacques's determined commitment to help Bourne find the truth about himself and his predicament. Dr. Geoffrey Washburn has found surgically implanted in the stranger a microfilm recording a Swiss bank name, an account number, and a signature that corresponds to his patient's handwriting. Working closely for months, doctor and patient piece together a portrait of the skills of a hired killer or a well-trained agent. Washburn trusts his patient's decency, but the latter's fierce attack on rough shipmates on a boat trip the doctor had meant as part of his recovery forces the amnesiac to depart for Marseilles. There, an accidental street encounter with a stranger informs enemies that he lives.

In Zurich, at the bank named in the microfilm, he discovers a name, Jason Charles Bourne, and great wealth, but his enemies, who expect him, lift his fingerprint from a glass he touches and force him to violence and flight. He seizes Marie St. Jacques to shield his escape, and enlists her help tracing vague snatches of puzzling memories. A waiter trembles fearfully in his presence. A paraplegic tries to kill him; after Bourne shoots through his throat in self-defense, St. Jacques crashes the car and mistakes pursuers for police. Bourne catches her would-be killer raping her; his selfless, generous rescue wins her support temporarily.

Part II (Chapters 10–22) follows their plan to discover Bourne's identity while evading a manhunt and pursuing killers, and ends with St. Jacques convinced that an ally is sending them a message. The two travel to Paris, where fragmented bits of memory help the bewildered Bourne recall his association with the Medusa Brigade, a covert CIA operation involving a ruthless band of murderers, thieves, and psychopaths paid well to terrorize the North Vietnamese enemy and given liberty to smuggle and bribe their way to greater wealth. Bourne decides his real identity is that of a ruthless killer seeking supremacy in the international criminal underworld.

A complicated reality gradually emerges. Bourne is really David Webb, whose Vietnamese wife and child had been killed by friendly fire. Deranged by his painful loss, Webb joined a special force and took wild risks to penetrate areas closed to the regular army. Code-named Delta, Webb walked a fine line between sanity and insanity on missions of questionable morality. When he led a force to rescue his brother, a POW in a North-Vietnamese camp being held as bait for the deadly Delta, Webb/Delta killed the real Jason Bourne for betraying the mission. Later, Treadstone head David Abbott, a father figure to Webb, arranged for him to replace the dead Bourne in order to track down the infamous

Jackal. The strategy was for "Bourne" to take credit for as many assassinations as possible to challenge and anger the Jackal, and trap him when he came in for the kill. The strategy backfired when Webb lost his memory and became Bourne, the outlaw-amnesiac. In other words, St. Jacques's instincts prove correct; Webb is a government agent acting for international interests. It takes, however, a great deal of action, travel, self-doubt, paranoia, and fear before the denouement. St. Jacques's support and practical advice help keep Webb sane and make him trust himself—even when newly acquired information could easily be interpreted negatively. Ironically, Webb's original allies believe him a rogue killer, responsible for his brother's death, and beyond redemption.

In Part III (Chapters 23–35) Bourne turns hunter, tracing Carlos to an expensive Parisian dress shop and tricking its manager, Jacqueline Lavier, to lead him to his prey. Disguised as a priest, Carlos meets his underlings in church confessionals. His longtime lover, Angélique, has married General André François Villiers, a respected, powerful military leader, whose son, unbeknownst to Villiers, died as a result of the treacherous Angélique's machinations. St. Jacques and Bourne initially believe Villiers a traitor, but he proves otherwise, strangling his wife and helping Bourne bait a trap that will lead to Carlos and the mysterious Treadstone agency.

Bourne hopes to prove his innocence and to rid the world of an evil predator, but Carlos plants the fingerprint surreptitiously obtained at the Zurich bank at the Treadstone Manhattan headquarters, so Bourne will be blamed for the deaths of Abbott's associates; in a night encounter in a graveyard, Carlos kills Abbott as well. Webb/Bourne's former associate and friend, Alexander Conklin, acting on the informal, hypothetical analysis of Dr. Morris Panov, believes him a psychopathic killer. When the protagonist traps Carlos in Webb's childhood home and battles him for survival and supremacy, Conklin intends to kill Bourne. St. Jacques, assisted by Dr. Panov and Brigadier General Crawford, interferes to save Webb. Carlos, injured, escapes; Webb/Bourne's trauma brings back the horrors of his first traumatic experience; Conklin is shocked into remorse at his misunderstanding of events; and Panov commits himself to restoring Webb to psychological health, a possibility ensured by the amnesiac finally remembering his own name.

## *The Bourne Supremacy*

The now happily married Webb and St. Jacques have settled in a quiet university town, where therapy, love, and normality have helped Webb daily regain psychological strength and, bit by bit, a sense of his lost self. This peace, however, is short-lived. The assassination of the Vice-Premier of the People's Republic in Kowloon, Hong Kong's sister city across Victoria Harbor, is marked by the scrawled message, "Jason Bourne is back!" Fear of what this might mean for the stability of the Far East leads high-level Washington political experts (aware that there is no real Jason Bourne) to kidnap St. Jacques to re-create for David Webb the trauma that originally plunged him into the Bourne identity, in order to find answers Washington cannot obtain. Government officials meet secretly in Central Colorado to brief Edward Newington McAllister, the government's contact with the Webbs. Although horrified at himself, McAllister initiates the kidnapping and the frame-up to plunge Webb into the conspiracies and treachery of Hong Kong, Kowloon, and Macao. Bourne recruits Conklin and Panov to help him plan his strategy. Following a carefully laid trail, Webb battles his better self to let his cold, calculating Bourne identity take charge.

Chapters 8–16 alternate between Webb/Bourne, who stirs the waters for clues, and St. Jacques, who plans and executes an escape from an official American "safe" house in Hong Kong. Bourne meets with a fake criminal warlord (a Hong Kong Special Branch officer in disguise), and follows clues neatly provided by cooperating British, American, and Hong Kong intelligence agents to the impostor-psychopath and his secret client—a sadistic politician who dreams of disrupting the West and marshaling Communist supporters to seize absolute power. Bourne's investigation in Red China and in Macao leads to the same answers St. Jacques discovers through a Canadian embassy friend, Catherine Staples; the dire situation demands dire deeds.

In Chapters 17–28, despite British and American pursuers, St. Jacques and Bourne turn hunters. Staples's intimate relationship with Inspector Ballantyne and her embassy position provide her insider knowledge that ensures St. Jacques's escape from the vigilant pursuit of Len Wenzu, the Head of the Hong Kong Special Branch. When Staples is made privy to the seriousness of the crisis, however, she joins government officials against her friend. Bourne traces leads to an airport assassination and prevents it, then rejoins Philippe d'Anjou to pursue more leads. St.

Jacques is attacked and nearly raped by street thugs, but is rescued by kindly Chinese. Her contact with Conklin marks a turn in the action as he and Panov come to her aid in Chapter 25, and together they try to contact Webb to save him from himself. Bourne and d'Anjou track the hidden power center to Peking, but walk into a Chinese trap at the Mao Memorial in Tian An Men Square, where d'Anjou is taken prisoner. Bourne mounts a rescue attempt, witnesses the sadistic behavior of an army of fanatics for whom human life has no value, and seizes his double. Repercussions in Red China and in Hong Kong require a final assassination to save Hong Kong from the ire of Peking. Government officials are in disarray as traitors are exposed and alliances change, and as Conklin and Panov spell out the implications of their deeds.

Chapters 29–32 record the final confrontation. As St. Jacques, Panov, and Conklin await word of him, Bourne (his double in hand) storms the American "safe" house compound. By Chapter 33 Bourne is in St. Jacques's arms, a psychological wreck, but safe. The government officials then do what they should have done from the beginning, that is, explain the nightmare possibilities reasonably and beg Bourne's assistance. In Chapter 37 Bourne destroys the megalomaniac who has precipitated the plot and in Chapter 38 Bourne is put aside as Webb returns to dominance.

### The Bourne Ultimatum

Five years later, an urgent telegram signed Jason Bourne leads Alexander Conklin and Dr. Morris Panov to a small-time carnival on the outskirts of Baltimore, just in time to witness an innocent bystander being shot in the throat. Carlos has thrown down the gauntlet, a final confrontation with Bourne is in the making, and the stalking has begun. They alert Webb, who puts his wife and two children (Jamie and Alison) on the next plane for the Caribbean to join Marie's brother Johnny in safety. Johnny, financed by Webb, has prepared for this eventuality by making his resort hotel an armed camp defended by high-tech security. The danger to his family revives the survivalist side of Webb's personality, and his deadly alter ego, Bourne, takes over. At the age of fifty he is not the lithe killer he once was, and his kindlier, more responsible personality, Webb, keeps coming to the forefront. Only the killer instincts of his self-contained Bourne personality, with its deadly competencies, however, can save Webb and his family from death.

A Prologue emphasizing the thirteen years since Bourne's original confrontation with the Jackal and an Epilogue in which Panov asserts, "It's really over now" (*BU* 662) frame the novel. In between is Bourne's final battle with the Jackal. Chapters 1–9 establish the situation, summarize the key background in the Carlos/Bourne conflict, and report strategy mounted and allies consulted or informed. Bourne plans his attack on Carlos as Carlos pursues Bourne's family to the Caribbean. A sequence of alternating scenes creates the same type of tension that worked so effectively in *The Bourne Supremacy*, when St. Jacques and Webb were separated.

The battle is in full swing in Chapters 10–27, with sidebars related to recent illegal Medusa activities. As he uses his intelligence agency sources to gather information and to verify guesses, Conklin uncovers a second source of trouble that later interlocks with the Jackal confrontation: a global cartel born twenty years before in Saigon. Former Medusa colleagues, now high in government and business in the United States and Europe, have regrouped to gain control of global financial centers and economies in multinational mergers and other manipulations. Shockingly, the cartel includes highly respected American senators, generals, and diplomats with ties to the Mafia. Bourne plans to infiltrate Medusa's new global operations and threaten key members with public exposure to force them to hire the Jackal to assassinate him. In the meantime, Bourne will keep tabs on his contacts so that he can prepare for the Jackal's attack. Bourne traces new Medusan activity to the country estate of General Norman Swayne, but a failed attack on Bourne's family by Carlos's agents brings both Bourne and Carlos to the Caribbean for a violent face-to-face standoff. The CIA and the Mafia unknowingly help Bourne track Carlos to Paris, where the danger from Medusa and the Mafia intensifies. The Mafia kidnap and chemically debrief Panov, and Carlos's men seize and interrogate Bourne, though both escape to safety. Chapters 25–27 add new twists and new dangers, including Jacqueline Lavier's sister, Dominique, whose message from Carlos prepares the final trap.

Discoveries in Chapters 28–35 help the Bourne team piece together events, thanks to the CIA's debriefing of a Mafioso *capo* (head), Panov's voluntary second chemical debriefing, and Russian assistance. A British intelligence film shows Bourne his younger self and the Russian Bryce Ogilvie in a base camp north of Saigon, evidence that the new Medusa organization and the Jackal had linked up earlier.

Just as Carlos traced Bourne to his origins in *The Bourne Identity*, in Chapters 34–41 of *The Bourne Ultimatum* Bourne traces Carlos to his origins in the KGB training school for terrorists and spies at Novgorod,

Russia, where Bourne and Carlos wage their final battle. This secret compound, like Nelson DeMille's in *The Charm School* (1989), duplicates a prototypical American community: Everywhere, USA, with streets, homes, entertainment, clothing, and so forth reproduced in meticulous detail, and with speakers of American English impressing American idioms and cultural conventions on trainees. The compound has a Maine waterfront village, a small Southern town, and a busy metropolis, each complete with appropriate structures and activities. A complex set of tunnels and locks between compound units allows rising water to figure prominently in the plot.

In Chapter 42 order is restored, the family is united, and life can proceed.

## CHARACTER DEVELOPMENT

Key characters recur, while others are limited to a single book. The villains are mainly one-dimensional: CIA operatives who have sold out to the opposition out of jealousy or greed; a corrupt general who made a fortune in Vietnam and who offers his statuesque wife to important business connections; a senile Frenchman enlisted in Carlos's army of the aged, who thinks he is still battling Nazis; a sadistic nurse, an "angel of death" who forces the head of her aged patient into flaming kerosene and who wields poison in her syringe. Jacqueline Lavier, one of Carlos's top operatives, is a little more complex. She heads the fashion house Les Classiques and controls every invoice. A tall, imperious woman, her face a "cold mask" (*BI* 212), Lavier is an experienced businesswoman committed to high fashion, personal comfort, and Carlos. Although she finances his secret accounts and faithfully does his bidding, Carlos kills her in a confessional because of a single act of disobedience. In *The Bourne Supremacy* her sister, Dominique, becomes Carlos's representative and go-between.

### Key Characters

*Carlos*. Venezuelan-born Ilich Ramirez Sanchez, also called "Carlos" or "the Jackal," is Bourne's infamous, deadly nemesis, a fictive character that Ludlum based on the real international assassin of the same name. A whole mythology has grown around this notorious, quasi-mythical villain: the Jackal has appeared in several popular fiction works, including Frederick Forsyth's *The Day of the Jackal* (1971), which captures his professionalism and expertise as he attempts to assassinate French president Charles de Gaulle. Legend has it that the real Carlos was trained by the Soviets at Novgorod and by Che Guevara in the field, that he has killed fifty to sixty important political and military figures, and that he was the unidentified second assassin who killed Kennedy. David Yallop's *Tracking the Jackal* (1996) traces the attempts by German prosecutors to extradite the Jackal from his reported residence in Syria. Overweight, balding, and drinking heavily in Khartoum, Carlos the Jackal was handed over to French officials by the Sudanese police on August 14, 1994. He appeared before France's top terrorist judge, and his trial was still pending as of 1996.

In historical fact the son of a rich doctor who was a committed Marxist, Ludlum's Carlos is more menacing than ideological; he is elusive and deadly, a narcissistic and greedy master terrorist who perverts and twists all he touches. Disguised as a Barcelonan priest, he sends his silent army of old men to carry out his will from the sanctity of a church. He turns the confessional into an abattoir; black-robed killer priests and deadly nuns with pious faces do his bidding. As Monsieur René Bergeron, he has created the fashionable House of René on Rue du Faubourg-Saint-Honoré in Paris. Despite clever disguises, Bourne recognizes him by his wide, heavy shoulders, tapered waist, dark skin, and catlike walk. His main disguise is as a well-known public figure frequently in the news. Carlos is a silent, deadly shark, whose hatred of Bourne becomes an obsession, "like a cancer in his aging brain" (*BU* 186); he blames Bourne for his failures, and vows to destroy him and his.

*Sheng Chou Yang.* The Red Chinese minister of state, Sheng Chou Yang in *The Bourne Supremacy* is a very bright and very ambitious hypocrite, who hides a diabolical reality behind a positive public image. A nationalist zealot with ideological roots in Taiwan and the dream of an economic *blitzkrieg* to seize Hong Kong, he is the first son of a very powerful Hong Kong *taipan* (boss), but he betrays both Red China and Hong Kong. His toying with East-West politics makes him potentially far more dangerous than Carlos. His fanatical followers crucify, slash, and burn not only enemies but also comrades who doubt or who fail their assigned tasks. He is a true paranoid, a Fu Manchu who chills Bourne's blood, and the world community sighs with relief upon his death.

Ludlum's protagonists and their associates are better developed than his villains.

*Webb/Bourne/Cain/Delta.* David Webb, alias Jason Bourne, Cain, and Delta, is the sympathetic, driven protagonist of the series. A decent man who does terrible deeds of destruction, a traumatized, divided personality, oddly quiet but unquestionably lethal, he is highly resilient and efficient, a professional with incredible endurance and a personal affinity for his work. Webb plunges into danger and violence to cope with seeing his family blown to pieces. Blaming the North Vietnamese (despite doubts), he volunteers for covert missions deep in Cambodia and North Vietnam, under the code name Delta. There he encounters the real Jason Bourne, a bloody, destructive, and treacherous man whose life he takes (on March 25, 1968) and whose identity he later uses. Ironically, whenever he or his are threatened, Webb finds himself slipping into a cold, calculating Bourne identity, the identity of a survivor whose highly developed skills and senses ensure success against seemingly impossible odds. Yet, the Bourne identity begins as a myth generated by Treadstone to challenge Carlos, with Bourne an agent provocateur, whose supposed assassinations are the work of faceless villains, happy to have their deeds attributed elsewhere.

Webb himself is a kindly university professor, a man of careful thought and precise words, not a man of action. Webb is the man St. Jacques loves; but the Bourne and the submerged Delta personalities are necessary for Webb and St. Jacques's survival. Webb/Bourne is "a walking encyclopedia" (434) of Washington's dirty secrets, which makes his potentially curable amnesia dangerous, and his instincts and skills as Jason Bourne make him a necessary tool in the battle against Carlos and Sheng Chou Yang.

*Marie St. Jacques.* Raised on a ranch in Ontario by Francophone parents, Marie St. Jacques is a highly trained English-speaking economist (a graduate of McGill University and Oxford University). Respected in her field, she has worked for the Canadian government since graduation. She is also beautiful, practical, affectionate, and daring, a tigress in the defense of those she loves. She can quickly size up a situation and project several scenarios. She is the feminine principle and life force in this series. Her gratitude to Bourne for rescuing her and her intuitive understanding of his vulnerability and need motivate her to nurture, protect, and then love him. She represents home, security, and health for Bourne, his "anchor" in "crashing seas," the prime motivator of his actions, and "the core of his emerging sanity" (*BS* 36). She also manages his finances and has the U.S. government's Zurich funds transferred to a secret account in the Cayman Islands. "Without Marie," Ludlum writes, Bourne would be "a loveless, discarded dead man," but with her he can find "the sun" again (*BS* 37). Just as Bourne's inherent goodness contrasts with Carlos's evil, so St. Jacques's wholesomeness, loyalty, and love contrast with the perverted lust and disloyalty of Angélique Villiers, Carlos's first cousin and lover since age fourteen, a terrorist willing to marry General Villiers in order to destroy his son and spy on him for Carlos. Angélique Villiers is evil personified, while St. Jacques is at times saintly in her devotion and love. Her willingness to repeatedly pursue Webb wherever his other self takes him is proof of her tough, resilient character and enduring love.

*Dr. Geoffrey Washburn.* Despite the debilitating alcoholism that has exiled him to Port Noir for killing a patient on the operating table, Washburn is a careful, caring physician. He fears the worst from Bourne's ramblings, but hopes for the best and leaves judgment and criticism for others. He starts Bourne on the road to recovery and prepares him for the slow return of his memory, believing that the physical must be healed before the psychological. Reading up on the latest theories in psychiatry, he initiates a procedure of testing to determine his patient's expertise and to trigger his memory. As Sherlock Holmes would do, he applies logic and reason to Bourne's situation. As his patient puzzles over his identity, Washburn comes to terms with his own problems and is better for the experience, facing the emptiness of his battle with alcoholism and longing to return to a more challenging life in Europe. Washburn's calm competence and thoughtful advice steady Bourne and guide his actions as he goes in quest of his memory; later Bourne rewards that friendship with 1,500,000 Swiss francs, enough money to help Washburn begin anew. Washburn's remade passport speeds Bourne on his journey of self-discovery. Washburn is mentioned in all three books because of his importance to Bourne's recovery.

*Alexander Conklin.* CIA operative Conklin, born Aleksei Nikolae Konsolikov, was a trusted friend of David Webb and his family. He recruited Webb for the Medusa organization, and inherited the Treadstone operation after its leading personnel were massacred. Conklin's career as a field strategist for Medusa ended when a land mine shattered his foot. His bitterness and his observations of the Delta personality's ruthlessness make him see Webb/Bourne as a crazed killer. His role in nearly killing Bourne leaves Conklin shattered and guilt-ridden; he drinks heavily, alienating colleagues. When St. Jacques is kidnapped and Bourne seeks Conklin's help (believing that Conklin drunk has sharper perceptions than most intelligence agents sober), he redeems himself. Bourne's confidence compels Conklin to respond with efficiency and insight and to exploit the intelligence network to trace St. Jacques. His insider knowledge and CIA contacts help him supplement guesswork with vital intelligence information, disseminate misinformation, and redirect intelligence operation tactics. He proves vital in forcing government agencies to do what is right. His friendship with his opposite number in Moscow helps defeat the Jackal.

*Dr. Morris Panov.* "Mo" Panov's hypothetical responses to Conklin's hypothetical description almost cost Bourne his life. Infuriated at having unwittingly furnished an erroneous analysis, Panov demands that the government allow him to assist in Bourne's treatment and recovery. He and St. Jacques become close friends and together they struggle throughout the series to restore Bourne's mental health and to protect him from his own government. Later Panov puts his own sanity on the line to recall information gleaned subconsciously while in enemy hands.

*Philippe d'Anjou.* D'Anjou, a former Delta who knew the dead Jason Bourne and who works for Jacqueline Lavier in *The Bourne Identity*, provides insights into the Vietnam and Cambodia operations as well as insider knowledge about Carlos's terrorist network; his recognition that Webb is not the ruthless Bourne he knew confirms the true Webb personality. In *The Bourne Identity*, after Bourne saves his life, he returns to Asia. In *The Bourne Supremacy* he reappears in Red China, where he and Bourne team up to capture Bourne's double and to oppose Sheng Chou Yang. After leaving Europe, d'Anjou capitalizes on Bourne's reputation remaining intact in Asia by creating a money-making assassin: a down-and-out, psychotic young Englishman, a former Royal Commando and escapee from a mental institution. D'Anjou teaches him the assassin's trade and makes him Bourne's double, but when the nameless psychotic swings out of control and acts for other principals, d'Anjou feels obliged to kill his monstrous creation. Bourne ends d'Anjou's torture at Sheng Chou Yang's mass political gathering, and later the memory of d'Anjou's comradeship helps him through difficult times.

*David Abbott.* Abbott, code-named "The Monk," created Medusa, Cain, and Bourne; he was the mastermind of the government's covert operations. Only he and a few close associates knew about Webb's Bourne commission, and even in high-level discussions he was loath to reveal operation parameters, in hope of trapping high-ranking traitors. Consequently, the murder of Abbott and his Treadstone team casts Bourne adrift, with no high-level American protectors who can intuit his situation. Abbott's lessons in survival, however, become the mainstay of Bourne's strategies and attacks, and throughout the series Bourne's on-the-spot decisions are the fruit of Abbott's teaching: "Crawl in closer . . . reduce the numbers. . . . The Monk had made that clear. Knife, wire, knee, thumb . . . points of damage. Of death." (*BI* 407).

*General Villiers.* The respected General of the French Army André François Villiers only appears in *The Bourne Identity*, where his high-level contacts and network open doors for the Treadstone trap. A proud man in his late sixties or early seventies, he has devoted his life to France. Now, he heads an organization of old soldiers who fought Nazis and Nazi sympathizers during World War II as leaders in the underground and who have again united to fight the traitors that still threaten their country. When his son died, Villiers took up his political mantle and fought, as his son did, against terrorists like Carlos. Bourne challenges Villiers to hunt Carlos with him, and Villiers admonishes him to strike swiftly, like a wolf pack. By making Carlos's plot to gather NATO secrets public record upon his death, Villiers helps undercut Carlos's network and power. He also provides Bourne an intelligence network to substitute for his lost Treadstone contacts.

*Cactus.* Cactus is an aging African-American, a former Treadstone specialist who intuits Bourne's troubled spirit and basic kindliness and empathizes with him. Bourne depends on him for disguises and fake identification in *The Bourne Supremacy* and *The Bourne Ultimatum*. He survives a bullet in the chest while assisting Bourne.

*Johnny St. Jacques.* Marie's brother, Johnny St. Jacques, is vital for plot development in *Ultimatum*. Bourne has saved him from a murder charge and has set him up in business on the island of Montserrat, about 300 miles south-south-east of Puerto Rico: he has a small hotel, a boat, and the essentials for a pleasant life. In turn, Johnny protects his sister and her family and aggressively wards off strangers.

## THEMES

The Bourne series is notable for its continuity as the kindly, academic David Webb pieces his life together, but is repeatedly forced back into survivalist roles as trained killer (Cain/Delta) and skilled undercover agent (Bourne), when necessity compels for national and international good. Recurring themes in this series are the importance of personal loyalty, the kindness of strangers, the healing power of love, the effectiveness of disguises at changing identity, and the negative effects of aging. As Bourne finds it harder and harder to engage in the type of combat that once came easily, he must rely more heavily on his acting skills, his loyal associates, and kind strangers to prevail. The acting and disguises suggest a broader concern with illusion and reality. Ludlum explores the conflicts between broad governmental strategies for the overall good of the nation and the welfare and rights of the individual citizen; the question of bad means versus good ends; and the responsibility of the individual who is part of a team or organization committed to broad policies, no matter what the cost in human terms is. He also investigates the nature of evil, whether in the form of an international terrorist, a hypocritical leader bent on personal aggrandizement and the acquisition of power, or a man who does what he knows is wrong for a cause that he believes is right. Human choices and human obligations are at the heart of this series.

Ludlum also addresses the realities of aging: a lessening of strength, a loss of resilience, and a hardening of personality traits. Since he follows the lives of Webb/Bourne and Carlos over some fifteen to twenty years, the topic is a natural one. What the two enemies did in their youth requires much more effort in their fifties. The sore muscles that were ready for action the next day at the age of thirty, remain sore for weeks at the age of fifty. Although Bourne discovers that some skills (like how to stalk and liquidate an enemy) return automatically in time of need, his body takes longer to recover from physical trauma; aching muscles, torn ligaments, and general pain are inevitable with age. He needs a hot shower and mild exercise to limber up, therapies that were unnecessary a few years before. In *The Bourne Supremacy*, when the protagonist battles a trained executioner, that champion of Macao feels dishonored at being bested by someone he considers an old man, that is, over thirty. In *The Bourne Ultimatum*, the Jackal has grown thinner and bald; his muscles are less defined, his agility lessened. Conklin too thinks wistfully of younger days and shining youth. Bourne breathes heavily and aches with pain from the "unused and abused" leg muscles when only a few years earlier he would have ignored them (*BU* 400).

Acting and role-playing drive Ludlum's vision of the espionage game. Moles burrow so deep that their roles almost become their reality, a phenomenon that leads to the Ludlum refrain, "They're everywhere." Villains and heroes require skillfully contrived disguises, changed roles, and new identities; both Bourne and Carlos prove capable of virtuoso performances. Under Abbott's direction, Webb underwent reconstructive surgery to make his features less distinctive and to allow him to more easily shift identities. Though an amnesiac, Bourne remembers Abbott's lessons about changing roles. His early disguises with stolen clothes help transform him into a new person, sometimes appearing rich and respectable, at other times seedy and dangerous. Using government funds, he consults a specialist (Cactus), who provides fake identification cards, contact lenses in different colors, glasses in various designs, and a new hairstyle and color, with packets of dye for future changes. These externals enable Bourne to become the "chameleon" of old, changing appearance sometimes several times in a day. His greatest asset, however, is his acting skill: his ability to change accents, body language, gestures, and even facial expressions to move into a new role. Sometimes the role is an aggressive strategy to intimidate and divide the enemy, as when he poses as a Taxation and Records investigator, Division of Fraud and Conspiracy; it can be a way to access secret information, as when he plays a knowledgeable, wealthy buyer of designer apparel; or it can be a way to infiltrate the enemy camp without suspicion, as when, wearing threadbare clothes and carrying a newspaper cone of smelly fried fish, he adopts the stooped posture and sad resignation of a longtime field worker. Bourne teaches St. Jacques his strategies so successfully that a change in hairstyle and makeup transforms her beauty to drabness.

Central to the series is the nature of loyalty and betrayal. Out of loyalty to his brother, Delta/Bourne assaults a North-Vietnamese prison camp, but two of his group, for whom immediate profit outweighs loyalty, turn the assault into a trap. Alfred Gillette, director of Personnel Screening and Evaluation for the National Security Council, proves treacherous out of class envy. Jealous of Washington gentry with houses in Georgetown, degrees from the right schools, and membership in exclusive clubs, he resents being relegated to "staff" and takes revenge by helping Carlos enter Treadstone. Even more treacherous is the brutal Czechoslovakian paraplegic, Chernak, who served the Nazis as a trilingual interrogator at the infamous concentration camp at Dachau; then, at war's end, he betrayed all trusts—even blackmailing his former Nazi associates. Conklin, in contrast, is a decent man who betrays his friendship with Webb because he fears the Bourne personality. Later, he acts to rectify his error and expiate his guilt, standing by Webb/Bourne in future operations and putting his reputation and life on the line. General Villiers, in loyalty to his son, aggressively fights terrorism, while his second wife, Angélique, has betrayed his love and trust, targeting him because of his impeccable reputation for honesty, his position of trust in the government, and his access to confidential materials. Fearing the vulnerability of his age, he trusts her with the literal key to his government's secrets, only to learn that she has been Carlos's tool from the beginning. Killing her with his own hands seems a fitting retribution. In contrast to Angélique's disloyalty is St. Jacques's repeated confirmation of her words to Webb, "I believe in you." Her trust and loyalty keep Webb sane, and her love helps Bourne recover his health and his identity. Conklin and Panov, influenced by her example, are steadfast in their loyalties.

Ludlum contrasts the greed, selfishness, and cruelty of his villains with the basic human decency of ordinary people, a decency born of common humanity and shared adversity. When they first meet him, Washburn and St. Jacques, recognizing Bourne's vulnerability, help him beyond the requirements of duty or gratitude. In *The Bourne Supremacy* St. Jacques's screams on the street bring startled strangers to assist her. Later, when attacked by thugs, kindly Chinese families rescue her, treat her wounds, feed her, and help hide her from her pursuers, including American Marines, Catherine Staples, and Edward McAllister. In *The Bourne Ultimatum* an old man's sense of right makes him protect St. Jacques and her children.

Ultimately, Ludlum argues, the individual is responsible for himself. Bourne provides Washburn a new chance, but Washburn himself must put his life back together or sink back into alcoholism. Conklin too must and does choose; despite the pain of withdrawal, he forces himself to become the competent professional again.

Ludlum depicts large, impersonal agencies using and abusing individuals, ignoring their rights, making them pawns in a larger game. Villiers, who has experienced the nightmare of his homeland invaded and his countrymen capitulating, fears that a free society can be undermined unless the guardians of democracy are vigilant. He argues that conspiracies abound—both from the left and from the right—and cannot go unchallenged. In contrast, Abbott pleads the difficulties of a democracy: stability and national security require continuity, yet democracy depends on a regular changing of the guard, with different people with different temperaments taking office. Some kind of fixed, long-range intelligence strategy is needed, but how can the J. Edgar Hoovers of the world be avoided or controlled if this is the case? McAllister, in *The Bourne Supremacy*, becomes a willing tool of his government; he disapproves of the human cost, but is convinced that the ends justify the means. Nonetheless, he finds the government representative who reminds him of his duty "the most immoral man" he has ever met (*BS* 112). Ludlum raises questions, identifies dilemmas, but provides no final answers. He does repeat in various ways that despite the sophistication of our intelligence apparatus, we as a nation fail to consider "the human quotient" (*BS* 21). That is, how human beings will react is always the unknowable factor.

## ALTERNATE READING: PSYCHOANALYTIC CRITICISM

Sigmund Freud's earliest work, *Studies in Hysteria* (1895), is a good place to begin a psychoanalytical approach to literature. A collaborative effort with Josef Breuer, it investigates the symptoms and causes of hysteria and the question of "unmasking" and discovery. In psychology, the term "hysteria" does not simply mean "emotional excitability," but rather a wide range of adaptive symptoms that hide a neurosis. Freud blamed hysteria on deeply disturbing, repressed, pathogenic memories, and believed that his task as psychoanalyst was to treat the physical symptoms by unmasking those memories, through bringing them to the patient's consciousness. In *Dora: An Analysis of a Case of Hysteria* (1905) Freud describes the drama of the psychiatrist as detective discovering the repressed parts of a mental life. For Freud, the effective psychiatrist, like a detective, must piece together the broken fragments of experience revealed through dreams and physical and psychological responses to stimuli, and must "translate" or interpret "manifest" neurotic symptoms into the more complete, but hidden "latent narrative" (Thompson 116).

Dr. Washburn thrusts Bourne into physical and psychological situations that parallel the stress and conflict that produced the original trauma in an attempt to trigger repressed memories and to evoke responses that will shed light on Bourne's other self. The readers' journey with Bourne in his search for his inner secrets is a journey through the corridors of psychoanalysis. The roughness of the fishing crew aboard the boat of Lamouche elicits automatic responses indicative of Webb's identity (his severely injuring three of the crew reveals his martial prowess and professional training). As outside stimuli trigger Bourne's instinctive responses and fragmented memories and bring him closer to discovering his complex inner self, the reader comes to appreciate the nightmares that have transformed his life and damaged his psyche and to condemn the callous indifference of a government that uses Bourne's weakness to further its own designs.

Although some critics doubt the value of psychoanalytical theory in casting light on literature, the amnesia and the multiple personalities of David Webb/Jason Bourne, and the attribution of these psychological problems to the stress and trauma of terrible personal loss and injury makes a psychoanalytical interpretation necessary to fully understand character and action. Psychological or psychoanalytical criticism involves using such theories to explain the value of a literary work or the general processes of literary creativity, to examine the structure or strategy of a work in terms of the intended reader response, or to investigate the thoughts and actions of a character in a literary work. In this case, a psychoanalytical approach seems justified to fully understand the nature of the main protagonist. Ludlum himself encourages this approach, since Webb/Bourne is clearly a disturbed personality, and a key figure and close family friend of the Webbs is the psychiatrist who did the original agency profile on Webb and who feels personally responsible for his recovery. Such a psychoanalysis would involve an identification of the causes and symptoms of Webb's amnesia, paranoia, and divided self, a consideration of activities or events that trigger retraumatization, an exploration of personality and motivation in terms of past case history and resultant private demons, and an understanding of the most effective means of treatment.

Ludlum, drawing on the expertise of relatives in the medical profession, provides plentiful details about causes, symptoms, and retraumatization, and suggests that love, loyalty, and inner strength, combined with psychotherapy conducted by someone the patient trusts deeply, promote recovery. Bourne is the deadly alter ego that Webb assumed to survive jungle warfare in Vietnam and Cambodia as a member of the Medusa Brigade; in times of stress this alter ego surfaces and the gentle Webb recedes. Unfortunately, Webb will never rid himself of the results of his initial trauma unless he can destroy the cause of retraumatization, specifically, the Jackal. The series explores Bourne's progression: amnesia and a divided personality resulting from debilitating psychological responses to trauma, then retraumatization, treatment, and gradual progress toward normality, followed by retraumatization, and a final working out of conflict that may result in a reintegrated, whole personality.

*The Diagnostic and Statistical Manual* of the American Psychiatric Association (1980) describes Post-Traumatic Stress Disorder (PTSD) as a constellation of characteristic symptoms that develop following a psychologically traumatic event; Scrignar, in *Post-Traumatic Stress Disorder*, characterizes this event as "generally outside the range of usual human experience," with the most common trauma involving "a serious threat to one's life or physical integrity; a serious threat or harm to one's children, spouse, or other close relatives and friends; sudden destruction of home or community; or seeing another person who has recently been, or is being, seriously injured or killed as the result of an accident or physical violence" (vi). Webb has experienced all of these: the sudden death of his wife and child; the bombing of their home; the injury and death of his friends and brother in Vietnam; the kidnapping of his second wife Marie in *The Bourne Supremacy*; the murder threats to her and their two children in *The Bourne Ultimatum*; murderous pursuit by killers and by friends who have turned against him; and the trail of blood that follows him wherever he goes. Scrignar, in *Post-Traumatic Stress Disorder*, describes war and the battlefield as a ghastly "microcosm of trauma," where all five senses are assaulted: the "terrifying cacophony" of discharging weapons, shrieking soldiers, and wailing wounded; the maniacal expressions on the faces of combatants, the broken bodies, the pervasive stench of death, and the other sights and smells engendered by weapons of destruction and the deaths and injuries they cause (2). The immediate symptomatic responses include heart palpitations or tachycardia, cardiac uneasiness or pain, headaches, giddiness, dimness of vision, and general neurological upset (exaggerated respiration, dilation of arteries, increased generation of adrenalin). The long-term effects include deep anxiety, depression, hysteria, dissociative reaction, depersonalization, neurasthenia, intense psychological distress when exposed to events resembling the initial traumatic event, and what psychologists call "covert mental processes": intrusive thoughts, flashbacks, and nightmares. There may be a feeling of detachment or estrangement from others, difficulty sleeping, persistent irritability or anger, hypervigilance, exaggerated startle response, guilt, episodes of terror or panic, difficulties making decisions, and a feeling that one's personality has changed. These are all effects that Webb/Bourne experiences at one time or another in the series.

Bourne's first doctor, Dr. Washburn, summarizes the medical and psychological studies he has consulted about Bourne, emphasizing the massive physical and psychological shocks that have affected him: "*Lobus occipitalis* and *temporalis*, the *cortex* and the connecting fibers of the *corpus callosum*; the *limbic system*—specifically the *hippocampus* and *mammillary bodies* that together with the *fornix* were indispensable to memory and recall" (*BI* 20). To this list he adds the subsequent hysteria that induced amnesia, and the mass of contradictions that suggest a personality at odds with his experience and training: suppressed violence rigidly controlled, pensiveness that unexpectedly yields to anger. The result is Bourne's apparently irreversible memory gap coupled with instinctive knowledge in times of danger.

The psychological effects of extreme trauma and stress may be temporary or permanent; recovery depends on the inner fortitude of the individual, the affection and support of family and friends, a nonthreatening environment, and productive work. St. Jacques constantly fears that her husband's defensive switch to the Bourne personality might be permanent and that the personality she loves—the gentle university professor—might be lost forever to the survivalist personality. Her battle throughout the novels is to remind Webb of their love and of his better self. There are times when he almost slips over the edge, especially when she has been kidnapped or goes missing for long periods, but her voice and touch help restore his memory and help him rediscover the Webb personality within.

Webb's own government takes advantage of his pathological anxieties in *The Bourne Supremacy* by manipulating environment and events (kidnapping his wife and sending him cryptic, threatening messages) to keep him on the run for its own purposes. Dr. Scrignar describes "the Spiral Effect" produced by retraumatization when the patient confronts environmental stimuli that he or she associates with or that resemble the initial traumatic event; Bourne is a textbook case of the negative effects of escalating anxiety. Retraumatization, says Scrignar, can last for a lifetime if untreated (24). Furthermore, part of the threat the CIA holds over Bourne in *The Bourne Supremacy* is public revelation of his medical records, with a distorted agency interpretation of the psychiatric diagnosis. Thus, Ludlum's conspiracy theories take on an even darker, more sinister edge when an individual's own government purposely manipulates the center of his being, his repressed memories and sense of self, for public purposes. There can be no greater invasion of privacy.

# 7

# International Cold-War Conspiracies

## *The Matarese Circle* (1979), *The Parsifal Mosaic* (1982), and *The Aquitaine Progression* (1984)

"The game is in progress . . . and the players on both sides know the score," Schellenberg said. ". . . [A] great and terrible game that, once started, is impossible to stop. The game controls us; we don't control the game. It's like a fairground carousel. Once it's in motion, that's it. . . . I'm trapped along with thousands like me."

Harry Patterson (Jack Higgins), *To Catch a King*

[I]t's the biggest game in modern history.

Joel Converse, *The Aquitaine Progression*

Unlike most Cold War stories, which depict Americans and British in conflict with Soviets, *The Matarese Circle*, *The Parsifal Mosaic*, and *The Aquitaine Progression* dramatize global conspiracies as products of past conflicts and villainy in place for generations. Right-wing fanatics, members of secret cabals bent on world domination and revenge for past wrongs, promote distrust, chaos, and instability. Their secret soldiers are zealots ready to sacrifice their lives for their cause, or corrupt officials ready to sell out to the highest bidder or to be easily blackmailed because of private perversions. American and Russian extremist groups exploit the situations to promote their causes, while decent people from different, even opposing nations, spurred on by self-righteous indignation and personal loss, use logic, instinct, and field-tested experience to put matters right—in part, for a time. Ludlum's storytelling here is top-notch, with credible, particularized characters engaged in fast-paced action to protect individualism and democracy; their refrain is "What kind of people are you?"

## GENRE CONVENTIONS

Jon Thompson, in *Fiction, Crime, and Empire*, enunciates the central conventions of espionage fiction. History is man-made, the outcome of human choices and action outside the public sphere; public events are either wholly fictitious or staged; the fate of nations and the course of history are at risk. The espionage novel purports to give the reader "a rare and uncensored glimpse" into behind-the-scenes realities (159). Character development is less important than the "labyrinthine complexity of events" (160). The plot presupposes a concealed truth with clues to be discovered and interpreted (112). The scale of deception is such that the protagonist's past social, political, and personal relations seem a "sham"—his life manipulated, his reality illusory (159). The individual, at personal cost, stands against the "monolithic organizations, institutions, and systems that regulate contemporary existence" (161) and that threaten "the democratic contract between the individual and his government" (162). The protagonist may overcome for the moment, or may be powerless in the grip of larger forces. Espionage fiction is by nature paranoic in its psychology, with its structure delineating the limitations of human action and its themes concerned with whether the real or the true is knowable or if it even exists.

In addition to the broad criteria established by Thompson, espionage fiction includes more particular conventions. Alienated heroes make personal sacrifices for the good of humanity and are sometimes pursued by their own side, as they play out covert activities with representatives of opposing nations or ideologies. The contest is most often between East and West, but may also be between members of the hero's own government, between organizations, or between worldviews. Sometimes traditional enemies join forces against a common deadly foe who threatens civilization. Their cooperation reinforces national differences but also commonalities. There are cat-and-mouse games with chase scenes, evasions, and narrow escapes, disguises, misdirections, and cryptic messages. Innocent bystanders become victims, dupes, or unwitting aids. Opposing sides plant misinformation or moles, and use double agents, codes, conduits, and drops. Action moves swiftly from one exotic setting to another; unpredictability, suspense, and uncertainty are key plot elements. The world is turned upside down, and sometimes righted, sometimes not. John le Carré's *The Spy Who Came in from the Cold* captures ironies typical of the genre, such as patriotic secret warriors dedicated to a cause because of its moral superiority, but betraying that very morality to defend their side. Control, the head of the spy services, confides:

> We do disagreeable things so that ordinary people here and elsewhere can sleep safely in their beds at night. . . . Of course, we occasionally do very wicked things. . . . I would say that since the war, our methods—ours, and those of the opposition—have become much the same. I mean you can't be less ruthless than the opposition simply because your government's *policy* is benevolent, can you now? . . . That would *never* do. (14)

*The Matarese Circle, The Parsifal Mosaic*, and *The Aquitaine Progression* gain strength from such Cold War spy conventions. They pit individuals against giant organizations, envision labyrinthian plots that threaten democratic values and hidden realities behind public facades, and assert the force of the individual in opposition to global conspiracy. Karas in *The Parsifal Mosaic* voices the traditional plight of the political operative: "we're always hiding. . . . We live in a movable prison" (6). Duplicity extends worldwide, and final enlightenment is an understanding of complexity, of labyrinthian plots, and of good and evil mixed.

Each novel ends with a temporary defeat of evil, but with the potential for further conspiracy, because the conflict is an ongoing one between opposing perceptions of reality and of the relationship of humans to government. In *The Matarese Circle* a common enemy, a secret, all-powerful third force, compels Soviet and American agents to cooperate, even as their own governments accuse them of treason for doing so and, even at the end, domination of the world by corporate interests remains likely.

Ludlum also adds his own twists to the genre. He sets the urban world of the Cold War novel in opposition to a Darwinian natural world and reverses traditional images of peace and trust. His heroes slither along mud banks, hide in stinking mounds of refuse while assaulted by stinging insects, and ward off vicious packs of Dobermans (one operative slits the throat of an attack dog that lands, teeth bared, at his crotch). Peaceful châteaux with acres of pastoral beauty prove hotbeds of conspiracies, and traditional victims (the elderly, the crippled) or representatives of the good (priests, pastors) prove tools of the opposition—in league with the devil.

## THE MATARESE CIRCLE

## Plot Development and Structure

*The Matarese Circle* alternates episodes by geographic location and theme: Key events occur in different parts of the world and, as a plot crux is resolved or complicated, characters face new places, problems, and insights. Some themes recur, but each of the three parts has its own thematic center. Part I alternates between the United States and Russia, with Washington, D.C., the final stage and distrust and hatred the main theme. Part II takes place in Corsica, Rome, Leningrad, and Essen, as a cause larger than their narrow national and agency interests compels the two rival U.S. and Soviet operatives to cooperate in an uneasy alliance. Part III begins in London but returns to the United States; Boston is the site of the resolution and of a new understanding of the international competition with which the book began.

Part I introduces the first manifestations of the Matarese conspiracy, the so-called Corsican fever secretly causing brutal assassinations of important political figures in the United States and the Soviet Union. "Mad Anthony" Blackburn, the Chairman of the Joint Chiefs of Staff, is gunned down in a New York brothel by a professional hit team, and then Dimitri Yurievich, a mildly dissident Russian physicist, is dispatched with equal efficiency while entertaining friends and family at a dacha, a Russian vacation house. The American and Soviet intelligence services see in each assassination the signature style of the opposition's best operative: the KGB's Vasili Taleniekov for the murder of Blackburn and Brandon "Bray" Alan Scofield, the U.S. State Department's Consular Operations man-of-all-dirty-work, for the murder of Yurievich. The leaders of both superpowers provide absolute assurances that neither country was involved in the assassination of the other's political figure.

Ironically, for all the mutual suspicions, Scofield and Taleniekov are burnt out, at odds with their superiors and the new political winds blowing through their agencies, and feeling their middle age and the narrowing of their prospects for a peaceful retirement. Both violate orders and instead do what they think is right, despite the consequences; both are disgusted with the bureaucrats they must work for ("Nothing ever changed much," is a mantra for them [96]); and both are stimulated only by the hatred they bear each other, for Taleniekov has had a brother killed by Scofield, in retaliation for the Russian's murder of the American's young wife in a Berlin sting operation.

This portrait of enervated and seemingly outdated spies, neatly handled in a chapter for each, changes when Taleniekov learns of the Matarese involvement in the murders. A dying secret police operative, originally a member of Stalin's NKVD, warns of the Matarese attempt to create chaos, but when Taleniekov tries the story out on important Soviet officials he is immediately branded a traitor to be shot on sight: the Matarese influence is everywhere. Taleniekov escapes Russia, concluding that the only way to expose the Matarese is to make common cause with his sworn enemy Scofield, who will be able to uncover the conspiracy on American soil and through U.S. government resources. The Russian contacts Scofield (code-named Beowulf Agate), himself recently retired forcibly from the State Department because of his rebellious behavior and surly attitude. Scofield naturally concludes his old enemy is trying to trap him, and sets a countertrap in a Soviet safe house in Washington. Chapters 7–10 trace the exciting cat-and-mouse competition between hunter and hunted in and around the hotel, with Scofield betrayed by his superiors. Circumstances finally force the two agents to call a personal truce when the Russian saves the American from death and both escape assorted killers and the Washington police. Scofield and Taleniekov hole up together in wary mutual suspicion before the former contacts his old mentor, Robert Winthrop, an old-school gentleman above suspicion of Matarese influence, and arranges a meeting in Washington's Rock Creek Park. The parties have only just gathered, however, when assassins appear in the darkness, and all scatter.

Part II begins in Corsica, where Scofield and Taleniekov travel separately to seek the source of the assassination fever in its founder, Guillaume de Matarese, a maniacal but successful entrepreneur who in 1911 organized a circle of professional killers guided by the Matarese Council. This legendary group, whose historical reality has been both dismissed as myth and accepted as a kind of Corsican Mafia, is singled out by Taleniekov's dying NKVD informant as the key to the current wave of killings; the old secret policeman even suggests that Stalin and Franklin Delano Roosevelt, among other world leaders who had outlived their

usefulness, had been assassinated by Matarese-for-hire at the behest of
their own governments. Scofield, who has visited Corsica before, connects with Taleniekov, whose pose as a scholar interested in Guillaume,
the ruined Villa Matarese, and local history leads to a murder attempt
by means of a Corsican Lupo shotgun, and then a manhunt into the dark
hills. Antonia Gravet, a young woman living far up in the hills, rescues
them and takes them to meet her great-grandmother, Sophia Pastorine,
now blind and ancient but formerly the mistress of Guillaume.

Guillaume, says the old lady, sought revenge on the European financiers who had tried to ruin him and who had caused the death of his
two sons. The *padrone* (Guillaume) invited the scions of five great European families similarly ruined by the financiers to join him in founding
the Matarese Council, an organization of professional killers based on
Arab assassin cults. All but one of the family representatives agreed to
join; he was killed, as were all the other witnesses, residents and servants
of the enormous Villa Matarese, in a *Götterdämmerung* including the
shooting of Guillaume by a young lad called the Shepherd Boy (an act
of planned suicide by the *padrone* himself) and the burning of the villa,
all to ensure secrecy. Only Guillaume's mistress survived by playing
dead in a horrific mass burial. She has recently heard the Shepherd Boy
on the radio—his voice "crueler than the wind" (226); he seems to have
risen to a position of importance, for he was giving a speech. The modern
Corsican villagers chasing the two spies are still bound by the original
oath of silence, and drive Scofield, Taleniekov, and Antonia from the old
lady's mountain farm, killing her in the process.

The threesome escape from Corsica, and Scofield and Antonia search
for descendants of the original Matarese Council. After being attacked
by a member of the Italian Red Brigades, a wildly radical terrorist group,
Antonia reveals to Scofield that she was a "drug [courier's] whore" for
the organization, a lure and pawn in their never-ending greed for drug
money. She confesses her naive acceptance of the leftist organization's
false idealism; she and Scofield, both corrupted and betrayed by their
political faiths, become lovers. Both are energized by their newfound
love, and Scofield sees a future for himself for the first time in years.
They attend a huge party at the Villa d'Este in Rome, where Scofield
confronts Count Alberto Scozzi, who is allied with the huge Paravacini
corporation. Accused of being an inheritor of the Matarese legacy and a
devotee of the Shepherd Boy, Scozzi runs, as Scofield had hoped, back
to his superiors, but is killed before any new information can be gained.

Antonia moves on to Paris, while Scofield goes to London to try to flush out another descendant, David Waverly, England's Foreign Secretary.

Meanwhile, Taleniekov has smuggled himself into Leningrad, the city of his youthful career at the University and of frequent visits during his rise in the ranks of the KGB. Chapters 22–27, the end of Part II, trace his search for records of the third Matarese Council member named by the old lady: Prince Andrei Voroshin, the head of an aristocratic Russian family considered piratical even by the czar before the Revolution. Taleniekov visits a former lover who has access to computer records, but she is killed by a Matarese assassin. An old professor named Yanov Mikovsky helps him search the revolutionary records of the fate of the Voroshin family, but the scholar too ends up dead. Taleniekov is further frustrated by the fact that the Matarese assassins—all of whom have a blue circle tattooed on their left chest and who repeat the phrase *Per nostro circolo* ("For our circle")—commit suicide rather than reveal any information. A hunch takes Taleniekov to Essen, Germany, where a lawyer friend, Heinrich Kassel, helps him discover that Voroshin changed his name to Verachten, which is the name of the family that controls the second largest corporation in the Ruhr Valley after the (real-life) Krupp corporation. In an exciting extended scene, Taleniekov breaks into the Verachten family compound only to see old Walther Verachten shot down by a guard when it seems he might talk. The Russian abducts Walther's middle-aged daughter, Odile (a leader in the corporation, who ordered her father's execution), but she too is killed and Taleniekov returns to Paris.

Part III is set in London and Boston. Chapters 28–30 follow Scofield's attempts to confront David Waverly, the British Foreign Secretary the team suspects of being a Matarese *consiglieri* (counselor). As the most politically distinguished of the inheritors so far, he is the hardest to get to, but Scofield arranges a meeting through a British intelligence contact. Waverly, however, is brutally assassinated before he can be interviewed by Scofield; Taleniekov and Antonia, who have met Scofield in London, are kidnapped. The American agent is told to return to Boston, if he wishes to save his friends; he is offered what amounts to a job interview if he would like to be a Matarese *consiglieri*. Chapters 31–37 focus almost entirely on Scofield in Boston as he prepares for his assault on the Matarese. He has learned that Trans-Comm Corporation of Boston owns much of the Verachten works of Essen and interlocks with Scozzi-Paravacini of Italy, and that these linked conglomerates are the brainchild of Nicholas Guiderone, the protégé of Joshua Appleton the Second. Guiderone is the Shepherd Boy who killed Guillaume de Matarese; he is the evil genius who has used the Appletons, a Boston establishment family and the last of the inheritors of the Matarese tradition, to further his own mad plan to replace world governments with international corporations. He is about to take control of the American presidency, for Guiderone's son, thanks to plastic surgery, has replaced Joshua Appleton the Third, a war hero and now a U.S. senator who is everyone's choice for the White House. Scofield finds proof of this substitution in the dental records of the real Appleton and his Matarese replacement, and uses them to deal for the freedom of Antonia and Taleniekov. His plan almost fails, however, when the important men to whom he has forwarded his proof—the Chairman of the Joint Chiefs of Staff, the director of the CIA, and the Secretary of State—turn up at Appleton Hall, all part of the Matarese conspiracy. Robert Winthrop, Scofield's old mentor, is still alive but a captive, so it is only a backup plan goading the Boston Police Department with a fake terrorist attack, complete with noisy bombs, that saves the day. Taleniekov, who had been seriously wounded in the kidnapping in London, sacrifices his life to help Scofield and Antonia escape. After debating the world takeover of corporate values with the Shepherd Boy, Scofield kills him, the fake Senator Appleton, and most of the other notables who are Matarese stooges; Appleton Hall burns to the ground, just as Villa Matarese did three quarters of a century earlier.

A brief Epilogue depicts Scofield and Antonia as charter boat owners in St. Kitts in the Caribbean, free of Washington skullduggery and hypocrisy. In the interest of corporate stability, the Matarese conspiracy has been hushed up worldwide, and bodies burned in Appleton Hall turn up in "innocent" plane crashes and car wrecks. A hopeful sign is that the U.S. president has taken charge and seems aware of the hypocrisies of his own government.

Throughout the novel the plot alternates between Scofield and Taleniekov, with Antonia a catalyst for Scofield's full acceptance and forgiveness of his old enemy. Although the Russian is a worthy character and fully Scofield's equal, the American dominates the plot by Part III. The general structural movement is from the United States to Corsica and Europe, and then back to the United States, with Taleniekov's investigations in the Soviet Union serving to heighten suspense and introduce parallel, but different, complications and adventures. As in an old film, Ludlum will frequently leave his hero hanging from a cliff (for example, Taleniekov shot at from close range in the hills of Corsica at the very end of Chapter 12) to crosscut to another character's activities (Chapter 13 follows Scofield for several pages before he meets up with the Russian, who has ducked away from the shotgun blast), thus adding suspense and maintaining interest. The parallels and differences between Russian and American agents are inherently interesting, and the focus on one begs for an equal focus on the other. Ludlum is also a master at ambushing the reader with a sudden, completely unexpected scene of violence and chaos, which results in constant tension and a sense of unease for the characters' welfare.

## Character Development

As the structure indicates, *The Matarese Circle* is a two-character book. Brandon "Bray" Alan Scofield, code-named Beowulf Agate, and Vasili Taleniekov, known to his friends as "the extraordinary Taleniekov" and to his enemies as "The Serpent," are almost perfectly matched in age, experience, outlook, and professional achievements. Much of Part I focuses on their feelings of anomie, of being middle-aged and having little left to prove; the sentence "Nothing ever changes" (86–87) applies equally well to each agent. Part II emphasizes how each reacts so similarly to a given situation that they need little discussion; though strangers, they think alike, as if they had worked side by side for years. They are not together much in Part III, when the plot dictates that the wounded Taleniekov leave the stage to Scofield, but their reconciliation speaks for itself: both have traveled a similar path from intense hatred and narrow self-interest to love and sacrifice for others.

Taleniekov and Scofield are classic Cold-War literary figures, representative of the modernist dilemma of committed ideological warriors losing faith in their cause. The great irony of the Cold War was that so much of it was fought by secret soldiers—agents and spies—who gave their whole lives over to causes that became, at least in their literary portrayals, less and less easy to distinguish, as ideological difference was flattened out by bureaucracy and as each side adopted the methods of its enemy. Both Scofield and Taleniekov are victims of department politics and changing styles; the battle tactics have become rigid and conventionalized, with no regard for casualties (their introductory chapters show both Scofield and Taleniekov disobeying orders to save hapless foot soldiers from destruction), and the overall strategy is less and less evident as the two superpowers become more alike. Scofield and Tal-

eniekov are equally competent, but worn down by their tarnished idealism and the terrible living conditions of the secret agent: the cheap
hotels, the constant travel, the absence of any stability, home life, or trust,
and the death of loved ones in secret and meaningless skirmishes. Both
the American and the Russian were brought into the secret life of spying
because of their bright intelligence, their aptitude for languages, and
their passionate curiosity; now, they have trouble feeling anything except
irony about their professions and contempt for their superiors.

Differentiating between Scofield and Taleniekov is not easy. Ludlum
suggests a greater passion on the part of the Russian and a greater reliance on cold reason by the American, a difference well in accord with
the general perception of their respective national characters. Scofield
keeps reminding himself to follow sequence, "always sequence" (483);
he believes that it is not the events themselves that shape the outcome,
but their timing and order. In contrast, Taleniekov asks for fire to follow
the explosions at Appleton Hall, and certainly his suicidal sacrifice is a
grand romantic gesture. Yet the Russian obeys a strict calculus to guide
his behavior, putting former lovers, old professors, and worthy friends
at risk in the interest of catching the Matarese. He is ready to kill Antonia
the minute she becomes a hazard to their search, and it is Scofield's
emotional intervention that saves her. The American, in turn, trusts his
instincts from the point of Antonia and Taleniekov's kidnapping to the
book's end, following sequence but also hunches and gut feelings. In
falling in love with Antonia he is the true romantic, far more so than the
Russian. He manages the classic escape to a charter boat in the Caribbean, while the Russian never gets to his small farm north of Grasnov,
instead sacrificing himself to the cause. Beyond this blurred difference,
Scofield and Taleniekov are a matched pair, and while Scofield is an
interesting, intriguing character, Ludlum deserves special praise for his
credible, sympathetic portrait of a KGB agent. Taleniekov feels real from
the inside; for all his superhuman heroics, he is a complete personality,
different from Scofield in national style, yet paralleling his professionalism. He is a well-defined character.

Antonia Gravet is also well defined, but cannot compete with the demands of plot once Scofield and Taleniekov begin circling their antagonists. Part II is Antonia's section, and she becomes increasingly
interesting as a character as we learn more of her: a mountain woman
with a Lupo shotgun who later appreciates Roman fashion and restau-
rants, an intellectual leftist who becomes involved with the Red Brigades,
a liberated woman who allows herself to be sexually exploited and en-
slaved, a seemingly strong personality faulted by seams of weakness.

The contradictions are both her own, those of a credible, well-rounded fictional character, and those of her culture, of an Italy superficially unified but in fact divided by regional, linguistic, political, social, and class differences. Unfortunately, once Antonia becomes emotionally attached to Scofield, these differences disappear, and in Part III she is little more than a damsel in distress to be rescued and protected.

In a sense, then, *The Matarese Circle* is a two-and-a-half character book, which focuses on Scofield and Taleniekov for three Parts, and on Antonia Gravet for about one and a half. This character focus is never apparent, however, for the novel is peopled with a wide range of interesting, convincing minor characters: Robert Winthrop, the well-meaning elder statesman in the U.S. government; Daniel Congdon, the sleazy Undersecretary of State; Aleksie Krupskaya, the old Istrebiteli/NKVD secret police agent; Sophia Pastorine, the old, blind ex-mistress of Guillaume de Matarese; Guillaume himself; Silvio Montefiori, the corrupt boat owner who smuggles the threesome out of Corsica; Lodzia Kronescha, Taleniekov's former lover, and Yanov Mikovsky, his old professor; Pietre Maletkin, the stupid and traitorous KGB man who helps Taleniekov in Leningrad; Heinrich Kassel, the radical lawyer turned Essen burgher; Roger Symonds, the British MI-6 man; and Dr. Theodore Goldman, the expert in interlocking conglomerates. Although many are types—for example, Montefiori and Kassel—they are given small defining details that particularize them and make them credible as characters. Even the unnamed dentist who supplies Scofield with the identity-confirming X-rays has a personality: he is "a man in a hurry" to treat as many patients as possible (475), smoking a surreptitious cigarette with Scofield in a workroom between clients: "Carcinoma loves company" (479).

Ironically, it is such minor characters who remain lively in the imagination long after the novel is finished. Most of the villains—Alberto Scozzi, Odile Verachten, and David Waverly—have very short life spans, and even the Shepherd Boy is only on stage briefly for a final set speech. The decision to include so many cameo parts by memorable minor characters is a wise literary decision, for these characters enliven and particularize, creating a believable context for the superhuman feats of the protagonists and the evil doings of the villains.

## Themes

The most provocative theme of *The Matarese Circle* is found in the thesis promulgated by the Shepherd Boy, Nicholas Guiderone, that national governments are obsolete and even dangerously violent; in their place Guiderone would put "the values of the marketplace [which] will link the peoples of the world" (516). Race, religion, social class, national character—all the characteristics that have defined the people of a specific region in the past are irrelevant to international corporations, which care only about productivity. Scofield answers Guiderone rather weakly, saying, "Give me an imperfect place where I know who I am" (516), but the final word comes from the president of the United States, an enlightened leader by this point, who nevertheless pays obeisance to corporate power: Scofield and Antonia read in a Barbados newspaper that the dead Guiderone's brainchild, Trans-Communications, has been reorganized, with the president saying, "a great American institution is in a position to export and expand American know-how and technology across the world, joining the other great companies to give us a better world" (535). The reader now knows, of course, that Trans-Comm is not an American institution at all, but has been a Matarese-controlled world conglomerate; whether the reorganization will make it American is a good question, with little to support a favorable answer.

The fall of Trans-Comm and Guiderone raises another important theme: that one dedicated person can make a difference. While the corporate power theme is subordinated to derring-do and the villainous Matarese, the power of the singular individual is evident throughout the book in Scofield, Taleniekov, and even Antonia. Scofield and Taleniekov may be burnt out, but they are equally skillful at evading and ultimately triumphing over their own bureaucracies, and at taking on the Matarese. Individuals inspire others: Antonia's love for Scofield motivates him to survive.

Ludlum's other recurrent theme is the danger of fanatics like the Italian Red Brigades, Guillaume de Matarese, and the Shepherd Boy. Such groups and individuals respect no human values when their interests are concerned. Quite apart from corporate depredation of cultures and nation-states, fanatics like Guillaume and the Red Brigades spring up throughout Ludlum's canon, using current circumstances to advance their insane agendas. They are, however, vulnerable to the committed individual who refuses to capitulate, as Scofield and Taleniekov demonstrate.

Finally, Ludlum's main theme is paranoia: hidden forces at work are the real story. From the gun battles in the Nebraska Avenue hotel and Rock Creek Park in Washington to the shoot-outs in Corsica, Rome, Essen, London, and Boston, the public story is always wrong, sometimes only partially so, but most of the time completely. This theme is most evident in the Epilogue: with the Matarese conspiracy put down and the conspirators killed or identified, governments, afraid of admitting their own possible obsolescence, choose silence, "the only [conclusion] that made sense in these insane times" (530).

## THE PARSIFAL MOSAIC

*The Parsifal Mosaic* is another exciting Cold War espionage story: fast-paced, tense, and fairly tautly told, with credible villains and a strong but emotionally torn hero. It led the *New York Times* best-seller list a week before its official publication, and sold 400,000 copies almost immediately (Adler 99). It is psychologically complex, and the trauma the protagonist faces is mythic: his beautiful and nurturing beloved is transformed into a demonic destroyer. The metamorphosis, however, proves an illusion, with both hero and heroine manipulated for devious ends by unknown forces. As in his other studies of democracies, Ludlum asserts the value of checks and balances and warns against placing too much power in the hands of an elite. He initially blames the enemy abroad, postulating an extremist group within the Russian KGB, only to then warn against a danger within: the American who fails to adhere to the wishes of the democratic public.

### Plot Development and Structure

The novel is divided into three books and an Epilogue. In Book I (Chapters 1–14) Czech-born U.S. State Department agent Michael Havelock, having been given seemingly indisputable evidence that his beloved Jenna Karas is a KGB double agent, arranges and observes her death, but is so shattered by the betrayal that he retires to teach college history based on his practical field experience and first-hand knowledge of war. Before classes begin, Havelock revisits cities his agency work never allowed him the leisure to enjoy (Amsterdam, Paris, and Athens)— his footsteps dogged by CIA and KGB agents suspicious of his motives. By accident, he glimpses a live Jenna Karas in a train station and traces her to the docks of Civitavecchia, Italy. He explodes with anger at a double sent to test him, but realizes that Karas is not dead (although he watched her body being riddled by bullets) and that she feels as betrayed by him as he by her. They have been manipulated into murderous distrust, and he must convince her of the plot against them before he can learn how and why.

The CIA, however, believes the official report, declares Havelock insanely dangerous, and sends CIA agent John Philip Ogilvie, code-named Apache, after him. In Rome, Havelock convinces Ogilvie of foul play, but Ogilvie is killed and Havelock must flee. As the CIA loses more agents to the activities of a high-placed traitor, Havelock traces Karas to a border crossing in the Alps and springs a trap for her, only to watch her pale face recede as she escapes by plane. In Chapter 13 Havelock tries to contact his mentor, Anthony (Anton) Matthias, the highly respected and much touted Viennese-born U.S. Secretary of State, only to be told by Matthias's neighbor Leon Zelienshi that Matthias no longer has time for old friends. A Russian who tries to recruit him confirms that Moscow orders kept Russians out of the area where Karas was supposedly killed. Thus, Part I ends with what had seemed a Cold-War conflict between Russian and American agents suddenly becoming something far more sinister: the possibility of a deep-cover mole or a traitor or even several traitors within the CIA or the American government at its highest levels. Because the point of view throughout Book I is that of Havelock (interrupted only briefly by that of CIA psychiatrists misdiagnosing his behavior as psychotic), readers share his anger, puzzlement, frustration, and dawning suspicions.

Book II (Chapters 15–25) provides a broader perspective that solves some puzzles and transforms what had seemed a personal conflict into a potentially disastrous national and international crisis. Chapters alternate between Havelock overcoming barrier after barrier in his personal hunt for Karas, and the President and his forces dealing with a crisis situation. Havelock uses a World War II French resistance network to search for Karas, and convinces Karas's friend of his integrity. The trail leads to New York and Jacob Handelman, a Nazi butcher from Prague whom Havelock kills; Handelman, disguised as a Jewish death-camp survivor, was using his respectable position to people a slave camp in Pennsylvania where Karas is being held. Captured by the Czech camp bosses, Havelock uses his knowledge of Handelman's operation to bluff his and Karas's way out. Finally together, the two share information: they postulate two intersecting plots at work, with one modifying the other. They approach Raymond Alexander, a writer for the *Potomac Review*, to find out about Matthias, whom they trace to a tightly guarded army island stronghold off the coast from Savannah, Georgia, where they discover an eerie replica of downtown Washington, D.C.

Interspersed among these events are chapters pulling together the different threads of investigation. A presidential conference absolves Havelock, analyzes past events from a new perspective, and discusses the government's fear of nuclear war. The trouble is threefold. Respected statesman and international diplomat Anthony Matthias has gone beyond his political brief to make secret diplomatic agreements unconfirmed by President or Congress. Working with a secret organization code-named Parsifal, Matthias has negotiated and personally signed nuclear first-strike treaties with both the Soviet Union and China, and if either side discovers the betrayal, nuclear war could follow. The *Voennaya Kontra Rozvedka* (VKR), an extremist branch of the KGB, has planted children in U.S. homes as *paminyatchiki* or deep-cover moles to grow up to be Soviet spies. One of these moles is a respected, highly placed State Department member. If this spy in the White House finds out about Matthias, all is lost. Meanwhile, Parsifal is demanding a blackmail payment of 800 million dollars to keep Matthias's insane agreements secret. The situation is so tense that, while the mole acts to cover his steps, the president approves Havelock's death for national security reasons. Before approaching the island prison, however, Havelock records dangerous, secret intelligence information and leaves the papers with Karas as blackmail security; when he is taken prisoner by the U.S. Army and discovers that Matthias is insane, he thus has a strong bargaining position.

In Book III (Chapters 26–39) events rush rapidly toward a climax, with an aftermath of violence and death. When Havelock meets President Berquist, he learns the full situation for the first time: how one man with power can produce global endgame scenarios. The staged death of Karas, their estrangement, and his retirement were part of a complex game plan to remove him from the international scene, where he might have recognized Parsifal, the secret manipulator behind Matthias and the originator of the doomsday agreements. As Karas and Havelock engage in a battle of wits with a mole called Ambiguity, whose identity they seek, their assistants are attacked, injured, and even killed. Among the victims are Undersecretary of State Emory Bradford, the doctor who performed the autopsy on the agent who wrote the CIA report on Karas's death, and Russian KGB Director of External Strategies Pyotr Rostov, who cooperated with Havelock to stop the VKR. As Jerry Adler remarks in "The Ludlum Enigma," legions of bystanders are "deadly pawns in a high-stakes poker game of international blindman's bluff" (100). Traps are reversed, and the most important mole is brought in on the president's team while others attack the Havelock team.

Once Havelock discovers the military zealot and China expert, Lt.

Commander Thomas Decker, who helped Matthias with the China policy, and once a captured mole has been debriefed, the State Department mole, Arthur Pierce, is finally identified and Havelock recognizes him as a participant in Karas's faked assassination. Parsifal is exposed as the brainchild of mad old men, fearful of the type of national lunacy they witnessed in World War II Germany and hoping to blackmail world powers into peaceful relationships by threatening global conflagration. Their benign motives have been driven by madness and manipulated by extremists, and Havelock and Karas must wage one last hunt before Matthias's explosive secret documents can be unearthed.

The Epilogue marks a return to normalcy. The world turned upside down is righted and the illusion of betrayal is replaced by the reality of love. Havelock, who as a child survived the nightmares of World War II, has survived the nightmares of the Cold War. Old lies and evasions have been exposed, and a lesson has been learned: the control of democracies should never rest in the power of a single individual, no matter how brilliant.

Geographically, the progression has been from Costa Brava, Spain, to Concord, New Hampshire, Amsterdam, Athens, and Paris, and then back to the United States, from New York to Pennsylvania, Savannah, Georgia, and Alexandria, Virginia.

## Character Development

Ludlum's hero, Havelock, and heroine, Karas, reflect many of the traditional characteristics of the warrior and his woman described in Sam Keen's *Faces of the Enemy* (133).

According to Keen, the warrior of traditional popular fiction has been hardened by experience; his role is to protect, to suffer, and to destroy. His reason dominates, although betrayal evokes rage, obsession, and risk-taking. He represses his fear and grief and channels it into aggressive action. Havelock fits this generic pattern. Born Mikhail Havlîcek in Prague, Czechoslovakia, Havelock, as a small child, returned from hunting rabbits to witness the Russian roundup and execution of all adult males in the town of Lidice, where his father worked. The women (including his mother) were conscripted for prostitution or slave labor, and the children were gassed or bayoneted. His mother killed herself the first night, and young Havelock lived like a wild animal in the forest until his father (a professor who secretly worked for British intelligence) found him and directed his energies toward resistance and revenge. By the age of ten he had learned to run and hide, lie low, and kill. When his father disappeared into a Siberian gulag (prison camp), Czech resistance fighters hid the young boy until the British MI-6 smuggled him to England, where an American colonel who had known his father adopted him. Then, with a fellow Czechoslovakian as his mentor, he devoted his life to Cold-War confrontations with the Russians.

As one of Keen's types of a warrior, Havelock is a strong, capable survivor who can transform ordinary objects into deadly weapons. A CIA operative for sixteen years, he has a reputation for integrity and competence, and an instinct for his job bred into him through rough experience. When angered, he is driven to perform extraordinarily well.

The traditional heroine, in turn, argues Keen, is expected to inspire, nurture, and heal, but circumstances conspire to force her to discover her powers of survival. Although she is normally warm and intuitive, when she joins the male world of political espionage, she leaves her role open to misinterpretation and soon becomes victim and suspected "demon," her every act interpreted as manipulative and aggressive. The beautiful, blonde Karas matches this generic type. A wonderful cook, she turns the CIA safe house into an intimate home through her power to produce mouth-watering Czech breakfast rolls. She understands Havelock's losses and heals his pain with her love and trust; yet she is intelligent enough and committed enough to work alongside him against their common enemy. Her decision to join Havelock's world of espionage, however, allows her to be manipulated and used against him. In over half of the novel she is a mysterious, shadowy figure, fleeing as Havelock pursues, perhaps the monster of his imagining, perhaps a frightened, much-wronged lover.

Beyond Keen's warrior categories, Ludlum's villains can also be classified into two types: the idealists who betray, lose, or subvert their ideals, and the fanatics who belong to ultraextremist cliques of already recognizably extremist organizations like the Russian KGB.

Anthony Matthias, the American Secretary of State whose meteoric rise has made him an international figure, is the idealist gone awry. He fled the Nazi invasion of Czechoslovakia with his family at the start of World War II, and started a successful new life. All went well, and his achievements were extraordinary. Respected for his humanitarian efforts, he was considered presidential material. Matthias is initially a figure of mythic proportions, seen through Havelock who reveres him as a superior, a consummate statesman, diplomat, and "man for all seasons"

(55). Later he becomes a figure of madness, a distorted reflection of the standard he could attain. A supposed defector whose loyalty Matthias had confirmed used the fact that he (the defector) had been funneling sensitive information to Moscow for years to blackmail Matthias into setting up a replay of the 1962 missile crisis, a geopolitical trap that drove Matthias over the edge into insanity. Although Matthias is humanized through the affectionate, respectful memories of Havelock, he mainly functions for purposes of plot and theme: he provides a motivation for the action and a warning against placing too much power in the hands of any one mortal. He is an American parallel to Stalin, says Pyotr Rostov: a gifted man with extraordinary capabilities and potential whose nation encouraged his madness.

Arthur Pierce is even more of an enigma. A VKR plant since childhood, trained to secrecy and deception, instilled with a fanatical belief in a motherland of the imagination, and committed to the destruction of the evil empire around him, he is the man of secrets Havelock describes, the mole who must be all things to all people and yet retain within himself a secret core. As his debate with Emory Bradford confirms (he claims to believe more in his system than Bradford believes in his), Pierce is committed to Communist ideology, despite his heroism in the American military and his successful diplomacy in the seeming service of America. He has schizophrenically separated his public and private selves and has served his organization well, subverting American diplomacy while seeming to promote it. Driven by fanaticism, he is the most difficult villain to identify and stop. Ludlum makes credible a character who has been raised to believe in his secret powers and secret mission against the only country he has ever known and to idealize the distant motherland of his imagination.

These characters, both positive and negative, attain greater depth through their mythological associations. Havelock's search for the truth becomes an "odyssey" of discovery (39). Arthur Pierce, the deadly mole, provides his own twist on events, calling Havelock "an ungrateful Ishmael" who cuts down his "Abraham" (679). Alexei Kalyazin captures Matthias's overweening ambition by describing him as an "Icarus" whose public took him too high and made him feel like a god, so that, "blinded," he fell to the sea (677). The Parsifal of the title refers to one of the great knights of King Arthur's Round Table, the one who used the spear that pierced Christ's side to heal Arthur's wounds, regenerate Britain's failing land, and restore the integrity of the Round Table. This is the image of himself Ludlum's Parsifal holds—the righteous wielder of a powerful weapon that can heal the world's wounds and bring international peace—but events prove the image false as the spear of Matthias's manuscript threatens to rip open the world's wounds and destroy rather than heal. Ironically, Pierce sees himself as a truer Parsifal—a Soviet hero who will use a deadly weapon to heal the sick capitalist world by bringing the regenerative powers of Communism to the American wasteland.

## Themes

*The Parsifal Mosaic*'s central theme is the danger of too much power in too few hands. Ludlum brings to life the old cliché, "Power corrupts and absolute power corrupts absolutely." Matthias's brilliant diplomacy turns sour when he is given free rein to wheel and deal in his country's behalf, and accolades to his superior understanding place pressures on him that destroy his reason and that lead him to betray the democratic ideals for which he originally struggled. Leon Zelienski and Alexei Kalyazin, two old friends who understand Matthias's power and his mental degeneration, determine to teach the world a sobering lesson: "to record the deterioration and collapse of a man with such power that he could plunge the world into the insanity that was down the road for him" and to convince mankind that "this must not be allowed to happen again; no one man should ever again be elevated to such heights" (660). This theme recurs as up and down the State Department chain of command individuals follow orders blindly, unquestioningly, because a superior issues them. Thomas Decker is typical: blinded by Matthias's prestige and position, he follows his dictates unquestioningly, even against his military training and code of ethics.

The failure to ask questions and to think carefully before obeying orders is a weakness of intelligence systems, one particularly unforgivable in a democracy, says Havelock. Erroneous interpretations by so-called experts have licensed agents to kill Havelock on sight; if they had succeeded, there would have been no one with the special knowledge and expertise to evaluate the situation, find the conspirators, and unravel the interwoven threads of a triple plot. Ironically, Havelock participated in the supposed assassination of Karas for similar reasons: high-level accusations, manufactured evidence that went unquestioned, guilt by pronouncement.

With puppetmasters manipulating evidence and interpreting apparent facts, who and what can be trusted? The KGB agent Rostov thinks he understands the betrayals of Western intelligence and the manipulations of the Russian VKR, but Havelock distrusts that view as limited. CIA psychiatrists see Havelock as a case study to be dissected and analyzed, and, from a few key details, imagine a "hallucinating schizophrenic" (102). Havelock's own agency believes psychological trauma and a lifetime of nightmare betrayals going back to his childhood in Czechoslovakia have distorted his perceptions. Havelock struggles to imagine the kind of people who would "put human beings on strings" like puppets and "blow them up . . . [like] mannequins in a horror show"; he asks "on whose stage and for whose benefit" the charades have been played out (54). His initial perceptions are limited to personal experiences, but new information provides a new perspective that reveals the larger pieces of the puzzle instead of the jigsaw pieces of his private corner. More knowledge allows for better guesswork and a better chance to intuit the full picture.

Ludlum explores a paradox. Knowledge and information guide perceptions, so keeping secrets can limit vision and produce erroneous interpretations and misjudgments. Yet, national secrets could endanger lives if exposed. President Berquist recalls Churchill's dilemma: he possessed the key to the German code machine Enigma, thanks to Allied intelligence, but if he had used that knowledge to prepare the city of Coventry for an upcoming bombing raid, England's breaking of the code would have been clear, Germany would have changed its code, and the Enigma secret could no longer have been used effectively to strike a decisive blow against the enemy. Berquist feels caught in the same situation: millions of lives depend on keeping secret Matthias's insanity, but if the government had revealed that secret sooner there would have been no problem. Later Havelock agrees that he too would have sacrificed individual lives to keep so significant and dangerous a secret. Yet knowledge of that secret would have allowed Havelock to solve the problem more quickly. In other words, secrecy also works for the opposition, and, in a democracy, words like "Top Secret, Eyes Only, Highly Classified, Maximum Clearance Required, Duplication Forbidden, Authorization to Be Accompanied by Access Code" (281) can prove dangerous. Berquist notes the irony of the prime objective of an "ever-expanding technology" being to divert the flow of accurate information (282).

Ludlum also asks how long a person can pretend to be what he is not. His answer is in the theater metaphors that dominate the book. He describes a deep-cover operative as "like an actor in a never-ending play, knowing that a wrong move could bring the curtain down and he'd be on unemployment" (Kisor 27). Unlike the actor, Ludlum notes, the agent is in extreme danger, and this is "the albatross" around the neck of everyone in intelligence: he can trust no one. When Havelock speculates about how difficult it must be for a mole to grow up with secrets that cannot be confided and to live his life as a patriotic American but beneath the surface be a dedicated Communist, Karas points out that he is describing someone much like himself: contained, self-sufficient, and secretive (537–38). By pointing out the contradiction of banning books, while trying to produce great scientists and engineers (497), Bradford calls attention to the Russian pretense of openness that has produced the consummate actor-hypocrite, Pierce.

In addition to these themes, Ludlum discusses the effects of aging on the human body, the lingering aches and pains that come from violent action, the obsessions of the past controlling the present, the intuitive understanding that exists between a man and a woman who love each other, and the importance of dogged persistence and of covering your back in the espionage trade.

## THE AQUITAINE PROGRESSION

*The Aquitaine Progression* grew from Ludlum's fears of Ronald Reagan giving a blank check to the Pentagon to do as it pleased. He describes the dangerous what-if situation he envisioned: What would happen if "capable commanders in the highest echelon of the military of various countries," former allies and former enemies, "got together and said the civilians don't know how to do it anymore—but we do"? (Kisor 26). In part, Ludlum brings to life the words of one of his favorite authors, George Bernard Shaw, in *Man and Superman* (1903): "When the military man approaches, the world locks up its spoons and packs off its womenkind" (Act 3). The *New York Magazine* reviewer W. Markfield calls *The Aquitaine Progression* "an arresting example" of Ludlum's "gift for tunneling into the American undermind and dredging out just the kind of paranoid perception that helps explain the harrowing complexities of modern history" (87). Even critic Alan Furst of *Esquire*, who denigrates the novel as "a comic book for adults," nonetheless is fascinated by the superwealthy, cultured, sophisticated fascists in the "dark, hushed corridors of secret power" (211).

The title derives from a region in southwestern France that extended from the Atlantic to the Mediterranean and north to the mouth of the Loire River; a mighty power in the first centuries after Christ, it was ruled by Charlemagne and his descendants for three hundred years, and, under the rule of Henry the Second of England and Eleanor of Aquitaine, included most of Europe. The generals have chosen the name Aquitaine to signify their secret alliance because, if England's later colonial empire were added to the territory, Aquitaine would encompass the territory of all nine of the countries they hope to unify under a military conglomerate.

## Plot Development and Structure

The novel follows a basic chronological pattern of forward-moving action that alternates between two opposing sides: American lawyer Joel Converse and, with time, those who support him; and the scheming generals and the minions who carry out their work. Intelligence dossiers on each of the generals and flashbacks to Vietnam provide background information, as Converse rediscovers rusty skills once honed for survival and calls upon past traumas to understand and endure the present terrors. Converse switches roles from hunter to hunted, and back again to hunter, to destroy those who would destroy. Geographically, the novel begins and ends in Geneva, with the action in between moving globally to wherever the generals are (France, Germany, Israel, and South Africa). Most particularly, the action follows the flight of Converse from Greece to France, Germany, Holland, and Switzerland, and his estranged wife Valerie Charpentier Converse's search for information from the American east coast to Colorado and Nevada, and in Europe from Germany to Switzerland.

The novel has three parts and an epilogue. Part I (Chapters 1–11) establishes the situation and Converse's search for evidence; Part II (Chapters 12–26) follows Converse on the run as the generals discredit him; Part III (Chapters 27–41) brings Converse and Charpentier together with support forces whose combined activities expose the conspiracy and topple its leaders; and the Epilogue returns to a pre-existent harmony, both international and personal.

In Part I Converse, engaged in legal action for his company, meets a schoolmate he has not seen in twenty years, Avery Fowler, now Press Halliday. Halliday, who has taken cautious steps to hide their former relationship, confronts Converse with a horrifying scenario—a neofascist conspiracy by an international cabal of retired military men planning to take over Europe, America, Canada, and most of Africa—and a challenge to accept an unprecedented assignment—to gather legal evidence to convict these schemers in court. The leader of the cabal is General George Marcus Delavane, "The Butcher of Danang and Pleiku" (21), whose barbarous acts and indifference to the loss of American lives in Vietnam earned him Converse's hatred, a hatred intensified by Delavane's having been directly responsible for Converse's time in a North-Vietnamese prison camp. After Halliday is attacked outside the lawyers' meeting and dies in Converse's arms, Converse goes to Mykonos, Greece, where he receives a set of *Mission-Impossible*-style dossiers and learns more about the Aquitaine network and its promulgators. His plan is to investigate and meet with each general in turn, starting with the French Jacques-Louis Bertholdier (Chapters 3 and 4), then the German Erich Stroessel Leifhelm (Chapters 5–11), and next the Israeli Chaim Abrahms (Chapter 11). The pattern is like that in *Trevayne*: a legal investigation moving from source to source seeking documented legal connections. During this period of investigation he is assisted by soap opera star Caleb Dowling, who helps him escape pursuers, and by navy lawyer Connal Fitzpatrick, who is Halliday's brother-in-law and who helps freeze Converse's military records so the cabal cannot access his denunciations of Delavane in a military hearing. Part I ends with a tantalizing glimpse of the civilian and army officers behind Converse's Mykonos contact and their fears for Converse and for the future.

In Part II the generals take the offensive, bringing internal military pressure to bear on Admiral Hickman and Lt. David Remington to open Converse's military records, murdering Converse's Mykonos contact (a Dr. Beale) and Remington, and meeting with Converse to discover who sent him. While the generals explain why they support a military takeover, Converse silently deplores their cold logic (290). After being drugged with a truth serum, interrogated, and imprisoned in a secret compound, Converse calls on his Vietnam POW experience to trick his guards, immobilize a pack of killer Dobermans that patrol the compound grounds, and escape by river. In the meantime, when Fitzpatrick goes after Hermann Göring's illegitimate daughter, Ilse Fishbein (the conduit or go-between of the generals), he is wounded and imprisoned on a secret island fortress (Scharhörn), and Fishbein is killed. The generals turn Converse's old friends and colleagues against him by framing him for murders he did not commit and by disseminating psychological evaluations that interpret his behavior as war-trauma psychosis. His face

appears in newspapers throughout Europe as the murderer of Walter
Peregrine, the U.S. Ambassador to Germany, and later as the terrorist
killer of other friends he contacts for aid. Converse must draw on his
wits, contrive disguises, and, like a chameleon, blend into the social situations around him, merging with crowds and holiday groups to avoid
the teams of searchers—which include, as in the Bourne series, bag ladies
and the other aged men and women who haunt bus and railway stations.
The generals seem unstoppable, eliminating Converse's allies and escape
possibilities, and blocking retaliatory action.

Part II also shows Converse's allies attempting to understand the situation and respond. Valerie Charpentier and Converse's father, Roger,
join forces, while Paul Stone, one of the team who originally set Converse
on his course, calls in an operative code-named Johnny Reb, who tracks
Fitzpatrick to his island prison. Caleb Dowling enlists Peregrine's secretary's aid to prove Converse did not kill the ambassador. The harrowing sequence of events in Part II suggests the generals' power and their
supporters' strength and number.

In Part III, Converse's team coalesces and progresses. Converse hires
a prostitute in Amsterdam to provide a quiet resting place, to obtain a
car, and to help him evade pursuers; in the meantime Charpentier first
contacts the respected Brigadier General Samuel Abbott in Colorado
(who was a POW in Vietnam with Converse) and then calls on the Resistance network her parents had been a part of for support. Disguised
as a priest, Converse rendezvouses with Charpentier, running, hiding,
and killing his way to her, while Paul Stone and Caleb Dowling contact
Charpentier. Their combined information confirms a countdown to disaster: The generals plot to turn an international peace conference into a
killing ground, assassinating the top leaders of nine nations and thereby
fomenting violent demonstrations that will require the military (led by
the generals or their representatives) to step in and take over.

Converse returns to his original venue to produce a well-documented
legal brief that will allow court action against the generals; he calls on
all involved to provide sworn testimony, including a knowledgeable officer (Prudhomme) of the Sûreté (the French equivalent of Scotland
Yard), Alan Metcalf (a friend of Brigadier General Abbott), Paul Stone's
team, and Charpentier. He also has the recorded testimony of three of
the generals (Bertholdier, Leifhelm, and Abrahms), whom he had kidnapped, interrogated, and set against each other. Fighting back also includes an assault on the island fortress, the rescue of not only Fitzpatrick
but also hundreds of other military officers, whose stolen identities were

to be used for the assassination plots, and the unlocking of the central computer containing the list of all members of the Aquitaine conspiracy worldwide. The list means that many of the assassinations can be prevented and that the military services of the nine key countries can weed out the traitors in their midst. Violence is not averted, but long-lasting chaos is.

The Epilogue returns to Geneva and to a Converse who is healed of his Vietnam trauma and ready to renew his marriage with Charpentier. The scenic locations, mind-boggling odds, countdown to disaster, and harrowing single-handed struggle of *The Aquitaine Progression* reflect the archetypal spy genre pattern. Unlike the genre heroes who save the world for little reward, however, Converse is a lawyer and, as such, bills the involved governments for his services for a total of $2.5 million.

## Character Development

Ludlum argues once again that one man can make a difference; in this novel that man is Joel Converse, an international corporate attorney and ex-Vietnam prisoner of war. As a Vietnam POW, Converse discovered within himself a toughness, resilience, and hard-headed determination that not only helped him endure harsh physical abuse (beatings, torture, starvation, injury) and isolation (in a bamboo cage set in the water and infested with river rats; in a dark, muddy, slime-filled pit), but also drove him to make two escape attempts, the last one a successful one-hundred-mile marathon to safety. As the story progresses, Converse evolves from a closed, self-contained workaholic to a more humanized and open individual who has faced his nightmares and come to terms with them, who has recognized his personal limitations and admitted his need for others and for love, and who has learned from experience. He repeatedly draws on past lessons learned through hard experience, but also adds new experiences to his repertoire: "He had just been taught a lesson, one he should not have had to learn. He knew it in a courtroom and in conference. Never explain what you don't have to" (101). His profession makes him a good choice for a Ludlum hero, for his instincts are to follow the "what-if" process that is so vital to legal thinking and so much a part of Ludlum's typical plot structure. Sometimes Converse feels like a puppet manipulated by unknown powers; other times he feels like an inept gladiator facing a stronger opponent in a Roman arena or a POW reliving the conflicts of his youth. He must be an effective actor, manufacturing his disguises and props out of a hostile environment. In the final analysis he is a deep believer in democracy and in individualism, doggedly determined to use the law against any who would undermine free institutions.

René Mattilon tells Converse he always thought of him and Valerie Charpentier, Converse's former wife, as "a matched pair" (82), and the action proves his insight true. They are matched in intelligence, honor, courage, and drive. Valerie is an artist who specializes in painting seascapes. She loved Converse dearly but found the traumas of war had left him so self-sufficient and so psychologically impenetrable that despite his good humor, self-irony, and earning power as a successful lawyer there seemed to be no room in his heart for love. His heart seemed icebound, so she left him. She has stayed close friends with his charming father, Roger, an ex-pilot still enamored with the romance of flight, and she has observed Converse's career from a distance, but at the beginning of the novel she has no hope or desire to renew the pain the limits of their relationship caused her. When she hears the lies about him and understands that even his closest associates believe him insane and capable of murder, however, she cannot stand idly by. She is committed to the truth, and ultimately the deepest truth proves to be her enduring love for him. She is finely drawn as competent and capable, with survival skills learned from her parents who were with the Resistance during World War II (her father French, her mother German).

Two other key characters, navy lawyer Connal Fitzpatrick (brother-in-law of Press Halliday/Avery Fowler) and actor Caleb Dowling, are necessary to the plot in a number of ways. Fitzpatrick's skill with languages (he speaks French, German, Italian and Spanish) make up for Converse's lack of languages, and his military connections are necessary to block access to Converse's files and to get Embassy support. He is headstrong and committed to action, a white knight defending his sister and searching for villains to charge. Converse recognizes him as a younger version of himself, before fear, loneliness, and experience tempered his boldness, bravery, and brashness. Fitzpatrick's capture and imprisonment parallel Converse's experiences in Vietnam, and his rescue leads to the penetration of the enemy's secret stronghold and the discovery of Aquitaine's computerized records. Dowling, in turn, is deceptively impenetrable, a successful soap-opera star who can assume a down-home country diction and style. He is intelligent, witty, and insightful. His wife survived the Nazi concentration camps and escaped through a German underground, but she still lives in terror of Germans; Dowling is committed to protecting her from further psychological trauma. A former marine who fought in Kwajalein, he is a man to be reckoned with. He recognizes Converse as someone in trouble, but trusts his instinct that he is basically decent and acting in a good cause. He provides Converse a safe haven in his hotel, sets up a meeting with the American Ambassador to Germany, and later helps prove Converse innocent of murder.

The villains are an international set of generals noted for their egoism, their hawkish obsessions with war and victory at any cost, their blood-thirstiness, and their firm belief that they would be better national leaders than the elected ones. Their leader and the instigator of the Aquitaine alliance is George Marcus Delavane, an infamous American general for whom the enemy body count was an obsession and who irrationally caused the deaths of hundreds of American pilots and thousands of soldiers by sending them into battle in impossible weather conditions. Warped and power-mad to begin with, he was further enraged by the loss of his legs to diabetes. His French counterpart, the fastidious General Jacques-Louis Bertholdier, was the same sort of murderous villain in Algeria. A Resistance fighter in World War II, he later set up an assassination attempt on General Charles de Gaulle and supported the Algerian generals as the only hope for a France he saw as enfeebled. He is an arrogant fanatic and a sexual pervert. Field Marshall Erich Leifhelm, the youngest general ever commissioned by Hitler, was a committed Nazi who made a sudden public reversal at war's end, associating himself with the attempts on Hitler's life to be able to carry on his Nazi vision of power undercover. A racist and a leader of the neo-Nazi movement, he envisions a Fourth Reich that will make Germany a ruling world power. An illegitimate child angered at his father's marriage to a Jewess, he is a psychopath who raped his half-sister and sent his father's legitimate family to Auschwitz. Chaim Abrahms, a Sabra (a native-born Israeli) with no sense of balance or compromise, is obsessed with Jewish survival and committed to battling the Arabs to the death; ironically, he finds common cause with people he should detest, simply because of their shared reputations for tough, no-nonsense militarism. He ends up killing his strong, brave wife and calling her death a suicide when she attacks him for betraying and endangering Israel. Less significant and far distant from the action are Jan Van Headmer, the South African Aquitaine leader, the Afrikaner "slayer of Soweto" (49) who provides the gold to finance the venture, and Derek Belamy, the secret British traitor with access to Interpol, NATO, and other Western intelligence networks. These violent, cruel killers all have in common a firm belief in the su-

periority of the military mind and of military organization; they also
believe that might makes right and that totalitarian regimentation is a
good way to rid the world of the crime and chaos produced by too much
liberty.

## Themes

Although Converse's Mykonos contact sympathizes with military
men—who are called on in times of national need to sacrifice life and
limb for the collective good and yet are shunted aside when their services
are no longer needed—Ludlum's major theme is a warning against the
authoritarian, disciplined military mind with its contempt for civilians
as weak, divided, inept, and ineffectual and its belief in order, privilege,
rank, professional training, and force. His generals are from very different ends of the political spectrum, but they are all convinced of their
personal superiority and of the superiority of a military solution to civilian problems from urban crime to government corruption. Their collective attitude is that the vacillations inherent in democracies are
inefficient and destructive, that numerous pawns may be sacrificed for
a higher cause, and that bloodshed and violence are necessary steps toward peace. The bloodbath they provoke in Northern Ireland to test their
powers confirms their callous indifference to human suffering and death.
   Another recurring Ludlum theme is the danger of fascism and the
need to learn from the past. The rise of the Nazis to power and the
horrors they inflicted represent the ultimate expression of fascism for
Ludlum, whose characters argue that in that history is a warning for the
future. If history repeats itself, the fault lies with those who had the
potential to study their past and to learn from it; Ludlum's heroes, men
like Dowling and Converse, are committed to making sure "it [the Nazi
rise to power] can't ever happen again" (133). Their memories of the
arrogant authoritarianism and barbaric inhumanity of the perpetrators
of the Holocaust and their wartime experiences in Korea and Vietnam
commit them to battling an international, totalitarian military takeover.
The dispassionate and quietly reasoned speeches about the waste, the
corruption, and the inefficiency of present political systems delivered by
the generals in support of their actions, backed by quotations from Vol-
taire and Goethe and by high-flown rhetoric, frighten Converse more
than anything else, for the thought that men of humor, wit, and intellect

could advocate the destruction of governments, the ruthless seizure of power, and the "shackling" of whole societies under the authority of a military state is unsettling (290). Charpentier calls Nazism "a national disorder rooted in arrogance" (468). Through his mad generals, Ludlum demonstrates the arrogance that could make fascism a global disorder.

Against fascist forces, Ludlum sets as the defender of democracy the lone individual, the educated American who is convinced of his values and who, instead of bending to force, stubbornly opposes it and is strengthened by that opposition. Ludlum's novels are paeans to the power of the individual who stands up and determinedly fights seemingly impossible odds as Converse does. His opponents call Converse "a hellhound," because the punishment inflicted on him and on the innocents around him steels him to his purpose. Ludlum also suggests the power of people of good will uniting in common cause against an enemy that threatens their values and way of life. When alone, Converse is kept on the run, but with a cadre of firm supporters he is a force to be reckoned with. Ludlum points to the effectiveness of the Resistance fighters in World War II, and envisions a secret Russian organization, accessed by a reference to Tatiana (one of the Czar's daughters, reputedly executed at Ekaterinburg in 1918), as another example of good people bound by trust acting in concert against destructive, evil forces, no matter what form they take.

A related theme is that, although decent people abhor violence, sometimes violence is necessary to counter violence. When people are trying to kill you, killing or injuring may be the only choice for survival. Converse is continually shocked at his own instinctive responses. He anticipates an attack and counters it. When he sees a two-way radio in the hands of one of Bertholdier's thugs, he acts instantly, thought blurred, to prevent more attackers being called in:

> With a sudden surge of strength he rammed his suitcase into the man's knees, tearing the radio away with his left hand, whipping his right arm out and over the man's shoulder. He crooked his elbow around the Frenchman's neck as he spun on the pavement. Then without thinking, he yanked Bertholdier's soldier forward, so that both of them hurtled toward the wall, and crashed the man's head into the stone. Blood spread throughout the Frenchman's skull, matting his hair and streaking down his face in deep-red rivulets. (103)

His actions disgust and appall him and he decries his own brutality, but he could not survive if he failed to act. Passive resistance to killers just means death.

Less central, but nonetheless a recurring theme, is the importance of learning other languages and thereby gaining insights into other cultures and other histories. Throughout his canon Ludlum has incorporated words, phrases, and even extended conversations in a variety of languages, often without translation. He does so to instill in readers a sense that they are missing something by not being skilled in languages. In his Cold-War novels, his most effective agents are well versed in languages, often knowing not just one or two but several. Fitzpatrick, in *The Aquitaine Progression*, underscores the importance of language learning with his useful versatility, particularly in contrast to the limitations imposed by Converse's failure to speak another language. Converse is repeatedly shut out of conversations, unable to cope without assistance; activities that could be carried out with ease if he could speak a given language become major impediments. Related is Ludlum's interest in national character and the distinctive values of different peoples. These unique national characteristics might prevent understanding and cooperation, but, if accepted and used in concert, they might also make for a stronger working force, providing different insights and perspectives that make for a better-rounded vision of reality. The value of knowing other languages and cultures is set against the racist generals and the genetic fallacies or stereotypes they voice. Monolingualism and monoculturalism are dangerous in an increasingly shifting world.

Minor themes include the ease with which both psychiatrists and ordinary people misinterpret human motives and behavior, and the unexpected sympathies produced by the Stockholm Syndrome, whereby stress causes prisoners to identify with their captors to discover commonalities. Ludlum also strikes at the destructive powers of negative journalism, which supersedes the rights of the courts and tries the accused in print with half-truths, innuendos, and lies. As usual, Ludlum extols the value of disguises and acting and notes the debilitating effects of aging on recuperative powers. He also brings up alcoholism, as he did in the Bourne series, this time with a positive model, Paul Stone, who overcame alcoholism and returned to a normal life but has to battle his impulse to drink every day.

## ALTERNATE READING: GENRE CRITICISM DECONSTRUCTED

As its name implies, genre criticism classifies and describes literary texts and studies the evolution of literary forms. It shows how the choice of a ready-made generic structure, with its own history of successes and failures, shapes the content and message of a particular author who works in that genre. In more recent times, structuralists have confirmed the validity of genre criticism but in new language. They point out that different types of literature, like different languages, have their own special "grammars" or structures through which to communicate meaning, and that communication depends on the reader being presented with recognizable, shared conventions that provide a basis for understanding and interpretation (Makaryk 82). Genre also establishes a frame of reference or guide for the reader and affects reader expectations; it suggests an order and coherence based on adherence to conventions or standard patterns of particular genres.

Genre is defined not only in terms of form—the novel, short story, poem, etc.—but also of attitude, tone, and purpose. Ludlum's tone and purpose are derived from the conventions of popular fiction. (See Chapter 2 for a discussion of conventions unique to the key genres on which Ludlum builds, and the introductory section on genre in this chapter, which enumerates formulas and conventions of the espionage genre.)

Genre conventions serve a double function. First of all, they provide writers a ready-made framework of plot schemes, conflicts, values, and patterns on which to build their individual concerns; and second, they provide readers the security and pleasure of familiar patterns that confirm a certain understanding of reality. The pleasure of a Ludlum Cold-War novel comes from a combination of the familiar with the new; genre patterns are employed and reinterpreted to provide new perspectives, insights, and surprises. In fact, Ludlum's use of genre conventions, which is far from simple, offers the possibility of deconstructing the sometimes uneasy fit of his ideas and attitudes and the literary vessels that contain his thoughts.

Since deconstruction (discussed in detail in Chapter 8) offers the possibility of variant and even opposing interpretations, deconstructing Ludlum's use of the conventions of the Cold-War novel can yield interesting results. While the genre requires unremitting opposition between East and West, Ludlum frequently relies on plots ultimately resolved by cooperation, and is drawn away from the Cold-War battle to other issues. In his works there is more in the world than simply Russian-American conflict and, in fact, the new world order sometimes requires cooperation between old enemies. Thus, in *The Matarese Circle*, the Russian and American agents who would normally be polar opposites in mortal conflict prove to have much in common and must work together for a common cause against a more dangerous enemy that threatens both their worlds. This meeting of opposites occurs both in *The Matarese Circle* and in *The Parsifal Mosaic*, where KGB and CIA agents work hand in hand to defeat the extremists in their own systems who threaten both their worlds—with the irony in *The Parsifal Mosaic* that the would-be peacemakers turn out to be the greatest threat to humanity. In *The Aquitaine Progression* it is America's allies that prove international threats, and a secret Russian organization, Tatiana, that offers assistance when the hero is in deepest need. This is a pattern for future interaction that will set men and women of goodwill worldwide in opposition to would-be tyrants everywhere. Thus, Ludlum is far from the committed Cold-War warrior, for all his dislike of the authoritarianism of the Soviet bloc; one scarcely needs deconstruction to see his attention focused far more enthusiastically on what the Left used to call bourgeois liberal sentimentalism, the idea that personal bonds can triumph over deep ideological differences.

# 8

# International Terrorism

## *The Icarus Agenda* (1988) and
## *The Scorpio Illusion* (1993)

> Three fundamental psychic experiences are essential to the creation of antidemocratic terror: fear and contempt; a passionate quest for almost total control; and an inordinate amount of unrepressed primitive impulses. . . . Basic distrust of the world underlies and presides over each [of the three elements of the terrorist stance].
>
> Eli Sagan, *The Honey and the Hemlock*

Ludlum's treatment of terrorism, begun in the Bourne series, continues in *The Icarus Agenda* and *The Scorpio Illusion*. Both start with Arab terrorism abroad; an Iranian-style taking of hostages at the American Embassy in Oman and an Entebbe-style rescue in *The Icarus Agenda*, and a Palestinian attack on an Israeli settlement in *The Scorpio Illusion*. They then face the possibility of terrorism brought home to America with attempted assassinations—of a congressman and a possible presidential candidate in the first novel and of the president himself in the second. Both involve several powerful cabals with tentacles extending worldwide, unscrupulous arms dealers, fanatical zealots, American traitors, and secret island bases outfitted with the latest technology. The heroes of both novels are driven by a desire for revenge and a hatred of senseless violence inflicted on the innocent. Their unifying themes are the irrationality and threat of zealots, "the arrogance of blind belief" (*The Icarus Agenda* 424), the vulnerability of public figures, and the presumption of those who would try to manipulate and dictate to a democracy. Both show the dispossessed, driven by childhood terrors and by racial, political, and religious hatreds, assaulting Americans and America as the rich symbol of their personal loss. In *The Icarus Agenda* disorganized, embittered young terrorists have their hatred, religious fervor, and raging hormones manipulated by powers beyond their understanding, while in *The Scorpio Illusion* a lone, daring, terrorist exploits the power of organized hate networks to seek revenge for childhood trauma and the violation of innocence.

## GENRE CONVENTIONS

Both *The Icarus Agenda* and *The Scorpio Illusion* are countdowns to disaster, timetables for terrorism. In the former the countdown of Book I is measured in human lives, and the deadline is the day of the next set of threatened executions if terrorist demands are not met; the countdown of Book II is less obvious, an election timetable for secret manipulators to promote or thwart a political candidate for the presidency. In *The Scorpio Illusion* the countdown is to the presidential assassination, as the terrorist evades an organized, international interagency network. The hunt spans continents and involves multiple disguises, sudden confrontations, and near misses, but the terrorist is finally trapped by a single individual committed to justice and revenge for the loss of innocent lives. *The Icarus Agenda*'s hunt for the secret controller, the Mahdi, also involves disguises, dangerous confrontations, personal injury, and cross-country travel, with a single individual intuiting who, where, and what.

Spy/adventure/terrorist stories often evoke images of fire, natural disasters, animals, insects, and mechanized/robotic humans to convey destructiveness and dehumanization. In *The Scorpio Illusion* Tyrell Hawthorne tells minisubmarine commander Catherine Neilsen that their lives depend on her becoming the machine, subordinating self to weapon to survive (341). When a member of the Scorpio organization ignites a match and burns a vital piece of paper in an empty wastebasket, "terror" spreads "like a gargantuan brushfire" set to ignite "a global conflagration" (592). The terrorist message of death, chaos, and anarchy will be sent across the world "like a monstrous, shattering bolt of lightning" (570). In *The Icarus Agenda* the Mahdi rises "from the raging fires of an earthbound hell," as terrorist bombs destroy whole families (93) before fleeing to the "cruel wasteland" that spawned them (111); Gerald Bryce, the White House computer expert, calls Evan Kendrick the lightning "bolt" that will blast the nation's enemies (221). Secret agencies and terrorist networks are like a "clandestine octopus, a mollusk with far-reaching secret tentacles" (*SI* 618); the searching hero treads a "maze," a "labyrinth" where danger and death await (*IA* 201). Villains are scorpions, serpents, and spiders spinning webs. In *The Scorpio Illusion* they reduce the Air Force surveillance plane to a smoking, disembodied fuselage, "its walls peeled back like the dismembered chest cavity of a huge, burning, upturned insect" (135). In *The Icarus Agenda* a ship owned by terrorists rises and falls "like an angry predator intent on feeding" (654), and Islamic zealots, "like starving locusts attacking the sweet leaves of trees," crawl over crates of weapons and rip them open (661). Kendrick circles his prey like a hawk (*IA* 201). Those wary of the motives of the *Scorpio Illusion*'s protagonist liken him to a rattlesnake striking a rat (205), while Bajaratt is "a serpent with glass eyes and a mouth filled with poison" (647); she kills as if swatting flies (354).

## THE ICARUS AGENDA

The Icarus myth tells of a young man (Icarus) given the power of flight with wax wings, but warned by his father Daedalus not to soar too high; the impetuous youth is so taken with his new powers, however, that he fails to heed the dangers and plunges to his death when the wax melts. In *The Icarus Agenda* would-be politicians have the potential power to soar above ordinary mortals, but, when they become ambitious and try to accrue powers invested in the vast and powerful democratic public, they can be burned by the sun of politics and create their own doom. This mythological Greek image becomes a modern warning about political ambitions. Evan Kendrick, the key protagonist, soars high, but controls his ambitions and uses his gift of power wisely, whereas the ambitious members of the secret cabals that seek to control him soar too high and produce death and destruction.

### Plot Development and Structure

*The Icarus Agenda* combines three stories in one. Book I is an exciting, fast-paced rescue story. Book II is a conspiracy story of competing, behind-the-scenes powers struggling to manipulate American democracy by reshaping its nature and by bringing terrorism to American soil. Book III, a sequel to the rescue/conspiracy stories, emphasizes the need for committed individuals to act responsibly to ensure the continuation of democratic rule.

The first book (Chapters 1–15) is a lively adventure novel in its own right. When 246 American embassy employees (and one deep-cover Mossad field director) are taken hostage by Muslim fanatics in Masquat, Oman, and then eleven are killed, wealthy Congressman Evan Kendrick volunteers his knowledge of the country and language and his local contacts to help out, as long as the President agrees to keep his role in the rescue a secret. Kendrick seeks revenge against an elusive villain who calls himself the Mahdi ("the guided one" or "the one who will lead the faithful to Paradise"), a holy name for the last appointed Imam and the title of the Muslim leader who overran the Egyptian Sudan and seized Khartoum from the British in 1885. In the past the modern Mahdi killed seventy of Kendrick's friends and employees, and now Kendrick traces the takeover of the U.S. Embassy in Oman to the Mahdi's stage management.

Kendrick darkens his skin, dons local attire, and, aided secretly by the much-respected young Sultan of Oman (Ahmat Yamenni) and an attractive American-Arab agent (Adrienne Khalehla Rashad), penetrates the opposition. Tossed in with the captured terrorists, he convinces them he acts directly for the Mahdi, effects the escape of himself and three terrorists, and is accepted into the Embassy compound. There he learns enough to track the Mahdi to Bahrain and to disorient and dispose of the Mahdi's real representative (an English turncoat, Anthony Macdonald). Injured in the process, he receives unexpected assistance from Washington/Cairo agent Khalehla and then from a Mossad rescue team guided by Emmanuel "Manny" Weingrass (Kendrick's longtime friend and father figure). An attempted rendezvous with terrorist agents results in Kendrick's capture. The Mahdi proves to be a sleazy, hypocritical African-American politician from Chicago, who is riding the waves of fanaticism to power and wealth. The Mossad rescues Kendrick, forces the Mahdi to cooperate, and frees the hostages. Kendrick, Khalehla, and the Mossad's roles are covered up, and all return to their separate worlds.

Book II (Chapters 16–44) follows Kendrick's rising career as an honest, direct congressman who wins the hearts of ordinary citizens through his intolerance of corruption and his willingness to speak his mind publicly.

Although he would rather spend his time at home in Colorado and plans to retire from public life at the end of his term, an organization known as Inver Brass has other plans for him. Inver Brass was the secret cabal behind Washington politics in *The Chancellor Manuscript* and Ludlum revives it here. It is a benevolent group of wealthy elitists concerned about the state of the nation. Like similar groups in *Trevayne* and *The Aquitaine Progression*, Inver Brass is determined to use the considerable influence of its members to provide the American public honorable, decent candidates for vice president and president. They have decided to give Kendrick opportunities to engage the public and, with the assistance of Milo Varak (the son of Anton Varak from *The Chancellor Manuscript*), have prepared a scenario for moving him into the public limelight. They admire Kendrick's personal courage, firm convictions, and hardheaded individuality; he is a man who cannot be bought. They do not expect to control him, just to launch him, and their major fear is that knowledge of their manipulation will backfire and drive him out of politics.

By making public Kendrick's role in the Oman rescue, they produce an overnight hero, but also awaken the suspicions and anger of their negative counterpart, a secret organization committed to perpetuating the military machine and its wasteful spending and to ensuring the reelection of the corruptible, greedy vice president. Supporters of this team attack the Kendrick problem with different strategies; they target Kendrick for assassination, bringing in teams of vengeful terrorists to assault his Fairfax, Virginia home, his Colorado ranch, and his office. The plot cuts back and forth between scheming groups, hunters, and hunted: the members of Inver Brass planning campaign strategy; the president, who wholeheartedly supports Kendrick; Kendrick and his friends, particularly Khalehla, with whom he has fallen in love; his father figure Manny, who is injured by both the terrorists and a doctor from the evil cabal; the vice president's murderous and grasping secret team and the terrorists they unleash; and Milo Varak searching for the traitor who has betrayed Inver Brass and Kendrick to the opposition. A complex web is spun and unraveled. Kendrick ends up a prisoner at the command center of the evil forces, but, with the aid of a poor Mexican, routs the enemy. The vice president is forced to give up his bid for reelection, and Milo Varak kills the traitor to Inver Brass, but dies in the process.

Book III (Chapters 45–47) unites the plots of Books I and II. Kendrick returns to the Middle East and, supported by the surviving Mossad team from Book I, Khalehla, and the Sultan of Oman, hunts the key financial supporter of Arab terrorism and of the American vice president's

schemes for power, Abdel Hamendi, a Saudi Arabian arms merchant
with ambitions to be the next Mahdi. In an interesting reversal of genre
patterns, Kendrick and his team hijack a terrorist ship transporting arms
to Yemen, replace the arms with sabotaged goods, and deliver weapons
that will backfire. As luck would have it, Hamendi is on hand to show
off his merchandise and is killed, along with the American lawyer who
ran the vice president's cabal. Kendrick is persuaded that, despite Inver
Brass's wrongheaded attempts to manipulate American politics, he is a
viable candidate who can right many wrongs and who is needed to
continue the battle against the organized forces of darkness. Thus, unlike
Trevayne in Ludlum's earlier novel, Kendrick is not the tool of a secret
cabal, and his rise to power is a boon and a blessing.

## Character Development

Evan Kendrick, a potential Icarus, flies close to the centers of power
but is not burned by the contact; his Daedalus, Manny Weingrass, has
taught him well. Though a congressman, Kendrick is free of political
ambitions and his dreams have practical concerns—building architectural structures that will improve the human condition. As head of the
ill-fated Kendrick Group, he had been a good employer, who insisted
on the best education for the children of his employees, an education
aimed at rearing "statesmen and stateswomen" like Disraeli and Golda
Meir (25). His recognition that education is the key to democracy reflects
Ludlum's own beliefs. Kendrick accepts personal responsibility for injustice and for the protection of innocents; he acts aggressively when the
occasion demands it, but his instinct is toward humanitarian sympathy
and good will. A man of personal courage with the will to endure, he
shows the Mossad team and Egyptian agent Khalehla Rashad how to
penetrate the enemy organization. He is intuitive about others and understands the motives that drive the terrorists he combats and the fears
that crippled their psyches. Kendrick knows the value and the limits of
disguise and carefully establishes a role that balances both—an Arab
with European ancestry. In addition, Kendrick, whose blue eyes reflect
"enigmatic reserve" (13), is an outdoorsman who engages in challenging
Class Five white-water rafting and who backpacks in the mountains. He
does not seek the limelight, but ordinary people trust him because of his
righteous indignation in the face of corruption and lies, his readiness to
battle hypocrites and fanatics, his individuality, and his ability to reduce
obfuscation to simple questions of right and wrong.

Kendrick is further defined by his friends. His closest companion and father figure is Manny Weingrass. Weingrass is typical of Ludlum's mentor figures: witty and self-deprecating, but a master architect, a Mideast expert, and a former Mossad agent. At the age of eighty-six and dying of lung cancer and of an incurable viral infection, he nonetheless continues to find pleasure in life, to pursue the ladies, and to protect the foster son he adores. He outwits the terrorists who attack Kendrick's Colorado home; he leads the Mossad team to Bahrain and effects Kendrick's rescue, and he arranges for an Israeli undercover agent to be on board the terrorist vessel Kendrick and his team hijack. His initial appearance is dramatic (waxed mustache, aquiline nose, sculptured head, rippling white hair, and colorful attire), but the key to his identity are his eyes. They are "green and alive, even in blank repose, the eyes of a wanderer, both intellectually and geographically, never satisfied, never at peace, constantly roving over landscapes he wanted to explore or create" (128). An eccentric and a wit, he applies intelligence and skill to achieve humanistic goals.

Another friend of Kendrick is Ahmet Yamenni, an Arab sultan wise in the ways of his people, and, though young, a clever statesman, who perceives the power of symbols. He maintains a balance between extremists in his domain in order to create a moderate middle way, but is courageous enough to provide valuable support in the fight against terrorism. His marriage to an American and their easy give-and-take confirm his enlightened perspective and his commitment to change.

A stranger at the beginning of the novel, Khalehla Rashad becomes the love of Kendrick's life. Her large brown eyes reflect intelligence, and her striking beauty is a foil to her expertise. Raped when she was an Israeli college student simply because she was an Arab, she used her contacts with her adopted uncle/father figure Mitchell Jarvis Payton to join the American CIA and to serve abroad, with Cairo as her base. She is committed to her work and proud of her competence—a weapons expert who speaks six languages fluently, she effectively infiltrates Arab social circles denied her countrymen—but her greatest pride is in saving lives and reducing the "malignant [political] immorality" she sees decent people constantly fighting (456).

## Themes

Like *Trevayne* (see Chapter 3), *The Icarus Agenda* explores a major political question: what kind of human being would make a good American

president? Ludlum's answer is Evan Kendrick: a person of personal courage and sacrifice, unfettered by racial prejudice or class distinctions,
guided by a sense of justice and humanity, and committed to the principle that a working democracy depends on the contributions of all its
citizens and that a ruling elite (no matter how benign) reflects an arrogance that could lead to injustice and tyranny. Kendrick has no ready
answers, but he acts responsibly. Through Kendrick and his friends the
novel praises the American potential to produce independent individualists, mavericks with deep-seated values, special competencies, and
stubborn persistence; these men and women would not normally seek
public office but, when compelled by personal outrage to step in and
drive the Pharisees out of the temple, will do so effectively.

President Jennings articulates a related theme: the strength of any democracy is its ordinary citizens. Jennings agrees with Britain's wartime
Prime Minister Winston Churchill that "democracy may have a lot of
flaws," but that it is "the best system man ever devised." He eulogizes
the basic American spirit as one of strength, greatness, and benevolence
(676), and attributes these values to the variety of people composing a
democracy: the racial, cultural, economic, and political mix. Like Trevayne, Jennings disapproves of elitist attitudes and argues:

> Whenever a select group of benevolent elitists consider them-
> selves above the will of the people and proceed to manipulate
> that will in the dark, without accountability, they've set in
> motion a hell of a dangerous machine. Because all it takes is
> one or two of those superior beings with very different, un-
> pristine ideas to convince the others or replace the others or
> survive the others, and a republic is down the drain. (673)

This is close to what happens in the story, as one man (Eric Sundstrom)
manipulates the seemingly benevolent activities of Inver Brass to achieve
his own malevolent ends.

Gerald Bryce, the computer hacker whose computer records punctuate
the action and who sets himself on a course to establish a new Inver
Brass with ties to the Middle East, equates Kendrick with the Vedic god
of fire, a messenger who will share valuable gifts with humanity. The
image, of course, is one Kendrick would reject, but it reveals the computer puppeteer's distrust of ordinary citizens and his belief that they
cannot discover truths for themselves. That distrust marks the limitations
of Bryce's vision and suggests that the battle against this type of mind-

set remains ongoing in a democracy. Democracy may be inefficient, argues Ludlum, and government committees exasperatingly tedious, but "those lower-class, troublesome committees on the Hill" represent the "Vox populi" and "the land is better for it" (286). With education and public disclosure, Ludlum believes the American populace can face harsh realities and deal effectively with them. Furthermore, subordinates who tell a president unpleasant truths are doing their country more good than those who simply say what they think a president wants to hear.

*The Icarus Agenda* asks wherein lie the roots of terrorism and who finances the fanatics who threaten violence. *The Scarlatti Inheritance* asked who financed the Brownshirts and the Nazi rise to power; here Ludlum asks who is financing modern terrorism and what they gain from doing so. How do terrorists get false documentation good enough to pass immigration checks? Who supplies them with what they need to operate in a foreign country: vehicles, weapons, ammunition, travel money, safe houses, travel reservations, appropriate clothing—the vital details that can make or break a mission? In answer, Ludlum envisions ambitious individuals, backed by the industrial networks that power and wealth can create, fostering instability in the name of stability and growth or employing the fanaticism of terrorists to further political or financial agendas.

Ludlum plays Arab against Jew to argue that the experiences that have fueled their racial and religious hatreds only emphasize their similarities. By having Kendrick work with a Mossad agent and a Muslim terrorist (both code-named Blue) who die violently and senselessly, Ludlum confronts the irony of Arab/Israeli conflict. Their rhetoric, their rationalizations and justifications, and their expressions of hatred sound alike; they are two sides of the same coin. The father of Azra the terrorist was a medical student in Tel Aviv, ousted to make way for an emigrating Jew and killed in an Israeli attack on a Lebanese refugee camp. The father of Yaakov the Mossad agent survived Auschwitz and the Wehrmacht only to be held hostage by terrorists; two of Yaakov's brothers were "butchered" in Sidon by Arabs (154). Azra led an attack on a kibbutz in Galilee, killing adults and children indiscriminately; he planted bombs in West Bank settlements and blew up an Israeli pharmacy to retaliate for "massacres" of Arabs at Jephthah and Deir Yasin. Driven by hatred, they stab, tear, and break each other, crying out their loathing. Kendrick tries to make Yaakov understand that Palestinians and Jews are both victims, and that the "terrible waste" (217) produced by their hatred must be stopped. In contrast to this hatred, Ludlum provides the immediate and warm friendship between Manny Weingrass and Khalehla Rashad and Weingrass's long-term brotherhood with Sabri Hassan and his wife Kashi from Dubai. These friendships demonstrate that common humanity can overcome and negate ethnic differences.

A less significant but nonetheless recurring theme concerns father-son relationships. *The Scarlatti Inheritance* has a very protective stepfather; *Trevayne* has a close father-son relationship where honesty and love bridge the generation gap; Kendrick in *The Icarus Agenda* has a warm relationship with his father-figure mentor. It is the loss of fathers and father figures that makes the terrorists Ludlum shows up close seem so vulnerable. But Ludlum also includes sons who betray their fathers' values and their relationship, who lie to their fathers and lash out at them. Alvin Partridge, Jr., helps set up his father for blackmail and makes deals with his father's enemies. The Speaker of the American House of Representatives has an illegitimate son by an Irish nurse whom he still deeply loves, but his son has become the provisional "wing commander" of the Irish Republican Army and opposes everything his father stands for. Thus, Ludlum implies that working together, sharing activities and responsibilities, and taking time to teach one's children one's own values and the reasons for them promote father-son harmony, while alienation and hatred result from separation and an absence of sharing.

## Alternate Reading: Deconstructionist Criticism

Deconstruction is a critical approach to literature based on a 1960s French school of metaphysical philosophy, led by Jacques Derrida, and made popular in the United States by the Yale school of criticism (Harold Bloom, Geoffrey Hartman, Paul de Man, and others). Deconstruction questions the validity of traditional means of analysis, and examines and tests the foundations, borders, and limits of systems of thought by seeking the opposites in play behind the written word. It argues that meaning is relativistic, a matter of interpretation reflecting the predispositions and self-interests of the interpreter, and that there are often plural and opposing implications behind even the simplest-seeming message. Deconstructionists thus look for contradictions or opposite positions in order to discover the indirect and often unwitting or unacknowledged divergences from the overt message behind the work, literary or otherwise. Michael Groden, in *The Johns Hopkins Guide to Literary Theory and Criticism*, describes the deconstructive method as a close reading of text focusing on a "binary opposition" (presence/absence, outside/inside, literal/"figural"), a line of argument or even a single word that reveals "radical incongruities in the logic or rhetoric" (186). The contradictions suggest "difference within unity" and show that words sometimes hide meaning. Thus, built into the language of the text are significant clues to different authorial attitudes hidden behind the words of his text, and the critical reader looks for this subsurface reality, often finding ambivalence, and perhaps even self-contradictory attitudes underlying the smooth surface of text and argument.

A deconstructionist studying *The Icarus Agenda* would carefully examine its overt statements about American politics to find a subsurface meaning revealed through binary opposites. For example, one cliché of democracy voiced throughout the novel is that a democracy depends on the involvement of *ordinary* citizens, whose *ordinary* voices we hear in reaction to television reports, yet the novel itself turns on *extraordinary* citizens. The protagonist Evan Kendrick is an *übermensch*, a superior person with extraordinary talents who engages in challenging physical feats, understands a foreign language and culture well, has high-level contacts, and does what no ordinary citizen could do: rescue hundreds of American prisoners from a terrorist stronghold. He is beyond being simply talented; he is a fantasy figure of extraordinary capability. These binary opposites (ordinary/extraordinary) suggest a basic underlying contradiction in the text. "It's the leaders who shape history," argue the leaders of Inver Brass (264), and the novel proves this true with examples from America's past; yet Inver Brass supposedly represents the negative forces in the novel, the underminers of democracy who negate its values by seeking an extraordinary potential leader, whom the ordinary citizens would ignore if not for the elitist organization's behind-the-scenes manipulations. In other words, the text's official voice asserts a trust in the ordinary and democratic and a distrust of elitism, but this belief in the power of the ordinary is negated by the novel's active depiction of the talent, strengths, and value of the extraordinary and elite.

The statements of the fictive United States President Langford Jennings further illustrate these inherent contradictions. "What I have is trust of the people because they see and hear the man [the presidential candidate]," he says, and adds, "I believe all those bromides about America being the greatest, the strongest, the most benevolent country on the face of the earth. Call me Mr. Simplistic, but I do believe. That's what the people see and hear and we're not so bad off for it" (676). Nonetheless, the same man admits, "I've seen too many brilliant, erudite men go down because they described the world as they knew it to be to electorates who didn't want to hear it" (464) and "there's not a single person in the entire White House staff of over a thousand who would say those things [hard negative truths] to me" (466). He also acknowledges the "river of corruption with so many tributaries there weren't enough scouts to pursue them in the canoes available" (247) and also the existence of what Weingrass denounces as "a government within the government, a bunch of servants running the master's house" (502). The contradictions are apparent: trust in the people/distrust of the people; strength from knowledge/a lack of reliable public information; the United States as the greatest, the strongest/corrruption and disorder within. The most significant contradiction is the reaction of the protagonist, a congressional representative of the people whose duty should be to reform what is wrong and to stand up for his constituents, but who instead says, "I don't like what I see. There's not supposed to be an oligarchy running this government and yet it seems to me that one has moved in. . . . I'm going back to the mountains" (271). The resultant image is indeed a set of binary oppositions: democracy versus elitism; involvement versus noninvolvement; the people's choice versus the choice of a secret elite; the greatest versus the most corrupt. Given this series of oppositions, then even "the most benevolent country" must be countered by the potential to be "the most malevolent."

In summary, a deconstructionist would argue that Ludlum, for all his rhetorical support of democratic principles, undercuts this piety by his choice of a superhuman protagonist and by inconsistencies in the voices of his spokespersons. These contradictions reveal an ambivalence toward the principles he espouses. Ludlum would probably reply that contradictory voices are a cornerstone of democracy.

## THE SCORPIO ILLUSION

In the Bourne series the real-life international terrorist, the Jackal, is part monster, part myth, the product of a wealthy Venezuelan Marxist family, a man for whom there can be no sympathy; in contrast, the divided Jason Bourne/David Webb is a man of honor and of good intentions, in spite of his deep-rooted psychological problems. *The Scorpio Illusion* provides an interesting departure from this pattern. Its international terrorist is the female counterpart to Carlos, with psychological problems as deeply rooted as those of Jason Bourne. She is a beautiful woman, Amaya Aquirre Bajaratt, whose traumatized childhood (her Basque parents were slaughtered before her eyes and she was raped at the age of ten) has warped her inner being and has committed her to the defiance and destruction of all authority. "Death to all authority!," she chants, a mantra against childhood terrors. While Ludlum studies the divided self of a heroic figure in the Bourne series, he examines the split personality of a terrorist in *The Scorpio Illusion*: the public image that could have been her reality and the private fanatic that reflects her twisted survival responses. The frenzied action at times gets out of control, but the study of teamwork in opposition to a lone-wolf terrorist and the psychoanalysis of that terrorist's motivation and methods keep the story interesting.

## Plot Development and Structure

The plot follows the hunted-hunter schematic that worked so effectively in the Bourne series, with Amaya Bajaratt circling in on her goal as Tyrell Hawthorne homes in on her. The Prologue describes the massacre that sets the revenge plot in action and ends with the introduction of the Scorpio organization. The name is born of the desert and symbolic of the poison its members inflict but also of their potential death, for, as the scorpion is alleged to do, in a frenzy of hostility and ambition they poison themselves. Thus, the Prologue prepares the way for the violence of the main action and the self-destruction of the villains. The Epilogue, in turn, uses fictive news clips and letters to provide a final summation and to contrast the public explanations with the private realities readers have seen at work in the body of the novel. Chapters 1–37 are a countdown to disaster, with Chapter 37 recording the time as events race toward climax: 6:55 P.M., 7:09 P.M., 7:32 P.M., 7:33 P.M., 7:51 P.M., 8:02 P.M.—a gunshot, a scream, "a ten-year-old child at peace" (650).

The first chapters (1–8) introduce the dueling pair, Bajaratt in the Caribbean, her hunters (French, American and British intelligence services) tracking her deadly course and providing a psychological profile and a composite of her deeds and assets to date, and Hawthorne in the Caribbean, competent, but still psychologically traumatized by past losses.

When Bajaratt's Palestinian husband is killed during a raid on Ashkelon, Israel, and she is the sole survivor, Bajaratt commits herself to a large-scale plan of revenge against the Western powers: the assassination of the president of the United States, timed to coincide with the assas-

sination of the British prime minister, the French premier, and the Israeli
prime minister. She draws on the resources of the fanatical revolutionary
forces assembled in the Baaka Valley (members of Hezbullah, the real
Lebanon-based and Iranian-supported "Party of God," as well as other
"soldiers of Allah"), resources with ties to an international organization
of "Scorpions," centered in the United States and including high-ranking
members of the CIA, the U.S. Senate, and personages close to the American president. Her first goal is to contact her millionaire patron and
revolutionary chieftain or *padrone*. To reach his isolated Caribbean island
fortress, she successfully weathers a hurricane and a tropical storm; then,
with his financial blessing and high-powered connections, she begins her
journey to the White House.

Her nemesis is Tyrell Nathaniel Hawthorne the Third, a disillusioned
former U.S. Naval Intelligence officer, who went to seed when his wife
was killed, supposedly by KGB operatives but possibly with the blessing
of his own superiors, and who has only recently come out of his alcoholic
haze and begun a deep-sea fishing operation with his brother. Hawthorne is recruited to help find Bajaratt because of his known expertise
and intuition in intelligence operations.

Bajaratt and Hawthorne meet in Chapter 4; Bajaratt, disguised as Dominique, makes love to Hawthorne and then orders his death. Hawthorne
uses his would-be killer to gain leads to Bajaratt, unaware she is Dominique. In Chapter 6 the AWAC II Air Force team arrives, and the hunt
begins in earnest. The attractive and competent Major Catherine Neilsen
and Lieutenant Andrew Jackson Poole assist Hawthorne throughout the
operation. A third crew member, Captain Salvatore Mancini, however,
has betrayed them to Scorpio and causes the early death of a young
enlisted man. With the Scorpios sabotaging wherever possible (for instance, blowing up the Air Force surveillance plane), revenge becomes a
key motivator—even more so when Hawthorne discovers in Chapter 16
that his beautiful and supposedly charitable lover, Madame Dominique
Montaigne, is really the infamous Bajaratt.

Chapters 9–14 contrast Bajaratt's successful inroads into Palm Beach
society as Contessa Cabrini with the Hawthorne team's assault on her
patron's island fortress. Bajaratt has rescued a handsome, aristocratic-
looking lad (Nicolo Montavi of Portici) from certain death on the docks
of Naples, and grooms him to step into a ready-made position as Dante
Paolo, *barone-cadetto* of Ravello, wealthy heir to the industrial wealth and
title of a favored Italian family. (Their real son died ignominiously, his
death unreported, and they have been saved from penury and elevated

to distinction by Baaka Valley funds, which buy support and silence.) As Bajaratt exploits the interlocked international terrorist networks, courts an American senator, involves her protégé Nicolo with the popular Italian-American soap-opera star Angel Capell to win needed publicity, and eliminates suspicious reporters to forward her attack plan, the Hawthorne team face death to gain vital information about her supporters and her goal. Chapters 15–30 emphasize how pervasive Scorpio is: they are everywhere. Nils Van Nostrand, the head of Scorpio, uses his high-level connections, including the easily duped Secretary of Defense, to arrange invisible means of escape and to disseminate disinformation about Hawthorne; he coldly disposes of operatives, regarded as human tools who prove liabilities, and sets a trap for Hawthorne. Thieves fall out in Chapters 17–29, as a shake-up of the top levels of Scorpio results in power plays and deaths, with David Ingersol killed, then the Secretary of Defense, next the Secretary of State, followed by Robert Ingersol and a CIA traitor named O'Ryan. Hawthorne obtains information from Vietnam veteran and Scorpio dupe Alfred Simon, and Nostrand plots to destroy Hawthorne. Meanwhile, Bajaratt has carried her publicity campaign to Washington, D.C., where the paths of Hawthorne and Bajaratt repeatedly intersect—first at Nostrand's private residence, where Hawthorne kills Nostrand, and then at the Shenandoah Lodge, where both spend the night. When Bajaratt kills the Secretary of Defense at the Shenandoah Lodge, Hawthorne is arrested as a suspect; later, when Bajaratt goes to pick up Nicolo after he has killed O'Ryan, they accidentally meet in a restaurant and Bajaratt shoots Hawthorne and Major Neilsen. The trail of deaths continues in Chapters 25–31, with Neilsen on the hospital's critical list and Bajaratt toying with Hawthorne. First Hawthorne's former European intelligence network chieftain, Captain Henry Stevens, is killed, and then the CIA director. Hawthorne is set up for the murder of Robert Ingersol, who has revealed to him the inner secrets and strategies of the Scorpios. Meanwhile, Bajaratt meets the powers behind the "Providers" (still another terrorist support group) and the Scorpios, eliminates a Mossad agent, and acquires the plastic explosive necessary to kill the president. Senator Nesbitt (a Jekyll-Hyde personality) proves an unsuspecting, highly vulnerable tool of Scorpio, and Senator Seebank and the Chair of the Joint Chiefs of Staff turn out to be top-level Scorpios.

In Chapters 31–37, the hunters converge on Washington, D.C., as various Scorpios are eliminated and as equal numbers of "good guys" fall prey to these indiscriminate killers. While Bajaratt uses position, positive publicity, and promises of big-time financial support to win a private audition with the president for the popular "Dante," the Hawthorne team's attempts to intercept her are repeatedly thwarted—first by the murder of Mossad antiterrorist agents, then by a breakdown of communications with London, and finally by the murder of the Secretary of State and of the key antiterrorist agent in Jerusalem. As Bajaratt moves closer to her target, the Hawthorne team trap the Chairman of the Joint Chiefs of Staff General Michael Meyers into exposing himself as the last elite Scorpio agent. Finally, with the aid of the Mossad and some intuitive guesswork, the Hawthorne team intercept Bajaratt seconds before the assassination is carried out. The final personal confrontation between Bajaratt and Hawthorne occurs in Chapter 37, when Hawthorne kills Bajaratt.

Thus, the structure alternates between hunter and pursued, with ever-closer encounters as they move toward the key target and a final showdown at ground zero.

## Character Development

The movement and the force of the plot depend on the love-hate relationship between the two main characters, Tyrell Hawthorne and Amaya Bajaratt. Both experience a divided self. Hawthorne is torn between love and revenge and between responsible commitment to a cause he believed in and disillusionment and distrust because of betrayal and loss. He had tried to drown himself in alcohol and, ironically, Dominique/Bajaratt helped him return to his senses and regain his life. Bajaratt, in turn, is divided between the public facade of the loving, caring woman she might have become if not for her childhood traumas and her hidden self, a twisted, vengeful terrorist committed to the destruction of all authority figures.

Labeled a "she-wolf" by international authorities, who consider her "the most accomplished terrorist alive" (16), Bajaratt is the vindictive and virulent Scorpio of the title. She is an expert on destabilization, a mercenary who sells her skills to the highest bidder, the female counterpart of the Jackal. A master illusionist who changes hair and eye color, clothing style, body language, and even weight (with the aid of body-suits) at will, she seems like three completely different women in the three known photographs of her, but her eyes, no matter their color, are always "enigmatically cold" (9). To counter hunters seeking the hidden, she is where they least expect her to be, disguised but highly visible—"in front of their eyes" (125). Yet Ludlum creates sympathy for her suffering. The ten-year-old Amaya Aquirre witnessed her parents beheaded with bayonets and the entire adult population of her Basque village executed. In defiance she recorded the deaths of her parents and signed her name Amaya el Baj, adopting the last name of her mother's killer, a sergeant Bajaratt, to always remind her of her commitment to destroy all authorities. Many of her aliases (like Madame Le*baj*erone of Paris or Madame *Bal*zini) include the three letters "baj" or an equivalent sound. A psychoanalyst describes her reaction as a form of the Stockholm syndrome, since she identified with the far stronger enemy and adopted enemy tactics in a subconscious attempt to outsmart them; the Freudians label her an "obsession-oriented" psychotic (59). She is a mentally disturbed woman whose sexual restlessness leads to numerous short-lived affairs, including one with Hawthorne at the time of his greatest vulnerability, just after his wife Ingrid was killed.

Her pursuer, Tyrell Hawthorne, is in his mid-forties, the son of a professor of American literature, a retired U.S. Navy Intelligence Lieutenant Commander, and the sole owner of Olympic Charters, out of the Virgin Islands. Memories of the political games that killed his wife lead him back into intelligence operations, and his outrage at being duped by Dominique/Bajaratt compels him to revenge. His inability to assuage his guilt at Ingrid's death spurs him to expose and stop Bajaratt. A further spur is his personal and professional commitment to pursue and destroy fanatics who prevent reasoned discourse between those with opposing ideologies. In the midst of the chase he falls in love with Air Force Major Catherine Neilsen, a quietly competent, affectionate team player, who has earned the respect of the crew she commands.

The other characters are sketchily drawn to meet plot needs. Captain Henry Stevens, who had Ingrid eliminated as a KGB agent when in reality she was CIA, is ridden by guilt but unable to make amends; his counterpart, CIA director Raymond Gillette, experiences similar guilt for his acts along the Ho Chi Minh trail in Vietnam. In contrast, Bajaratt's patron, an ambitious and wealthy recluse code-named "Mars," and his homosexual lover, Nils Van Nostrand, code-named "Neptune," feel no guilt, despite being responsible for numerous deaths. Both enjoy the power their support of terrorist activities and their involvement in the Scorpio organization bring. Nicolo Montavi is a handsome, pliable, basically decent youth, grateful for having been rescued from dock thugs who threatened his life, wishful for an ordinary life with a respectable girl his age, and necessary stage-dressing for Bajaratt's assassination scheme. Louisianian Andrew Jackson Poole, a self-proclaimed "techno-nerd" (130), promotes the Hawthorne-Neilsen romance and provides the technological wizardry Hawthorne lacks. Ludlum's affection for his own pets shows through in Poole's concern for the *padrone*'s guard dogs and his refusal to leave the island until they are looked after.

## Themes

Ludlum weaves themes from the Bourne series (see Chapter 6) with new concerns.

One recycled theme is aging. Hawthorne was fourteen years younger when an intelligence operative, and he says he was not a young man then. Now it is harder for him to engage in physical conflict without pain, and his reflexes are not quick enough to compete with Major Neilsen in operating a minisubmarine. He is behind on technology, and he distrusts the high-tech machinery his subordinates are at home with. He is far more cautious than the younger members of the Air Force team, who ride him about having been away from intelligence work for too long. He says, "I'm history" (362), yet he brings the experience and instinct the younger professionals lack, and is the only person who can pull together disparate threads to see a unifying pattern and who can anticipate to some degree the moves of the enemy.

Ludlum also contrasts the new world of computers, laser beams, access codes, and other technological wizardry with "the human quotient," to argue that personal relationships, personal experience, and intuition or a feeling in the "gut" remain more valuable than "steel whirligigs" (138). Determined individuals can outthink and outmaneuver Mars's seemingly impregnable mechanical fortress or the White House's elaborate, mechanized security system. A network of international computer systems cannot do what Hawthorne can: anticipate Bajaratt's moves and respond on instinct to intercept her. Related to this focus on the power of the individual is the argument that individual intuition and drive can be enhanced by teamwork, if that team is competent and committed and shares values and goals.

Another recycled Bourne theme concerns acting and disguises. In the Bourne series the hero was the master illusionist; in *The Scorpio Illusion* the villain is. Bajaratt can transform herself from a sophisticated beauty to an ugly matron, with a plump, sagging body, darkly shadowed eyes, lined and weary flesh—a mask of age and decay. She can be a frumpish ex-pilot for the Israeli Air Force or the Countess Cabrini, graceful and wealthy and utterly charming. Bajaratt is so convincing in her role as the generous Dominique Montaigne, protector of orphans and supporter of relief agencies for the abandoned children of Somalia and Ethiopia, that Hawthorne cannot connect her to Bajaratt, despite a close description and the coincidence of their encounter. Even the street-smart Nicolo is to some degree taken in by the projected image of herself, although his visual evidence that she kills too easily makes him suspect her motives. Robert Ingersol, however, argues that "we're all actors" appearing on the stage of life and that Hawthorne's success as a hunter is due in part to his instincts as an actor who can penetrate the disguises of others (519).

Still another Bourne theme is love and betrayal. Hawthorne must resolve the suspicions surrounding the loss of his wife Ingrid. He must also expiate the guilt he feels about his affair with Dominique when he discovers her true identity by dedicating himself to her destruction. At the same time, his respect and attraction for Catherine Neilsen grows as her affection, competence, and honesty prove genuine under fire. Ludlum attacks government corruption, particularly competitive generals and admirals with grandiose schemes of self-aggrandizement and government bureaucrats on the take, flying "on military aircraft to Caribbean resorts beholden to army engineers or naval coastal surveys" (260). He calls them the enemy at America's heart. The Secretary of State bemoans America's "government of opportunists," "benign reformers," and "predators" (397). Hawthorne and Ludlum's answer to lack of accountability, secret chains of command, and paranoid possibilities is for government officials to "go public," to publicize the truth, no matter how unpleasant it is (660).

As in the Bourne series, Ludlum explores the causes of terrorism, citing varied and differing motives. Mars is "evil incarnate" (172), malevolent and wicked, delighting in chaos and power. Neptune shares Mars's evil vision and acts out of lust, egotism, and a personal delight in manipulating and outsmarting others. Some agents act out of racial hatred: Arabs against Jews, Blacks against Whites. Some, like Bajaratt, act in response to personal nightmares that warped their lives. Others, like David Ingersoll, are weak and easily blackmailed into participation through extortion tempered with financial reward. Still others, like the CIA operative O'Ryan, believe they deserve more credit and greater rewards for their achievements. Many are greedy and like the financial rewards, or have private dreams of personal gain and dominance over those they see as inferiors. Related to this theme is the vulnerability of public figures, in this case the ease with which a determined terrorist could threaten the American president.

Geoffrey Cooke, who recruits Hawthorne for the Scorpio mission, argues a key issue of Ludlum's most recent books: that the West no longer has the "luxury of known enemies," that the Cold War moles, double agents, and old-style spies based on competition for power or for geo-political influence are gone, their place taken by a fanatical breed that does not think "anything like the way we used to think" (46). Cooke proclaims, "The whipped of the world are turning, their age-old frustrations exploding, blind vengeance paramount" (47). These hate-driven schemers are "everywhere" and, like the Scorpios of this novel, "know everything we do" (114). Furthermore, terrorism has become capitalistic, as fanaticism finances worldwide businesses devoted to destabilization and dependent on Swiss bank accounts, Japanese satellites, and French and Libyan arms merchants.

## Alternate Reading: Freudian Analysis

Originated by Viennese physician Sigmund Freud in the 1890s, Freud-ian analysis provides systematic methods for researching the inner ex-periences of the human mind and for treating psychological and emotional disorders through psychoanalysis, a method of dream analysis and similar devices to help the patient discover unconscious memories and desires and adjust mental conflicts. Traditional psychoanalytical the-ory asserts that subconscious drives for sexual pleasure and for aggres-sion propel behavior and that traumatic experiences weaken the psyche and cause abnormal compulsions and personality disorders. Freud sought to trace adult disorders, hysterias, and neuroses to childhood roots, particularly to sexual seductions by adults. Freudian literary critics apply the theories of the subconscious and of psychoanalysis to the study of fiction, searching for clues that explain the behavior of characters within a work and for symbols reflective of the inner psychology of the author. In *The Scorpio Illusion* Ludlum consciously draws on Freudian theory to lend depth to his treatment of the two dominant characters, a psychotic woman, driven by childhood traumas to emasculate dominant males and to destroy all symbols of male hierarchical power, and her opponent, a weakened, age-conscious male reaffirming his masculine strengths.

Having been raped as a child, Bajaratt sees all authority figures as sharing in that violation. Consequently, sex must always be associated with danger for her, for sex is both a compulsion to repeat the patterns that have created her personality and a weapon with which to control men. Her initiation into sex, a rape at the age of ten after witnessing the destructive violence of males assaulting and penetrating her village and home, ended in a victory over the male destructive principles as she "plunged a hunting knife into the Spanish soldier who was hungrily, furiously breaking her virginity" (530). As an adult, sex continues to be a weapon wielded against the male world: her partners range from a fanatic whose destructive methods she emulates to victims or enemies that she intends to kill. The CIA psychiatric profile emphasizes her "emotional intemperance"; in effect, she becomes a rapist herself, repeatedly violating and destroying the man who violated her at the age of ten. Weapons are extensions of her ego, Freudian symbols of warped sexuality. When she kills with a bayonet, she feels like a girl of ten again, taking pleasure in the knife plunging into her adult violator (530), and when she kills with a gun she fondles the steel and gains satisfaction from its discharge.

Ludlum's fictional psychiatrist, a specialist in children's disorders, argues that a male child who experienced the psychosexual trauma Bajaratt underwent would write "Death to all authority" and sign his full name to assert primacy and commit himself to vengeance, his method to "outmuscle" his enemies. A young female, instead, would not reveal her full name because her method would be secrecy and a carefully plotted vengeance achieved through mental, not physical, combat (21). Taking her mother's killer's name is a manifestation of the Stockholm syndrome, a child in brutal circumstances determined to become as loathsome a killer as the one she watches. Her choice of aliases containing clues to her identity, however, reflects the child's attempt to leave a part of her as evidence of her commitment to revenge. Her chameleon-like role-playing and careful orchestration of events are tactics "to outwit and strike" (300); her pleasure comes from "penetrating" the strongholds and the secrets of dominant males. She tells the U.S. president shortly before she tries to kill him, "In many ways I am still a child, sir, a child who remembers many things" (642).

Her code name "Little Girl Blood" reminds readers of her childhood violation, her baptism in blood. It is appropriate that her father figure is an aged homosexual bound to a wheelchair, vitriolic in his hatreds. It is also fitting that her secret weapon is a golden rose with hidden thorns and a deep dark orifice at its center filled with poison: "a golden thorn red with blood, its tiny orifice dark . . . open" (209)—a weapon she tries to use on Hawthorne in their final confrontation.

Her key male opponent, Hawthorne, is also driven by Freudian impulses: to reassert male dominance and to revenge himself on her for using his weakness and vulnerability against him. He claims that she had "ripped him apart in a way no human being should ever do to another" and that she had taken his love and mocked it, "trading the innermost secrets of the manipulated for lies from the manipulator" (417). This personal violation, worsened by her shooting his new love, is a deep psychological spur to hunt her down and destroy her.

Hawthorne sees Bajaratt in Jungian terms (see Chapter 3) as the mythic, destructive female force, the *Belle Dame Sans Merci*, the dark lady without mercy whose sexuality pulls men to their doom—in contrast to his beloved Catherine, whose gentle heart wins love and respect. Bajaratt is the demon lover of legend, a succubus or a Circe, a terminal femme fatale seducing young males, distracting them from duty and social function, and consuming their life force. She chooses the young and the strong, and leaves death in her wake. Her terrorist lover, incited to ever more daring feats by her passion, dies on an alien shore. Her American lover feels the bite of her bullets and the sting of her wrath. Her youthful Italian lover has been lured into her arms as bait for destroying a more powerful male. Her ego feeds on her seductive powers, and even as she engages him in mortal combat, she sends Hawthorne sexually alluring telephone messages that twist his heart. Yet, ironically, her most effective disguise is as a nurturer, a bountiful tender of orphans and a supporter of charitable causes among the world's poor.

# Ludlum As a Cultural Phenomenon
## *The Apocalypse Watch* (1995)

> The conquest of the earth, which mostly means the taking it away
> from those who have a different complexion or slightly flatter noses
> than ourselves, is not a pretty thing when you look into it.
>
> Joseph Conrad, *Heart of Darkness*

Ludlum says *The Apocalypse Watch* grew out of a personal confrontation
in Munich, Germany, in 1993, with Ludlum proud of having stood his
ground when he and an associate encountered four or five young neo-
Nazis, wearing swastika armbands, sporting orange crew cuts, and dominating the pavement. The title contains a sinister threat. The word
"apocalypse" suggests both an unveiling of the hidden, a disclosure or
revelation, and a biblical vision—as in the book of Revelations—of the
end of the world as we know it. The word "watch" also carries a double
possibility: a division of time, particularly nighttime military duty, and
a state of being on the lookout, of vigilant watching, as if on sentry duty.
Thus, Ludlum threatens doomsday if we fail to stay vigilant and heed
the warnings implicit in his unveiling of hidden possibilities.

Throughout his writing career, Ludlum has depicted the Nazis as em-
bodying the barbarous nature in mankind, the forces of darkness against
which we all must battle: fascism, totalitarianism, racism, sexism, and

inhumanity. Placed at the beginning of *The Apocalypse Watch*, David Ansen's *Newsweek* statement about the unfathomability of the "systematic evil the Nazi regime perpetrated . . . a moral black hole" sums up Ludlum's own view. Ludlum's early books dealt with World War II Nazis and his later books often incorporated a figure with a Nazi mentality or a Nazi heritage. A mad general in *The Aquitaine Progression* was one of Hitler's key officers; in *The Parsifal Mosaic* a former Nazi perpetuates modern-day concentration camps for illegal aliens. In *The Apocalypse Watch*, Ludlum captures the worst Nazi nightmare of all: Hitler enthroned in a secret shrine, a living monument to the Nazi dream of power; a new Führer acting with the blessing of the old to topple former Allies, burn Paris and the Bundestag (the democratic German parliament building), poison large numbers of supposedly genetically inferior people, and bring to power a new order of genetically pure *Sonnenkinder*, whose superior intellects and Aryan genetic traits will ensure their leadership worldwide.

## GENRE CONVENTIONS

Ludlum builds on the standard conventions of espionage fiction: undercover agents in the enemy camp, long-term moles with secret missions spelled out a generation before, traitors bought or blackmailed, hunters and hunted, disguises, international cooperation between high-level secret services with resulting leaks, unsafe safe houses, armed fortresses, midnight assaults by specialized teams, surprise attacks, secret codes and passwords, cyanide tablets, death in a dozen or more ways, and the fate of the free world in the hands of a small group of patriotic men and women, tested in the fires of experience and innovative and daring when faced with doomsday. High-ranking allies play a double game. Interrogations follow good cop/bad cop routines, and prisoners plan strategies to confuse and misdirect captors. Telephone lines are tapped, rooms bugged, computer networks penetrated, and master lists sought.

From terrorist fiction Ludlum draws kamikaze fanatics, terrorist threats to kill large numbers in terrible ways, and a countdown to destruction, with the days, hours, then minutes ticked off as the good try to figure out the strategies of the bad. Often revenge motivates the fight against terrorism, as it does for French Deuxième Bureau Inspector Claude Moreau, whose younger sister was forced into narcotics addiction and prostitution to punish him personally. The conventions of romance in such fiction throw men and women together in adverse situations; tested by adversity, they discover the seeds of a deep love, but, despite fleeting moments of passion, are not truly free to commit to this love until their mission is accomplished.

Ludlum adds his own innovations: the mythical *Sonnenkinder*, whose intelligence, physical perfection, and undercover training have raised them to power through Europe and America; the patterns of history repeated with variations in modern events; and the most beautiful, pastoral areas—like a quiet valley in the Swiss Alps or a lovely French chateau in the Loire Valley—as secret, camouflaged centers of enemy activity. Science fiction meets espionage in the secret computer breakthrough—a microchip brain insert whose electrical impulses change memories, so that an enemy agent can think he is untainted when, in fact, his memories have been restructured in significant ways. The description of preprogrammed radio and television sets transmitting information to patients with implanted microchips recalls Aldous Huxley's *Brave New World*, in which youngsters are preconditioned for their roles in life through subliminal messages received during sleep.

## PLOT DEVELOPMENT AND STRUCTURE

*The Apocalypse Watch* is more loosely structured than Ludlum's other novels, with two false starts and false climax after false climax in a dramatic final sequence of repeated tension and release, as one disaster is averted or one threat contained and another materializes. The novel brings together elements or patterns from Ludlum's earlier books, and echoes, in particular, the themes and concepts introduced in the early Nazi and neo-Nazi novels. Frequently, Ludlum seems to be playing games with readers, setting up avenues of exploration that prove dead ends and teasing us with details whose significance is only clear hundreds of pages later.

The Prologue begins "high in the Austrian Hausruck," in a secret Alpine hideaway and training camp for The Brotherhood of the Watch— "the progenitors of Germany's Fourth Reich"—a hideaway that multilingual deep-cover CIA agent Harry Latham, code-named Sting, has penetrated under the alias Alexander Lassiter (1). Latham's disguise is reminiscent of *The Scarlatti Inheritance*—a big-time arms merchant making huge sums selling weapons illegally to third-world nations—while the story he is told of the *Sonnenkinder*, distributed throughout the Western nations and paving the way for a Fourth Reich, echoes *The Holcroft Covenant*. Latham drops radioactive pellets and plants a transponder in the snow to guide fellow agents to this neo-Nazi camp, but is exposed as an infiltrator and used as a guinea pig in a scientific experiment in mind control. His escape with a list of neo-Nazis and his assurance of mission accomplished puts in motion the queries that dominate the rest of the novel. He has nine to twelve days before a telltale rash will appear and the microchip embedded in his brain will implode, but by then his usefulness to the neo-Nazi cause will be over.

The first chapter points in a very different direction: an attempted assassination of a Nazi leader (a high-ranking French collaborator) by a man bent on revenge for the death of his beloved wife and children. The opening is like a scene out of Geoffrey Household's *Rogue Male*: the would-be assassin, Jean-Pierre Jodelle, a seventy-eight-year-old former leader of the Resistance, who has stalked his prey for nearly fifty years, has the monster he has tracked in his rifle sights, only to be thwarted by interfering guards. Jodelle's public suicide in the theater where his son is performing Shakespeare's *Coriolanus* shocks Jean-Pierre Villier, France's finest, most popular actor and, as he learns for the first time, Jodelle's only surviving son. In an intriguing sequence, Villier draws on his acting repertoire to disguise himself and, like Jason Bourne, moves comfortably through shadowy streets among the silent armies of the down-and-out—a "chameleon" who merges with his environment (31). Villier connects his father's oppressors with the Loire Valley and draws out an assassin whose capture confirms the realities of a neo-Nazi conspiracy. The detailed buildup of family, historical background, and personality makes readers expect Villier to be Ludlum's first actor-hero, but he then disappears until the very end, when his discovery becomes important to the final sequence of events.

The next chapters focus on Drew Latham, Harry Latham's younger brother (parallels are repeatedly drawn to the elder Latham) and a special officer for the U.S. Intelligence special branch called Consular Operations, which is responsible both to the American State Department and the CIA. Drew has become the focus of an all-out search-and-destroy effort by the neo-Nazis, who fear that seeing his brother Harry up close will arouse Drew's suspicions and foil their game plan. Thus, hit team after hit team assaults Drew, at first singly (a fake chauffeur) and then in growing numbers.

Drew cooperates with the French foreign office (the Quai d'Orsay) and the Deuxième (the secret service), first with Henri Bressard (First Secretary of Foreign Affairs for the Republic of France) and later with Deuxième Inspector Claude Moreau. Karin de Vries, a multilingual NATO-vetted researcher, personally processes Drew's research request in order to avoid the normal channels that she fears are compromised. Drew initially suspects her motives, but later comes to respect her commitment to battling the neo-Nazis and her understanding of how deeply they have penetrated the intelligence networks of several nations. Her former husband, Frederick de Vries, was a brilliant undercover agent who worked for the Americans against the Gestapo and who taught his wife invaluable tricks of the trade. With time, Karin and Drew fall in love.

When a bullet finally kills Harry Latham, Drew takes his place, pretending he himself has died and Harry lives on. By this point, however, Harry's doctor and neo-Nazi contact Gerhardt Kroeger has decided Harry must die, so the attacks continue. At one point Karin's quick reflexes save Drew's life. Another time masked neo-Nazis with grappling hooks assault the safe haven of CIA Colonel Stanley Witkowski. The surviving attackers who do not commit suicide fall at the hands of Nazi moles in the system, but piece by piece information is gleaned and traitors exposed. Inspector Moreau, who has played a dangerous double game, heads to Munich to check on Dr. Hans Traupman, the Chief of Cranial Surgery at Nuremburg and the doctor who invented the microchip procedure used on Harry, while Washington agent Wesley Sorensen goes to Centralia, Illinois, to confirm that the wife of the American Ambassador to France is a *Sonnenkinder*. A carnival hides a secret Nazi rendezvous, and a Lutheran priest with pitbulls and a predilection for choirboys proves a dangerous adversary. Karin is kidnapped, rescued, knifed, and shot, but continues gamely, arranging safe passage and aid for a young addict/prostitute in return for admission to Traupman's fortress home and later confronting the new Führer Jager. The final action involves a series of false climaxes: the thwarted kidnapping of Traupman from his residence and his successful kidnapping from his boat (Chapter 36); the kidnapping of neo-Nazis at a restaurant gathering, where Führer Jager and his foreign supporters are filmed (Chapter 37); revelations about the neo-Nazi mission named Water Lightning (Chapter 38); Drew's rescue of Karin from a mad and frenzied Jager (Chapter 39); the action to stop Water Lightning (Chapter 40); the trapping of a high-ranking French collaborator (Chapter 41); the plans for a night attack on the Loire Valley chateau, "the Eagle's Nest" (Chapter 42), with the attack

carried out (Chapter 43). The continued action confirms widespread ag-
gression and deep neo-Nazi infiltration of top-level positions in the secret
services of several nations.

As in *The Scorpio Illusion*, a key villain is a sexually obsessed homo-
sexual, a "sculptured Mars," and the code name Daedalus, associated
with Icarus, evokes once again the mythological imagery that dominated
*The Icarus Agenda*. The Mafia, which was so important in *Trevayne* and
*The Road to Omaha*, appears briefly in a rather unnecessary section on
New Orleans, in the character of a Mafia chieftain who acts for the Nazis;
Ludlum had in mind the 1992 Louisiana elections, in which self-
proclaimed Nazi admirer and racial bigot David Duke ran for governor.

The Epilogue reveals the true computer list Harry Latham sought in
the Prologue and ends the story in a fairy-tale way: Drew inherits millions from his dead brother and he and Karin settle in the Rocky Mountains; five thousand neo-Nazis are condemned to a penal colony where
they are taught tolerance and forced to watch films of World War II Nazi
atrocities. As in the Road series, a military man (Colonel Witkowski)
shows up with advice about designing Drew and Karin's house and
about future missions.

## CHARACTER DEVELOPMENT

The nature of the plot does not allow for much in-depth development
of character. Instead, readers get a series of thumbnail sketches aimed at
quick insights.

The two main characters are Drew Latham (Harry Latham's younger
brother) and Karin de Vries (the wife of Frederick de Vries, who is pre-
sumed dead). In response to his cerebral brother, Drew has developed
his physical skills. A former hockey star, he is a belligerent individualist
with a certain animal brutality, but his heart is in the right place, and
his military training is vital to accomplishing a task his brother failed at.
He is possessive, aggressive, and easily angered. He is embarrassed by
the dye job Karin gives him and by the constrictions of the French military uniform disguise (particularly the tunic), and fears they make him
look effeminate. Once he overcomes his suspicions of her, Drew is
quickly enamored and amorous, but Karin keeps the focus on primary
objectives as long as she can. Karin is clever, intelligent, and cynical. She
has been an abused wife and is horrified at the extremes to which her

long-missing husband has gone. She bravely endures physical injury and rape, persists in the hunt, and proves a worthy ally.

Ludlum develops a myriad of minor characters that are too numerous to detail here, each with a history, delineated motives and values, and revelations about either how their past could be misread and twisted or how their present reality hides a hidden self. Characterized by their skills, their political histories, or the dichotomy between their appearance and their reality, they either serve the plot or further themes. Typical is François, a minor background figure. François drives like the maniacal sportscar racer he once was, transporting Drew, Karin, and Moreau from rendezvous to rendezvous, a silent but trusted team member. His family's unexpected appearance at a carnival with neo-Nazi connections enables *Sonnenkinder* Janis Courtland to escape capture. Later, Drew discovers that François killed a man out of jealous passion and has been blackmailed into secretly working for the opposition; his contact is Jacques Bergeron (Moreau's right-hand man and next in line for the inspectorship). François's plight emphasizes the strategies by which the neo-Nazis enlist personnel in key positions; it also allows Latham to track down Moreau's killer and expose the mole in the Deuxième. François is one of many characters developed to this degree in *The Apocalypse Watch*.

## THEMES

Ludlum warns about fascism, fanaticism, neo-Nazis, and the dangers of an authoritarian mentality. He emphasizes the fanaticism of the original progenitors of Nazism, the secret funds channeled to Argentina, Brazil, Paraguay, and other nations that took in large numbers of fleeing Nazis, and what he sees as an historical pattern of strong German nationalism coupled with efficiency, competence, and social pressure to conform. As an historian, Ludlum believes in history's power to change the future if its lessons are understood and heeded. A study of the rise of the Nazi regime should teach readers to recognize the signs that people of the time ignored. Thus, Ludlum's modern Nazis reflect the values and repeat the patterns of their predecessors, with modern variations. They still quote Nietzsche about "perfectibility through self-assertion" and the "moral glorification of the supreme rulers" (249); they still like giant rallies at huge outdoor stadiums, at which large crowds are whipped to a frenzy; they still respond to manipulative rhetoric that plays on emotions and prejudices and to an hysterical oratorical style with forceful crescendos. They still pride themselves on their inventiveness—like the development of the giant gliders of the 1930s, used to circumvent treaties prohibiting a German air force, and the decision to use the poison Zyklon B for mass executions in the death camps during World War II; and they still advocate genetic cleansing and racial and masculine superiority. Ludlum denounces all who would devote themselves to a cause that asserts the genetic superiority of one group over the masses of human beings, that is founded on racism, sexism, and intolerance, and that promotes militaristic totalitarianism over democratic freedoms. In *The Apocalypse Watch* he captures a battleground on which "the insanity of the crazed McCarthy period" meets "the Nazi madness of the late thirties" and the fanaticism of today. He envisions demonic leaders "screaming exhortations" to mindless robots marching in "lockstep" to a litany of hatreds (352). His final warning is that defeating fascist fanatics must be an ongoing effort: "There are always others waiting in the wings. Their names may be different, the culture different, but the common denominator is always the same: 'Do it our way, under our authority, no deviations permitted'" (745).

Ludlum also returns to the fears voiced in works like *The Chancellor Manuscript* about secret lists of names in secret files, lists that accuse and condemn without benefit of the courts or the justice system. He has often denounced the destructiveness of McCarthy-like accusations that produce a climate of intimidation, suspicion, and distrust, and that rely on innuendo and guilt by association to destroy decent people. Here he cleverly reverses the McCarthy pattern, so the list is of secret fascists—neo-Nazis who have supposedly penetrated the government, the media, and important industries. Neo-Nazi scientist Gerhardt Kroeger enunciates the strategy: "the frenzied Red-baiting of the forties and fifties" paralyzed the nation with fear and paranoia and weakened it within; ironically, the Communists used this fear, secretly channeling in money and misinformation in order to taint thousands of innocents with "the Soviet brush"; now the neo-Nazis will do the same (59). If the list is accurate, the president is ready to forgo democratic niceties to purge the country of these extremists, and he sets in motion FBI and CIA investigations of individuals who previously seemed beyond reproach. Their privacy is invaded, their garbage searched, their friends and neighbors interrogated. Ludlum's investigators view medals of honor from the Korean War, for example, as proof one is anti-Communist—a Nazi trait, is it not? In other words, every facet of these individuals' lives is scrutinized and twisted to confirm the interpretation suggested by the list, but turning McCarthyism on its head since the target is now the right wing.

The plot at times seems weighed down by story after story of investigations of this sort (an MBC News anchorman, a chairman of the board of an electronics company that deals internationally, a Rush Limbaugh–style radio and television impresario, liberal senators, members of the British House of Lords, Deuxième officials, and so forth), but this is because Ludlum so fears the danger of master lists silently accusing individuals who can never confront their accusers nor face a jury of their peers, but are judged in absentia. On the one hand, one must fight the Nazi mentality, wherever it appears; on the other hand, one must not sacrifice individual rights and the judicial system that protects those rights in the name of efficiency or out of fear. Thus, the list that Harry Latham brings back is an ingenious study in disinformation, with some genuine neo-Nazis who are stealing secrets and destroying vital computer databases included but also with a far larger number of innocents whose effectiveness as citizens will be ended by a Nazi taint, no matter how false it is.

Another theme is the vital contribution actors made to World War II, and their continued value in matters of espionage. Julian Villier, the actor who adopted Jean-Paul when his family was killed, describes "artists drawn together against an enemy that would destroy all art" (15). He enumerates the varied ways stage people drew on the skills of their trade to dupe and defeat the Germans. For example, the musicians inserted melodic phrases into musical scores to pass along codes; the illustrators employed coded colors and images to send messages in the daily and weekly posters the Germans demanded they produce; the actors corrupted texts to include secret messages and even to provide saboteurs with direct instructions. Jean-Paul's wife, Giselle, a talented actress in her own right, notes that it is easy for actors to merge with crowds and to lose an enemy agent who pursues them. A talented actor, says she, can enter a building looking like one person and reappear on the street looking like someone else entirely, just by changing their walk or rearranging their clothing (63). Karin de Vries later proves this true, drawing on her husband's disguises and cosmetics, tricks of coloring and clothing, to change Drew's appearance.

Ludlum is not all seriousness, however. As in his Road series, he engages in mildly satiric portraits and dialogue. For example, one of his characters jokes about the Hamptons, with its beaches filled with would-be artists of both sexes, "either very thin or very fat," who carry "galleys to prove they're writers," and with its candlelit cafés a haven for egotists extolling "their unprintable scribblings" and deriding "unwashed publishers" who fail to recognize their genius (184). Ludlum's Arnold Argossy (a play on Jason and the Argonauts' Argosy) is a parody of a Rush Limbaugh–type "hysteria-prone ultraconservative" media person, who engages in "singularly vicious attacks" on all things liberal and thrives on name-calling—"libbo-Commies, Female-Fascists, Embryo-Killers, Homeless-Suckers" (189). Argossy's radio talk show ("Hello, America, you true, red-blooded sons and daughters of giants who carved a nation out of a land of savages and made it sweet" [189]) echoes a satiric put-down of "just folks" the down-home American, anti-Communist, racist language that Paul Newman mockingly delivers in the 1960s film *W.U.S.A.* (based on Robert Stone's 1967 *Hall of Mirrors*) and draws just as strong a racist response from the right-wing fringes. Ludlum's denunciation of a current right-wing media celebrity, Oliver North, as a "sanctimonious," "self-serving" "liar," however, seems deeply and personally felt, the author's own persona intruding.

The theme of youth versus age, so seriously treated in earlier works, takes on the quality of popular science fiction film such as *Logan's Run* (1976), in which the greatest crime is turning thirty. Ludlum's neo-Nazis eulogize physical perfection and pride themselves on their youthful reflexes and superbly trained bodies. "Old men" of thirty are looked on with contempt, as somehow not reliable, not fit enough for the feats demanded of them. In one episode, a rebellious and disgusted thirty-year-old assassin complains about an underling, calling him a "mad teenager who acts . . . before he's thought things out" (248). The neo-Nazi youth cult is set in opposition to the defenders of freedom and democracy, most of whom are over forty—some of the most respected ones (in positions of authority) ranging from fifty to eighty. The marines who assist Drew Latham joke about his age in contrast to their youth, but are impressed by his military prowess. It is tempting to see in this generational competition Ludlum's possible frustration with younger people of the late twentieth century, whose politics and lifestyles have deviated significantly from those of their baby-boom elders.

Less developed themes grow out of the central ones. For example, with so many killings, an obvious question is "Are these deaths justified?" Ludlum's answer, in the words of Drew Latham as he consoles Karin de Vries, is that the opponents of an insidious, destructive, and evil conspiracy are caught in a classic liberal dilemma, because their opponents are willing to use any means to destroy them, so vigorous self-defense is a matter of survival. Latham points out that he and his team do not kill unless it is necessary (their hope has been to take prisoners), but that, if they do not kill when they must, "ten thousand times the killings will take place" (302). Another minor theme is the similarity between the extreme political left and the extreme political right. Ludlum's Nazis argue that "book-burning religious fundamentalists" and extreme Russian nationalists have so much in common with the neo-Nazis that their "agendas could have been written by Hitler and Goebbels" and that both groups secretly approve of the concept of ethnic cleansing (317). Ludlum also attacks religious hypocrisy, particularly Catholic priests and Lutheran pastors who supported the Nazi regime, and clergymen who engage in perverted sex, corrupting choirboys or obsessing over prostitutes. His new Führer wears a clergyman's collar, and among his supporters are genuine priests who are racial and moral bigots. A final theme is the distinction between the German people and the Nazis and neo-Nazis who are sometimes mistakenly equated with them. Ludlum carefully balances his disgust with the Nazis with images of Germans who are as horrified by the Nazi mentality as Ludlum and with characters like Elke Mueller Traupman, who urges Drew to save Germany from the fanatics who will be the death of the nation (365).

## ALTERNATE READING: READER-RESPONSE CRITICISM

Reader-response criticism depends on studying a fictive work in terms of explicit audience experience: what strategies authors use to appeal to readers, how readers feel as they read, how they respond to the literary text, and why they respond the way they do. It emerged as a critical approach in the 1960s and 1970s, but had its roots in the approaches to reading poetry of earlier critics like I. A. Richards and Louise Rosenblatt. The German Hans Robert Jauss in the late 1960s lectured on the reader's "horizon of expectations," while the American David Bleich taught literature by encouraging individual reader responses. Stanley Fish wrote of an "interpretive community" of shared understandings and of "affective stylistics" as a reader's responses change in relationship to time and order, and Norman Holland applied psychoanalysis to explain variant reader interpretations. Bleich and Holland defined reading as "a form of covert wish-fulfillment" (Cuddon 771–72). Such critics distinguish between the intended audience and the real audience; with older texts their critical activity is to recreate the values, prejudices, and assumptions of readers with a culture, mind-set, and worldview very different from our own, while with contemporary texts they ask how readers participate in texts or make meaning from texts, and why readers respond as they do.

Reader-response critics would be interested in the satisfaction that comes from Ludlum's use of familiar genre conventions, but also in his departures from them to surprise or shock his audience—as when a daring hero like Harry Latham is captured and transformed into a *doppelgänger* of his former self before the very first chapter. They would also find intriguing the psychological force that compels even denigrators of Ludlum's novels to keep turning pages until the late hours of the night to find out what will happen next. The human sympathetic nervous system programs readers for the rush of physical response to a scary story—to be startled by the imaginative twig snapping in the silent imaginative darkness, to squirm in anticipation of the expected attack on the hero from an unknown direction, to squeal silently at the threatening figure intruding into his space. If readers are caught up in a story, such reactions can be largely physiological; as the American psychologist William James pointed out, it is not that we see the tiger, are afraid, and then run, but rather that we see the tiger and run—an instinctive or behaviorally programmed response—and then feel the fear, which is a reaction to the adrenaline rushing through our body.

Ludlum uses this phenomenon to provide pleasure, since readers are intellectually aware that the threat is synthetic and can be walked away from; but the fear of conger eels swarming over the hero's vulnerable body or of enraged Dobermans snapping at his heels also touches deep bodily responses. As with young predators playfully practicing hunting and killing skills, the activity is not confused with real violence, yet going through the motions persuades the body to react realistically. Ludlum's signature chase scenes, descriptions that lead readers to compulsive page turning even as the intellect questions their realism and credibility, stimulate the reader's sympathetic nervous system: the words and the mental imagery they evoke heighten the fight-flight response, and readers empathetically share the hero's excited if nervous anticipation of attack and possible obliteration. In other words, Ludlum creates a gut-level sense of threat, but in the safety of prose; the roller-coaster makes our juices flow even as our brain tells us we are perfectly safe.

Apart from Ludlum's mastery of technique, reader-response critics would be interested in him as a popular phenomenon, would note the gap between the negative comments of professional reviewers and the broad-based popularity of Ludlum's books, and would question this difference in reader response, asking what makes Ludlum so popular with the general reader. Reviewers, of course, tend to take as their standard "high culture" and, as a group, tend to be contemptuous of "popular culture" or, even worse, "mass culture," yet commercial success is relevant as the judgment of countless readers. Ludlum writes in a popular culture tradition aimed at the tastes, fears, hopes, and expectations of ordinary people. Furthermore, he equates popular culture with democratic culture and sees himself as building on the popular mythologies of our culture. His distrust of large corporations and large governments, his contempt for fanatics, his fear of conspiracies, and his trust in the power of an educated, informed, and motivated individual, touch a nerve deep in the American psyche. His latest works appeal to the reader's fantasy of a split self in the Walter Mitty fashion: the domesticated, middle-class suburbanite who, of necessity, becomes a James Bond–type hero, battling evil forces but still retaining his safe identity. Their complex plots, exotic settings, and in-depth exploration of politics, psychology, and culture, please readers brought up in an age of conspiracy. The topicality of his novels and their peculiar mix of the familiar and predictable with the new and intriguing provide a satisfying sense of being on top of things and of sharing in the behind-the-scenes realities of daily events. Headlines become real as Ludlum's heroes charge across the page, battling the amorphous, multitentacled organizations that would seem to negate the power of the individual, a power intrinsic to the American sense of self and to the mythology of democracy: one vote can make a difference, one individual can avert disaster, one individual can save a nation or even the world. His books reinforce the basic myths and values of U.S. culture: the individual can control his or her fate, loners can join groups that support them, yet remain individuals, weaknesses and faults can be overcome and triumphed over, and happy endings are still possible.

Ludlum's broad appeal is also based on his careful balancing of values and perspectives, so that his negative attacks on military authoritarianism will be balanced with a positive portrayal of a sympathetic soldier, and a denunciation of Nazis will be offset by a description of kindly Germans smuggling Jews out of danger. His readers can find satisfaction in his confirmation of middle-class values: his heroes save the world, but get paid too. Converse makes two million dollars; Latham inherits a fortune; the Hawk and Devereaux make enough to live comfortably the rest of their lives. Ludlum combines the appeal of the fast-paced action comic book with the surprises and strategies of the theater and the appeal of the Harlequin romance—a fantasy relationship that pits a strong man and a nurturing woman against the world. As in romance novels, a formulaic approach promises familiarity and escapism, while new settings, characters, and plots provide variety.

More important, while offering sops to political correctness, Ludlum appeals to our most deeply rooted fears. The urban environment creates new threats in direct relation to its size and complexity, and it is just this environment in its most recent form that is Ludlum's territory. Skill at reading and unraveling deceit becomes part of the repertoire of social interaction as the number of possible encounters with strangers—potential enemies—increases. Reading the intentions of people little known to us is part of city life, and since such readings are by nature interpretive, they will be incorrect at times, leading to stress and a constant need for feedback: Am I understanding this person correctly? Is the stated motive the real one? What are other possible advantages that can be taken of me that I don't perceive? Ludlum touches our worst fears about modern society, that secret and evil forces are manipulating our lives.

# Bibliography

All references to Ludlum's texts are based on the Bantam paperback editions.

## WORKS BY ROBERT LUDLUM

### Novels

*The Apocalypse Watch*. New York: Random House, 1995.
*The Aquitaine Progression*. New York: Random House, 1984.
*The Bourne Identity*. New York: Richard Marek; London: Granada, 1980.
*The Bourne Supremacy*. New York: Random House, 1986.
*The Bourne Ultimatum*. New York: Random House, 1990.
*The Chancellor Manuscript*. New York: Dial; London: Hart Davis MacGibbon, 1977.
*The Cry of the Halidon* (as Jonathan Ryder). New York: Delacorte, 1974; London: Weidenfeld and Nicolson, 1975.
*The Gemini Contenders*. New York: Dial; London: Hart Davis MacGibbon, 1976.
*The Holcroft Covenant*. New York: Richard Marek; London: Hart Davis Mac-Gibbon, 1978.
*The Icarus Agenda*. New York: Random House, 1988.
*The Matarese Circle*. New York: Richard Marek; London: Hart Davis MacGibbon, 1979.
*The Matlock Paper*. New York: Dial; London: Hart Davis MacGibbon, 1973.

*The Osterman Weekend*. Cleveland: World Publishing; London: Hart Davis MacGibbon, 1972.

*The Parsifal Mosaic*. New York: Richard Marek; London: Granada, 1982.

*The Rhinemann Exchange*. New York: Dial, 1974; London: Hart Davis MacGibbon, 1975.

*The Road to Gandolfo* (as Michael Shepherd). New York: Dial, 1975; London: Hart Davis MacGibbon, 1976.

*The Road to Omaha*. New York: Random House, 1992.

*The Scarlatti Inheritance*. Cleveland: World Publishing; London: Hart Davis MacGibbon, 1971.

*The Scorpio Illusion*. New York: Random House, 1993.

*Trevayne* (as Jonathan Ryder). New York: Delacorte, 1973; London: Weidenfeld and Nicolson, 1974.

## Article

"James at 30." *Entertainment Weekly* (19 June 1992): 78–79.

## Audio Cassette Tapes

*The Apocalypse Watch*, read by Michael Prichard for Books on Tape; read by Edward Herrman for Talking Books, 1995.

*The Aquitaine Progression*, read by Robert Lansing for Random House Audio Books, 1986.

*The Bourne Covenant*, read by Robert Ulrich for Random House Audio Books, 1990.

*The Bourne Identity*, read by Darren McGavin for Bantam Audio, 1987.

*The Bourne Supremacy*, read by Michael Prichard for Books on Tape, 1986.

*The Bourne Ultimatum*, read by Michael Prichard for Books on Tape, 1990.

*The Chancellor Manuscript*, read by Michael Moriarty for Bantam Audio, 1984.

*The Cry of the Halidon*, read by Robert Foxworth for Dove Audio, 1996.

*The Gemini Contenders*, read by Anthony Heald for BDO Audio, 1989.

*The Holcroft Covenant*, read by Michael Moriarty for Random House Audio Books, 1988.

*The Icarus Agenda*, read by Michael Prichard for Books on Tape, 1988.

*The Matarese Circle*, read by Martin Balsam for Bantam Audio, 1987.

*The Matlock Paper*, read by Rod Steiger for Random House Audio Books, 1994.

*The Osterman Weekend*, read by Robert Loggia for Random House Audio Books, 1990.

*The Parsifal Mosaic*, read by Michael Prichard for Books on Tape, 1983.

*The Rhinemann Exchange*, read by Michael Prichard for Books on Tape, 1984.

*The Road to Gandolfo*, read by Joseph Campanella for Random House Audio Books, 1991.

*The Road to Omaha*, read by Martin Shaw for HarperCollins Audio Books, 1992.
*The Scarlatti Inheritance*, read by David Dukes for Random House Audio Books, 1989.
*The Scorpio Illusion*, read by Michael Prichard for Books on Tape, 1993.
*Trevayne*, Braille Institute of America, 1989.


## Film Adaptations

*The Apocalypse Watch*, a miniseries made in London, produced by Robert Halmi and expected to be telecast in 1998.
*The Bourne Identity*, a 1988 Roger Young television miniseries, starring Richard Chamberlain, Jaclyn Smith, Anthony Quayle, Donald Moffatt, and Denholm Elliott.
*The Holcroft Covenant*, a 1985 British movie directed by John Frankenheimer, starring Michael Caine, Anthony Andrews, Victoria Tennant, and Lilli Palmer.
*Osterman Weekend*, a Sam Peckinpah film released by EMI/Twentieth-Century-Fox in 1983, starring Rutger Hauer, John Hurt, Craig Nelson, Dennis Hopper, and Burt Reynolds.
*The Rhinemann Exchange*, a three-part, six-hour NBC television miniseries, telecast in March 1977 as part of NBC's *Best Sellers* series.


## WORKS ABOUT ROBERT LUDLUM

### General Information

Adler, Jerry. "The Ludlum Enigma." *Newsweek* 99 (19 April 1982): 99.
"Alfred Coppel." In *Contemporary Authors, Autobiography Series,* edited by Mark Zadrozny, vol. 9:1–6. Detroit, Mich.: Gale Research, 1989.
Andrews, Peter. "Momentum Is Everything." *New York Times Book Review* (30 March 1980): 7.
Bandler, Michael J. "The Ludlum Mosaic: A Thriller Writer Who Escapes in History." *Book World, Chicago Tribune* (18 April 1982).
Baxter, Susan, and Mark Nichols. "Robert Ludlum and the Realm of Evil." *Maclean's* 98 (9 April 1984): 50–52.
Block, Lawrence. "The Ludlum Conspiracy." *Writer's Digest* 57 (September 1977): 25–26.
Brandt, Bruce E. "Reflections of 'the Paranoid Style' in the Current Suspense Novel." *Clues: A Journal of Detection* 3 (Spring/Summer 1982): 1, 62–69.
Carcaterra, Lorenzo. "The Ludlum Solution." *New York Sunday News Magazine* (2 May 1982): 14–15, 17, 22.
Christy, George. "The Great Life." *Hollywood Reporter* (8 April 1982): 23.
Donaldson-Evans, Lance K. "Conspiracy, Betrayal, and the Popularity of a Genre:

Ludlum, Forsyth, Gerard de Villiers and the Spy Novel Format." *Clues: A Journal of Detection* 4 (Fall/Winter 1983): 92–114.

Edwards, Thomas R. "Boom at the Top." *New York Review of Books* (8 May 1986): 12–13.

Flashner, Graham. "Instant Replay." *New York* 21 (28 March 1988): 32.

Harwood, Richard. "Hooked on the Lure of Ludlum." *Washington Post Book World* (23 March 1980): 3.

Hinckley, Karen. "Ludlum, Robert." In *Twentieth-Century Crime and Mystery Writers*, edited by Leslie Henderson, 685–86. Chicago: St. James Press, 1991.

Holt, Patricia. "Ludlum Dashes Through." *San Francisco Chronicle* (5 April 1982): 41, col. 1.

Hunt, Christopher. "Places I Love: An Interview with Robert Ludlum." *Travel & Leisure* (July 1983): 126.

King, Stephen. "The Ludlum Attraction." *Washington Post Book World* (7 March 1982): 1.

Kisor, Henry. "Robert Ludlum, Merrily Stirring a Stew of Spies." *Chicago Sun-Times* (7 March 1982): 24–27.

Klemesrud, Judy. "Behind the Best Sellers: Robert Ludlum." *New York Times Book Review* 82 (10 July 1977): 38.

Leonard, John. "Paranoia Versus Greed." *New York Times* (5 April 1977): 31.

"Ludlum on Ludlum: An Interview with Robert Ludlum." New York: Bantam Audio Publishing, 1986.

"Ludlum, Robert." In *Contemporary Authors*, vol. 33–36: 526. Detroit, Mich.: Gale Research, 1978.

"Ludlum, Robert." In *Contemporary Authors, New Revision Series*, vol. 41: 283–86. Detroit: Gale Research, 1989.

"Ludlum, Robert." In *Contemporary Literary Criticism*, vol. 22: 288–91. Detroit, Mich.: Gale Research, 1978.

"Ludlum, Robert." In *Contemporary Literary Criticism, New Revision Series*, vol. 43: 273–79. Detroit, Mich.: Gale Research, 1983.

"Ludlum, Robert." In *Current Biography*, 247–50. Bronx, N.Y.: H. W. Wilson, 1982.

"Ludlum, Robert." In *International Who's Who*, 963. London: Europa Publications, 1994.

"Ludlum, Robert." In *Who's Who in America, 1980–1981*, 2082. Indianapolis: Macmillan, 1981.

"Ludlum, Robert." In *World Authors, 1980–1985*, edited by Vineta Colby, 554–55. New York: H. W. Wilson Co., 1991.

Lynah, Charlie. "Robert Ludlum: Master of Intrigue." *Connecticut Today* (3 May 1982): 4–5.

Macdonald, Gina. "Robert Ludlum." In *Contemporary Novelists*, edited by David Mote, London: St. James Press, 1997.

Massa, Ann. "Ludlum, Robert." In *Twentieth-Century Crime and Mystery Writers*, edited by John M. Reilly, 970–71. New York: St. Martin's Press, 1980.

Nekriach, Tatiana. "Zagadki populiarnosti: Politicheskie romany Robert Ladlema." *Literaturnoe Chozrenie: Organ Soiuza Pisatelei* (October 1986): 10, 31–35.

Penzler, Otto. "Collecting Mystery Fiction: Robert Ludlum." *Armchair Detective* 4 (Fall 1989): 382–84.

Sandomir, Richard. "The Ludlum Identity." *Compass* (14 March 1982): 1–7.

Skarda, Patricia L. "Robert Ludlum." In *Dictionary of Literary Biography Yearbook: 1982*, edited by Richard Ziegfeld, 305–16. Detroit, Mich.: Gale Research, 1983.

Stanley, Deborah A. "Robert Ludlum." In *Authors and Artists*, vol. 10: 117–24. Detroit, Mich.: Gale Research, 1993.

Thomas, Phil. "Ludlum Says His Books Popular Because of 'Age of Conspiracy.'" Associated Press (11 April 1982).

Wallace, Charles P. "The Military Minds and a World Obeys." *Los Angeles Times Book Review* (11 March 1984): 3.

## REVIEWS AND CRITICISM

### The Apocalypse Watch

Jones, Steve. "Paranoia and Power: The Stuff of a Robert Ludlum Novel." *USA Today* (9 June 1995): D–14, col. 1.

"The Apocalypse Watch," *Publishers Weekly* 242 (17 April 1995): 37.

Wilkens, Mary Frances. "The Apocalypse Watch." *Booklist* 91 (15 April 1995): 1452–53.

### The Aquitaine Progression

*Book List* 80 (15 January 1984): 697.

Cornish, Sam. "Robert Ludlum's Newest Is More Than a Mere Thriller." *Christian Science Monitor* 76 (27 March 1984): 22.

Furst, Alan. "Thrilled to Death." *Esquire* 101 (April 1984): 211–12.

*Kirkus Review* 51 (15 December 1983): 1269.

Lehmann-Haupt, Christopher. "The Aquitaine Progression." *New York Times* 133 (16 March 1984): 22.

*Maclean's* (9 April 1984): 50–52.

Markfield, W. "The Aquitaine Progression." *New York Magazine* 17 (26 March 1984): 87.

*New York Times Book Review* 89 (22 April 1984): 14.

*Publishers Weekly* 225 (6 January 1984): 78.

*Virginia Quarterly Review* 60 (Summer 1984): 97.
*West Coast Review of Books* 10 (July 1984): 29.


## *The Bourne Covenant* (Audio)

*Publishers Weekly* 237 (2 February 1990): 50.


## *The Bourne Identity*

Andrews, Peter. *New York Times Book Review* 85 (30 March 1980): 7.
*Book List* 76 (15 April 1980): 1180.
*Books of the Times* 3 (May 1980): 210.
*Book Seller* 40 (May 1980): 55.
*Book World* 10 (23 March 1980): 3.
*Critique Studies in Modern Fiction* 39 (December 1980): 4.
Demarest, Michael. "The Bourne Identity." *Time* 115 (14 April 1980): 101.
*Economist* 28 (19 December 1981): 87.
Haynes, M. A. "The Bourne Identity." *Library Journal* 105 (15 April 1980): 1003.
*Kirkus Review* 51 (15 December 1983): 1269.
*Kliatt* 15 (Spring 1981): 10.
Lehmann-Haupt, Christopher. *"The Bourne Identity."* *New York Times* (20 March 1980): 210–11.
*Listener* 104 (13 November 1980): 665.
*New Republic* 185 (25 November 1981): 39.
*New York Times Book Review* 86 (1 March 1981): 31.
Postman, Andrew, and Tom Spain. "Audio Reviews: *The Bourne Identity.*" *Publishers Weekly* 233 (22 January 1988): 73.
*Publishers Weekly* 217 (8 February 1980): 65.
*Publishers Weekly* 219 (23 January 1981): 123.
Walker, Martin. *New Statesman* 99 (17 June 1980): 972–73.


## *The Bourne Supremacy*

"Audio Reviews: Fiction." *Publishers Weekly* 235 (3 March 1989): 77.
*Best Sellers* 46 (May 1986): 35.
*Book List* 82 (1 February 1986): 778.
*Books* (May 1987): 33.
Demarest, Michael. *Time* 127 (10 March 1986): 74.
Edwards, Thomas R. "Boom at the Top." *New York Review of Books* 33 (8 May 1986): 12–15.
Isaacs, Arnold R. "Jason Bourne Returns." *Book World, The Washington Post* 16 (9 March 1986): 4.
*Kirkus Review* 54 (15 January 1986): 80.

Lehmann-Haupt, Christopher. "The Bourne Supremacy." *New York Times* (6 March 1986): C25.

Lochte, Dick. "The Bourne Supremacy." *Los Angeles Times Book Review* (23 March 1986): 3.

Michaud, Charles. "The Bourne Supremacy." *Library Journal* 111 (15 March 1986): 78.

Steinberg, Sybil. "Fiction: The Bourne Supremacy." *Publishers Weekly* 229 (31 January 1986): 363.

*Time* 127 (10 March 1986): 74.

*USA Today* 4 (26 February 1986): 6D.

*Virginia Quarterly Review* 62 (Summer 1986): 94.

*Wall Street Journal* 207 (19 March 1986): 28.

*West Coast Review of Books* 12 (January 1986): 24.

Wiltse, David. "Chopping Down a Forest of Bad Guys." *New York Times Book Review* 91 (9 March 1986): 12.

### The Bourne Ultimatum

*Book List* 86 (July 1990): 150.

*Book List* 86 (August 1990): 2194.

*Books* 3 (March 1990): 18.

*Book World* 21 (18 March 1990): 9.

Callendar, Newgate. "Spies & Thrillers." *New York Times Book Review* (11 March 1990): 33.

Campbell, Don G. "Storytellers: New in April." *Los Angeles Times Book Review* (18 March 1990): 8.

Glynn, Lenny. "Bourne Again." *Maclean's* 103 (2 April 1990): 67.

Gross, Ken. "Picks & Pans: Pages, *The Bourne Ultimatum*." *People Weekly* 33 (16 April 1990): 43–44.

*Kirkus Review* 58 (15 January 1990): 72.

*Kliatt* 25 (Spring 1991): 12.

*Los Angeles Times Book Review* (10 March 1991): 10.

Steinberg, Sybil. "Fiction: *The Bourne Ultimatum*." *Publishers Weekly* 237 (2 February 1990): 75.

*Wall Street Journal* 215 (22 March 1990): A12.

*West Coast Review of Books* 12 (January 1985): 24.

### The Chancellor Manuscript

"Audio Reviews: Fiction." *Publishers Weekly* 234 (2 September 1988): 71.

*Best Sellers* 37 (June 1977): 71.

*Book List* 73 (15 May 1977): 1401.

*Book World* (26 February 1978): E4.

Freedman, Richard. *New York Times Book Review* (27 March 1977): 8.

*Kirkus Review* 45 (15 January 1977): 57.

*Library Journal* 102 (1 April 1977): 834.

*New Statesman* 99 (27 June 1980): 973.

*New York Times* 126 (5 April 1977): 29.

*New York Times Book Review* (29 January 1978): 37.

*Observer* (3 July 1977): 24.

Phillips, Barbara. "*Chancellor Manuscript*: New Thriller." *Christian Science Monitor* 69 (31 March 1977): 27–31.

*Publishers Weekly* 211 (24 January 1977): 327.

*Publishers Weekly* 213 (2 January 1978): 63.

*West Coast Review of Books* 3 (May 1977): 32.

### The Cry of the Halidon

Callendar, Newgate. *New York Times Book Review* (4 August 1974): 26.

*Publishers Weekly* 205 (8 April 1974): 76.

### The Gemini Contenders

*Best Sellers* 36 (June 1977): 71.

Binyon, T. J. *Times Literary Supplement* (1 October 1976): 1260.

*Book List* 73 (15 May 1977): 1401.

Heldman, Irma Pascal. "*The Gemini Contenders*." *New York Times Book Review* (28 March 1976): 18.

*Kirkus Review* 44 (1 January 1976): 28.

McCray, Nancy. "*The Gemini Contenders*." *Booklist* 89 (15 May 1993): 1716.

*New York Times* 125 (30 April 1976): C17.

*New York Times Book Review* (10 April 1977): 35.

*Publishers Weekly* 209 (12 January 1976): 50.

*Publishers Weekly* 211 (7 February 1977): 94.

### The Holcroft Covenant

"Audio Reviews: Fiction: *The Holcroft Covenant*." *Publishers Weekly* 237 (2 February 1990): 50.

*Best Sellers* 38 (June 1978): 70.

*Book List* 74 (15 April 1978): 1324.

*Kirkus Review* 46 (15 February 1978): 775.

Leonard, John. "Books of 'The Times': *The Holcroft Covenant*." *New York Times* 127 (13 March 1978): C19.

*Library Journal* 103 (1 April 1978): 775.

Postman, Andrew, and Tom Spain. "Audio Reviews: *The Holcroft Covenant*." *Publishers Weekly* 233 (22 January 1988): 73.

*Publishers Weekly* 213 (20 February 1978): 105.

*Publishers Weekly* 211 (25 December 1978): 58.

Ryan, Allan A., Jr. "Triple Word Score." *Book World, The Washington Post* (19 March 1978): H3.

*West Coast Review of Books* 4 (May 1978): 29.


## The Icarus Agenda

*Armchair Detective* 22 (Fall 1989): 401.

*Book List* 84 (1 January 1988): 739.

*Books* (February 1988): 21.

*Book World* 18 (21 February 1988): 1.

Diehl, Digby. "Separating Fact from Fiction." *Modern Maturity* 31 (April 1988): 96–98.

Johnson, Julie. "Five Rich Rotters." *New York Times Book Review* 93 (27 March 1988): 16.

*Kirkus Review* 56 (15 January 1988): 79.

*Library Journal* 113 (15 February 1988): 179.

*Library Journal* 114 (August 1989): 178.

*Publishers Weekly* 235 (6 January 1989): 100.

Rafferty, Terrence. "Books: Beeg." *New Yorker* 64 (20 June 1988): 90–92.

Robertson, Peter L. "Ludlum's Lightening Pace Keeps 'Icarus' Flying High." *Chicago Tribune Books* (28 February 1988): Section 16, p. 7.

Steinberg, Sybil. "Forecasts: The Icarus Agenda." *Publishers Weekly* 233 (22 January 1988): 102.

*Wall Street Journal* 215 (5 July 1988): 18.

*West Coast Review of Books* 15 (April 1990): 35.

Woodward, Bob. Review. *Washington Post Book World* (21 February 1988): 1.


## The Matarese Circle

*Best Sellers* 39 (May 1979): 48.

*Book List* 75 (15 March 1979): 1131.

*Book World* (18 March 1979): E3.

Freedman, Richard. "Killer Thrillers." *New York Times Book Review* (8 April 1979): 14.

*Kirkus Review* 47 (15 January 1979): 80.

Lekachman, Robert. "Of Killers and Thrillers." *New Leader* 62 (23 April 1979): 17–18.

*New Republic* 62 (23 April 1979): 17.

*New York Times Book Review* (27 January 1980): 35.

Postman, Andrew, and Tom Spain. "Audio Reviews: *The Matarese Circle.*" *Publishers Weekly* 233 (22 January 1988): 73.

*Publishers Weekly* 215 (15 January 1979): 116.
*Publishers Weekly* 216 (10 December 1979): 68.
*School Library Journal* 216 (September 1979): 167.
*Wall Street Journal* 193 (2 April 1979): 26.
*West Coast Review of Books* 5 (May 1979): 25.


### The Matlock Paper

*Books and Bookmen* 18 (July 1973): 135.
Callendar, Newgate. *New York Times Book Review* (6 May 1973): 41.
*Esquire* 79 (May 1973): 66.
Fitzpatrick, Kelly J. *Best Sellers* (15 April 1973): 41.
*Kirkus Review* 41 (15 February 1973): 209.
*New York Times Book Review* (12 May 1974): 18.
*Publishers Weekly* 203 (26 February 1973): 123.
*Publishers Weekly* 205 (25 March 1974): 58.
*Times Literary Supplement* (3 August 1973): 911.


### The Osterman Weekend

*Book List* 87 (15 September 1990): 245.
*Book World* 12 (February 1991): 8.
Hill, William B. *Best Sellers* 32 (1 April 1972): 5.
*Kirkus Review* 39 (1 December 1971): 13.
*Library Journal* 97 (1 March 1972): 903.
*Observer* (6 August 1972): 25.
*Publishers Weekly* 201 (3 January 1972): 65.


### The Parsifal Mosaic

Adler, Jerry. "The Ludlum Enigma." *Newsweek* (19 April 1982): 99–100.
Barkham, John. *Middletown* (Conn.) *Press.* (30 March 1982).
*Book List* 78 (1 February 1982): 681.
*Book World* 12 (7 March 1982): 1.
Hunter, Evan. "Reincarnation and Annihilation." *New York Times Book Review* 87 (21 March 1982): 11.
*Kirkus Review* 50 (15 January 1982): 87.
Lehmann-Haupt, Christopher. "Books of the Times." *New York Times* (2 March 1982): 10.
*Library Journal* 107 (15 March 1982): 651.
*Publishers Weekly* 221 (29 January 1982): 56.
*Publishers Weekly* 223 (4 February 1982): 27.
*Time* 119 (5 April 1982): 78.

*Wall Street Journal* 199 (29 April 1982): 28.
*West Coast Review of Books* 8 (May 1982): 27.
Winks, Robin W. *New Republic* 187 (20 September 1982): 43–44.
———. *New Republic*. 187 (27 September 1982): 43–44.

### The Rhinemann Exchange ✓

*America* 131 (16 November 1974): 302.
*Best Sellers* 34 (15 September 1974): 280.
*Book List* 71 (15 December 1974): 407.
"Briefly Noted: *The Rhinemann Exchange*." *New Yorker* 50 (14 October 1974): 202–3.
Callendar, Newgate. "*The Rhinemann Exchange*." *New York Times Book Review* (27 October 1974): 56.
*Kirkus Review* 42 (15 July 1974): 759.
*Publishers Weekly* 205 (22 July 1974): 64.
*Publishers Weekly* 207 (9 June 1975): 65.
*Publishers Weekly* 21 (1 March 1991): 49–50.
Veit, Henry C. Review. *Library Journal* 99 (1 October 1974): 2504.

### The Road to Gandolfo

*Publishers Weekly* 207 (10 February 1975): 52.
Veit, Henry C. *Library Journal* 100 (1 April 1975): 694–95.

### The Road to Omaha

*Book List* 88 (15 May 1992): 18.
*Books* 6 (March 1992): 13.
Buck, Mason. "The Road to Omaha." *New York Times Book Review* (12 April 1992): 18.
*Chicago Tribune Books* (29 December 1991): 6.
McCray, Nancy. "The Road to Omaha." *Booklist* 88 (15 May 1992): 1708.
*New York Times Book Review* 97 (12 April 1992): 18.
*Publishers Weekly* 239 (2 March 1992): 28.

### The Scarlatti Inheritance

*Best Sellers* 31 (1 June 1971): 122.
*Best Sellers* 32 (1 May 1972): 71.
*Book List* 87 (15 November 1990): 600.
*Critical Review* 219 (October 1971): 215.
Frakes, J. R. "Popcorn Fiction." *Book World* 5 (21 May 1971): 11.
*Kirkus Review* 39 (1 January 1971): 21.
Levin, Martin. "Reader's Report: *The Scarlatti Inheritance*." *New York Times Book Review* (4 April 1971): 49.

*Library Journal* 96 (15 April 1971): 1387.
*Library Journal* 116 (1 February 1991): 109.
*Publishers Weekly* 199 (11 January 1971): 60.
*Time* 97 (8 March 1971): E3.

### *The Scorpio Illusion*

Glaviano, Cliff. *Library Journal* 118 (1 September 1993): 242.
McCray, Nancy. 90 *Booklist* (1 November 1993): 557–58.
Polk, James. "The Scorpio Illusion." *New York Times Book Review* (20 June 1993): 16.
*Publishers Weekly* 240 (19 April 1993): 48.
*Publishers Weekly* 240 (2 August 1993): 30–31.
Seaman, Donna. "The Scorpio Illusion." *Booklist* 89 (1 April 1993): 1387.

### *Trevayne*

Ainsser, John. "Audio Reviews: Fiction." *Publishers Weekly* 237 (3 August 1990): 50.
*Books* 4 (June 1990): 22.
Callendar, Newgate. *New York Times Book Review* (28 January 1973): 20.
*Publishers Weekly* 237 (3 August 1990): 50.
Stevens, Karen E. *School Library Journal* 19 (May 1973): 100.

## OTHER SECONDARY SOURCES

Ambler, Eric. *The Dark Frontier*. London: Fontana, 1940.
Anderson, Perry. "Modernity and Revolution." In *Marxism and the Interpretation of Culture*, edited by Cary Nelson and Lawrence Grossberg, 317–33. Urbana: University of Illinois Press, 1988.
Atkins, John. *The British Spy Novel: Styles in Treachery*. London: John Calder, 1984.
Arendt, Hannah. *Eichmann in Jerusalem*. New York: Penguin, 1963.
Becker, Ernest. *Escape from Evil*. New York: Free Press, 1975.
Bennett, Tony. "Marxism and Popular Fiction." In *Popular Fiction: Essays in Literature and History*, 214–27. London: Methuen, 1986.
Bettelheim, Bruno. "Individual and Group Behavior in Extreme Situations." *Journal of Abnormal Social Psychology* (October 1943): 417–52.
Borklund, Elmer. *Contemporary Literary Critics*. London: St. James, 1977.
Breuer, Josef, and Freud, Sigmund. *Studies in Hysteria*. New York: Basic Books, 1957.
*British Mystery and Thriller Writers Since 1940, First Series*. Vol. 87 of *Dictionary of Literary Biography*. New York: Bruccoli Press, a division of Gale Research, 1989.

Buchan, John. *The Thirty-Nine Steps*. Edinburgh, Scotland: Blackwood; New York: Doran, 1915.

Callinicos, Alex. *Against Postmodernism: A Marxist Critique*. New York: St. Martin's Press, 1990.

Campbell, Joseph. *The Hero with a Thousand Faces*. New York: Pantheon Press, 1949.

———. *The Power of Myth*. New York: Doubleday, 1988.

Cawelti, John G. *Adventure, Mystery, and Romance: Formula Stories As Art and Popular Culture*. Chicago: University of Chicago Press, 1976.

Cawelti, John G., and Bruce Rosenberg. *The Spy Story*. Chicago: University of Chicago Press, 1976.

Condon, Richard. *The Manchurian Candidate*. New York: McGraw Hill, 1959.

Conrad, Joseph. *Heart of Darkness*. New York: Viking Penguin, 1905.

Cremer, R. D., ed. *Macau: City of Commerce and Culture*. Hong Kong: UEA Press Ltd., 1987.

Cuddon, J.A.A. "Reader-response Theory." In *A Dictionary of Literary Terms and Literary Theory*, edited by J.A.A. Cuddon, 770–72. Oxford, U.K.: Basil Blackwell, Ltd., 1991.

Deighton, Len. *Billion Dollar Brain*. London: Cape; New York: Putnam, 1967.

———. *The Ipcress File*. London: Hodder and Stoughton, 1962.

DeMille, Nelson. *The Charm School*. New York: Warner Books, 1989.

Denning, Michael. *Cover Stories: Narrative and Ideology in the British Spy Thriller*. New York: Routledge & Kegan Paul, 1987.

Duncan, Robert (James Robert Hall). *The Q Document*. New York: Morrow, 1964.

Egleton, Clive. *The Eisenhower Deception*. London: Hodder and Stoughton, 1981.

———. *In the Red*. London: Hodder and Stoughton, 1993.

———. *The Mills Bomb*. London: Hodder and Stoughton, 1978.

Eysteinsson, Astradur. *The Concept of Modernism*. Ithaca, N.Y.: Cornell University Press, 1990.

Fast, Howard. *Mirage*. New York: Fawcett, 1965.

Finney, Jack. *The Body Snatchers*. New York: Dell, 1955.

Flowers, Betty Sue, ed. *Joseph Campbell: The Power of Myth with Bill Moyers*. New York: Doubleday & Co., 1988.

Follett, Ken. *The Eye of the Needle*. New York: Morrow, 1978.

Forsyth, Frederick. *The Day of the Jackal*. London: Hutchinson, 1971.

———. *The Odessa File*. London: Hutchinson, 1972.

Fowler, Robert, ed. *A Dictionary of Modern Critical Terms*. New York: Routledge & Kegan Paul, 1987.

Freedman, Carl. "Towards a Theory of Paranoia: The Science Fiction of Philip K. Dick." *Science-Fiction Studies* 11 (1984):15–24.

Freud, Sigmund. *Dora: An Analysis of a Case of Hysteria*. New York: Collier Books, 1963.

Frye, Northrop. *Anatomy of Criticism: Four Essays*. Princeton, N.J.: Princeton University Press, 1957.

Gintsberg, L. I. "National Socialist Party." In *Great Soviet Encyclopedia*. Vol. 17, edited by Alexandr Mickhailovich Prokhorov. New York: Macmillan, 1970.

Gintsberg, L. I., and A. I. Mukhin. "Germany." In *Great Soviet Encyclopedia*. Vol. 6, edited by Alexandr Mickhailovich Prokhorov, 340–79. New York: Macmillan, 1970.

Goldman, William. *Marathon Man*. New York: Dell Publishing, 1976.

Groden, Michael, and Martin Kreiswirth, eds. *The Johns Hopkins Guide to Literary Theory and Criticism*. Baltimore, Md.: Johns Hopkins University Press, 1993.

Hall, Adam. *The Quiller Memorandum*. New York: Dell, 1975.

Hall, Stuart. "Notes on Deconstructing 'The Popular.' " In *People's History and Socialist Theory*, edited by Raphael Samuel, 227–40. London: Routledge & Kegan Paul, 1981.

Harris, Wendell V., ed. *Dictionary of Concepts in Literary Criticism and Theory*. Westport, Conn.: Greenwood Press, 1992.

Higgins, Jack. *Cold Harbor*. New York: Simon and Schuster, 1992.

———. *The Eagle Has Landed*. London: Collins, 1975.

Hilfer, Tony. *The Crime Novel: A Deviant Genre*. Austin, Tex.: University of Texas Press, 1990.

Hitchens, Christopher. "On the Imagination of Conspiracy." In his *For the Sake of Argument: Essays and Minority Reports*, 12–24. London: Verso, 1993.

Hitler, Adolf. *Mein Kampf*. Translated by Hurst and Blackett. Las Vegas, Nev.: Angriff, 1996.

Hofstadter, Richard. *The American Political Tradition*. New York: Vintage, 1988.

Household, Geoffrey. *Rogue Male*. London: Chatto and Windus, 1939.

Hsiang-Lin, Lo. *Hong Kong and Western Cultures*. Honolulu: East West Center Press, 1964.

Huxley, Aldous. *Brave New World*. London: Chatto and Windus, 1932.

Huyssen, Andreas. *After the Great Divide: Modernism, Mass Culture, Postmodernism*. Bloomington: Indiana University Press, 1986.

Jacobus, Mary, ed. *Women Writing and Writing about Women*. London: Croom Helm, 1979; Totowa, N.J.: Barnes and Noble Books, 1979.

Jameson, Fredric. *Marxism and Form: Twentieth-Century Dialectical Theories of Literature*. Princeton, N.J.: Princeton University Press, 1974.

Johnson, Steven. "Paranoid's Delight." In a *MacAddict* feature called "Filter," May 1995, in INLINE (http://www.macaddict.com)

———. *The Political Unconscious: Narrative As a Socially Symbolic Act*. Ithaca, N.Y.: Cornell University Press, 1981.

———. *Postmodernism, or the Logic of Late Capitalism*. Durham, N.C.: Duke University Press, 1991.

Jung, Carl G. *Man and His Symbols*. New York: Doubleday & Co., 1964.

Kahn, David. *The Codebreakers: The Story of Secret Writing*. London: Weidenfeld and Nicholson, 1967.

Kaplan, Harold I., and Benjamin J. Saddock. "Personality Disorders." 7th ed., 731–751. In *Synopsis of Psychiatry: Behavioral Sciences/Clinical Psychiatry*. Baltimore, Md.: Williams and Wilkins, 1991.

———. "Psychotherapies." In *Synopsis of Psychiatry: Behavioral Sciences/Clinical Psychiatry*. 7th ed., 1134–1154. Baltimore, Md.: Williams and Wilkins, 1991.

Keen, Sam. *Faces of the Enemy: Reflections of the Hostile Imagination*. San Francisco: Harper & Row, 1986.

Kernig, C. D., ed., "National Socialism." In *Marxism, Communism and Western Society: A Comparative Encyclopedia*. Vol. 1. New York: Herder and Herder, 1972.

Khokhlov, A. N. "Hong Kong." In *Great Soviet Encyclopedia*. edited by Alexandr Mickhailovich Prokhorov. Vol. 25, 66–67. New York: Macmillan, 1980.

King, Frank H. *The History of the Hong Kong and Shanghai Banking Corporation*. 3 vols. Cambridge, U.K.: Cambridge University Press, 1988–1990.

Kipling, Rudyard. *Kim*. Harmondsworth, U.K.: Penguin, 1987.

Klein, Fritz. "Vorbereitung der faschistischen Diktatur durch die deutsche Grossbourgeoises (1929–1932)." *Z. Gesch.-Wiss*. 1 (1953): 872–904.

Knight, Stephen. *Form and Ideology in Crime Fiction*. Bloomington: Indiana University Press, 1980.

Lane, Kevin P. *Sovereignty and the Status Quo: The Historical Roots of China's Hong Kong Policy*. San Francisco: Westview Press, 1990.

le Carré, John. *Call for the Dead*. London: Gollancz, 1961.

———. *The Honourable Schoolboy*. New York: Knopf, 1976.

———. *The Spy Who Came in from the Cold*. London: Gollancz; New York: Dell, 1960.

Levin, Ira. *The Boys from Brazil*. New York: Random House, 1976.

Macdonald, Andrew. "Frederick Forsyth." In *British Mystery and Thriller Writers Since 1940*, vol. 87 of *Dictionary of Literary Biography*. Eds. Bernard Benstock and Thomas F. Staley, 125–135. Detroit, Mich.: Bruccoli Press, a division of Gale Research, 1989.

———. "Forsyth, Frederick." In *Twentieth-Century Crime and Mystery Writers*, 598–600. Edited by John M. Reilly. New York: St. Martin's Press, 1980.

MacInnes, Helen. *Above Suspicion*. Boston: Little, Brown, 1941.

MacLean, Alistair. *The Guns of Navarone*. London: Collins, 1957.

———. *Where Eagles Dare*. London: Collins, 1966.

Makaryk, Irena R., ed. *Encyclopedia of Contemporary Literary Theory*. Toronto: University of Toronto Press, 1993.

Marchetti, Victor, and John Marks. *The CIA and the Cult of Intelligence*. New York: Dell, 1975.

Marshall, S.L.A. *Men Against Fire*. New York: Morrow, 1967.

Marx, Karl, and Friedrich Engels. *The Communist Manifesto*. Harmondsworth, U.K.: Penguin, 1967.

Merry, Bruce. *Anatomy of a Spy Thriller*. Montreal: McGill Queen's University Press, 1977.

Miller, Arthur. *All My Sons*. In *Arthur Miller's Collected Plays*. New York: Viking, 1957.

Mommsen, Hans. "National Socialism." In *Marxism, Communism and Western Society: A Comparative Encyclopedia*, edited by C. D. Kernig, vol. 1: 65–74. New York: Herder and Herder, 1973.

Monoghan, David. *The Novels of John le Carré: The Art of Survival*. Oxford, U.K.: Blackwell, 1985.

Morgan, W. P. *Triad Societies in Hong Kong*. Hong Kong: Government Press, 1960.

Mote, David, ed. *Contemporary Popular Writers*. London: St. James Press, 1997.

Neville, Katherine. "Behind the Reign of Terror." *The Washington Post* (19 December 1993): 3.

Newquist, Roy, ed. *Counterpoint*. Chicago: Rand McNally, 1964.

Okuley, B., and F. King-Poole. *Gambler's Guide to Macao*. Hong Kong: South China Morning Post, 1979.

Palmer, Jerry. *Thrillers: Genesis and Structure of a Popular Genre*. London: Edward Arnold, 1978.

Panek, LeRoy. *The Special Branch: The British Spy Novel, 1890–1980*. Bowling Green, Ohio: Bowling Green University Popular Press, 1981.

"Paranoid Personality Disorder" and "Schizoid Personality Disorder." In *Diagnostic and Statistical Manual of Mental Disorders: DSM-IV*. Washington, D.C.: American Psychiatric Association, 1994.

Parish, James Robert, and Michael R. Pits. *The Great Spy Pictures*. Metuchen, N.J.: Scarecrow Press, 1974.

Patterson, Harry (Jack Higgins). *To Catch a King*. New York: Fawcett, 1979.

——. *The Valhalla Exchange*. New York: Stein and Day, 1976.

Penzler, Otto. "Collecting Mystery Fiction: Robert Ludlum." *Armchair-Detective* 22 (Fall 1989): 382–84.

——. *The Private Lives of Private Eyes, Spies, Crime Fighters, and Other Good Guys*. New York: Grosset and Dunlap, 1977.

Polan, Dana. *Power & Paranoia: History, Narrative, and the American Cinema, 1940–1950*. New York: Columbia University Press, 1986.

Porter, Dennis. *The Pursuit of Crime: Art and Ideology in Detective Fiction*. New Haven, Conn.: Yale University Press, 1981.

"Reader-Response Criticism." In *The New Princeton Encyclopedia of Poetry and Poetics*, edited by Alex Preminger and T. V. F. Brogan, 1014–16. Princeton, N.J.: Princeton University Press, 1993.

Reilly, John M., ed. *Twentieth-Century Crime and Mystery Writers*. London: Macmillan, 1980, 1991.

Rowan, Richard Wilmer, with Robert G. Deindorfer. *Secret Service: Thirty-Three Centuries of Espionage*. New York: Hawthorn, 1967.

Sagan, Eli. *The Honey and the Hemlock*. New York: Basic Books, 1991.

Sanford, Nevitt. *Sanctions for Evil*. San Francisco: Jossey-Bass, 1971.

Sauerberg, Lars Ole. *Secret Agents in Fiction: Ian Fleming, John le Carré and Len Deighton*. New York: St. Martin's Press, 1984.

Scrignar, C. B. *Post-Traumatic Stress Disorder*. New Orleans, La.: Bruno Press, 1988.

Shapiro, David. *Neurotic Styles*. New York: Basic Books, 1965.

Shaw, George Bernard. *Man and Superman*. New York: Viking Penguin, 1950.

Stevenson, William. *A Man Called Intrepid: The Secret War*. New York: Harcourt Brace, 1976.

Sutherland, John. *Best Sellers*. Boston: Routledge & Kegan Paul, 1981.

Symons, Julian. *Bloody Murder: From the Detective Story to the Crime Novel: A History*. London: Viking, 1985.

Thompson, Jon. *Fiction, Crime, and Empire: Clues to Modernity and Postmodernism*. Urbana: University of Illinois Press, 1993.

Tsai, Jung-Fang. *Hong Kong in Chinese History*. New York: Columbia University Press, 1993.

Twitchett, Denis, and John K. Fairbank. *The Cambridge History of China*, vol. 11. New York: Cambridge University Press, 1980.

Van Dover, J. Kenneth. *Murder in the Millions*. New York: Frederick Ungar Publishing Co., 1984.

Wistrich, Robert S. *Who's Who in Nazi Germany*. London: Routledge, 1995.

Yallop, David. *Tracking the Jackal; The Search for Carlos, the World's Most Wanted Man*. New York: Random House, 1996.

Zentner, Christian, and Friedemann Bedürftig, eds. *The Encyclopedia of the Third Reich*. 2 vols. New York: Macmillan, 1991.

# Index

## About the Author

GINA MACDONALD is Visiting Assistant Professor of English at Loyola University in New Orleans, Louisiana. She is the author of *James Clavell: A Critical Companion* (Greenwood, 1996), and has published well over a hundred articles in periodicals and books on popular fiction, detective fiction, and popular culture. She is also co-author of a text for bilingual writing students and a freshman composition text.

**Other Titles in**
**Critical Companions to Popular Contemporary Writers**
Kathleen Gregory Klein, Series Editor